MAR 1 9 2002

Working In Show Business

BEHIND-THE-SCENES CAREERS IN THEATER, FILM, AND TELEVISION

LYNNE ROGERS

BACK STAGE BOOKS
An imprint of Watson-Guptill Publications/New York

Editor: Dale Ramsey
Designer: Bob Fillie, Graphiti Graphics
Production manager: Hector Campbell

First published in 1997 in the United States by Back Stage Books,
an imprint of Watson-Guptill Publications,
a division of BPI Communications, Inc.,
1515 Broadway, New York, NY 10036-8986.

Library of Congress Cataloging-in-Publication Data for this title can be
obtained by writing to the Library of Congress, Washington, D.C. 20540

Manufactured in the United States of America

ISBN 0-8230-8842-1

1 2 3 4 5 / 01 00 99 98 97

To Tim, Jim, and Amanda—with love always.

ACKNOWLEDGMENTS

"When you need to get something done, ask a busy person," must be an ancient show business saying. I am indebted to these very busy, very generous people: Gerald and Barbara Alden, Stephen Adler, Brandy Alexander, Jean Block, Sandra M. Bloom, Judy Boals, Mel Bourne, Julianne Boyd, Bob Branigan, Albert Brenner, Fern Fields Brooks, Mark A. Burley, Daisy Carbeon, Ann Cattaneo, Casey Childs, Steven Cohen, Nancy Coyne, Lenore DeKoven, Maria di Dia, Jo Ann Emmerich, Paul Erbach, Debby Falb, Kathryn Finnefrock, Carol Flemming, Jim Flynn, Nancy Ford, Sally Gifft, Sol Glushak, Joanne Goodhart, Albert Hague, Renée Orin-Hague, Bill Hanauer, John Handy, Laurence Heath, Abe Jacob, Albert and Trudy Kallis, Jan Kastendeick, Alan Kimmel, Isobel Robins Konecky, Herb Lager, Bruce Lansbury, Bruce Lazarus, Paul Libin, James Lipton, William Ivey Long, Kevin MacCollum, Sara Martinez, Sally Ann Meares, Brian Meister, Ben Mordecai, Robert Moss, Andrea Naier, Dorothy Olim, Don Padgett, Jim Parsons, Patrick Plevin, Loren Plotkin, Dale Ramsey, Phyllis Restaino, Richard Seader, Harriet Slaughter, Jack Spencer, Dawn Steinberg, David Stone, Frederic B. Vogel, Sharon Waldman, Ric Wanatek, Berenice Weiler, Marc Weiss, Barry Weissler, Josleen Wilson, Jack Wood . . . and Mari Lyn Henry.

Contents

FILM 111

TELEVISION 177

CLOSING SHOT 211

APPENDIX 213

Introduction

FADE IN:

THE SCREEN IS DARK.

VOICE OVER
(in the style of <u>Law and Order</u>)

In the alluring world of show business, which lies
somewhere between Oz and The Twilight Zone, there are
three communities—Theater, Film, and Television.

(CUE SOUND AND FADE IN PICTURE)

From far away, we can see their bright lights and
hear the constant buzz of high-powered activity. As
we move in closer we hear laughter, and in the fore-
front we glimpse crowds of attractive people, exquis-
itely groomed, beautifully dressed. Other people, men
and women, move about behind them. We can't quite
make them out. Everyone is very busy. The shiny ones
in the pretty clothes are smiling, waving at us. It
would be so exciting to join them, wherever they live
in that show business world.

FREEZE FRAME

SOUND OUT

But, face it, we are not dazzling people. Do we
belong here? And who are those people behind them?
That's what we'll have to find out.

THEME UP

HOW MANY TIMES HAVE YOU THOUGHT about, maybe even dreamed about, a show business career? If you mentioned it to your friends or family, didn't some well-meaning, unbearably honest person say, "What do you want to do, be an actor and wait on tables?

The answer to that is: "Who says you have to be an *actor*?"

For every working actor, there are dozens more people working behind the scenes—at theaters, in studios, and at locations all around the world. It may not be common knowledge, but many of them are powerful, secure, and as sought-after as the most bankable star. They are the skilled professionals who help talented performers make demanding work look easy.

Media coverage of the world of show business is devoted almost exclusively to stars—big, little, up-and-coming, or used-to-be stars. While it may be fun to get the intimate details about a celebrity's personal stay-in-shape routine, or learn how fabulous it was to work with so-and-so, the glut of celebrity news provides no real information about the *business*—not a hint of what it's all about.

Without information, it's hard to envision the intricate activity backstage, off-screen, or in the studio. Without information, we are unable even to fantasize about where there might be room for us in a world where everybody's job is, ultimately, to make the "magic" happen.

Why a career in show business? Consider the fact that it is arguably the single major industry in which American products are recognized as the best and are sought after throughout the world. As *Fortune* magazine declared, "Pop culture is our hottest export."

Broadway theater alone is a billion-dollar-a-year industry, with an estimated attendance (in 1997) of 10.57 million people. That's almost twice the number of people who buy tickets to local football, baseball, and hockey games. Theater beyond Broadway is a thriving industry; touring shows in more than ninety cities across the continent attract double the New York audience and generate twice the income. The works of American playwrights, in English and in translation, enthrall audiences around the world: *Fiddler on the Roof, Death of a Salesman,* and *A Chorus Line,* modern classics of the American theater, are always playing somewhere. In fact, at the premiere of *Death of a Salesman* in Tokyo, playwright Arthur Miller was stunned by the number of Japanese who thanked him for so movingly describing and dramatizing family relationships in Japanese society.

According to the Bureau of Labor Statistics, the motion picture business is currently one of the top ten growth industries in the United States. American films influence and entertain audiences everywhere. Batman, Braveheart, and even Disney's animated Quasimodo were heroes in Barcelona as well as in Amarillo. *Pretty Woman,* the 1990 movie that made Julia Roberts a star, was the number-one film in Sweden and Israel.

In their heyday, *Dallas* and *Dynasty* were as popular with television viewers in Capetown and London as in the United States. Today, *Baywatch* is the most widely syndicated television show in the world, followed closely by *Melrose Place, 90210, Seinfeld, Friends, Roseanne,* and *Murphy Brown. The Bold and the Beautiful* intrigues daytime audiences in Corfu, and children in Eastern Europe adore the Muppets.

Technological advances have altered our universe. As recently as 1992, the information superhighway was, for most of us, a dimly grasped concept on a distant horizon. In what seems a finger snap, it is here on a global scale. Programming-on-demand via satellite, capable of delivering more than 150 channels, is already available in limited markets to millions. The need for new and original material to satisfy these audiences is not going to diminish; it can only grow. Clearly, we are going to need qualified people to carry on—and go further.

The question now remains: If you're not going to be an actor and wait on tables, what are you going to do? To answer that you need some idea of what the career possibilities are.

Show business is the practice—the art and method—of getting the show on. The following pages will walk you through the process, explaining who does what, and when, in the course of developing a play, a film, and a television show from an idea to a reality. Joining us on this exploration will be a host of working professionals. What they have to say may open your eyes to careers you didn't even know about, to bright new opportunities.

And in unexpected places. Recent employment figures show that the highest rates of job growth in the industry have been in Las Vegas, Atlanta, Chicago, Phoenix, Dallas, and Provo. It's conceivable that pursuing a show business career no longer means transplanting oneself to New York or Los Angeles.

What wages can you expect to earn? Even though many people insist that their age and salary are two numbers they never mention, *Working in Show Business* will give you a fair picture. What your working conditions will be like and what sort of training you'll need before you can embark on the career that most attracts you are also explored.

One thing is certain: In this territory, the level of anticipation is always high. Whether it's a play, a movie, or a TV show, everybody working on every project wants it to be more than great—an audience-pleaser, a hit, an award-winner. No one in this business can afford to do less than terrific work. Hours can be long, and schedules are often irregular. Doing your best is taken for granted.

Some words of warning before we begin: For all the excitement, anticipation, collaborative effort, and commitment, the outcome is always unpredictable. Just as the most meticulously fitted airplane can take an unexpected nosedive, mistakes can be made, and they have been, frequently by the most highly respected inhabitants of this territory. In *Not Since Carrie*, Ken Mandelbaum entertainingly describes events leading up to forty of the most spectacular flops in Broadway history. *Heaven's Gate, Waterworld,* and *Cutthroat Island* are but three of a multitude of eagerly awaited films that were launched with outrageous fanfare, sank like rocks, and disappeared within weeks after opening. And trivia books are cluttered with titles of TV series that were canceled after one episode.

What goes wrong? Who can say? Tastes change. Some totally unforeseen incident occurs and the project is suddenly irrelevant. Everyone becomes too caught up in the process, too close to see intrinsic flaws. Producer Richard Seader remembered this incident from his early days as company manager of the original 1962 production of *A Funny Thing Happened on the Way to the Forum*:

> The final run-through prior to moving the show to New Haven, for the then-customary out-of-town tryout, was on a Sunday night for an audience of theater people working in all the other Broadway shows. They loved it. They laughed, they cheered. There was, literally, dancing in the aisles. They told us we had a hit. We opened in New Haven and we got blasted. They hated us! We were in shock. What had gone wrong? We didn't know. There were rewrites after every performance, cast changes, and still nothing—maybe a few

laughs, but really, nothing. We told ourselves that it was New Haven. They didn't know what it was all about. Wait till we get to Washington, they'll get it.

But in Washington, it was the same. Bad reviews, unresponsive audience, maybe a few laughs. We were dying. And the word was getting to New York: It would be a disaster.

George Abbott, the director, said, "We are all too close to this to see what the trouble is. We don't know how to fix it. I think we should ask Jerry Robbins to take a look at it. [The director and choreographer Jerome Robbins's theater credits at the time included *Bells Are Ringing, West Side Story,* and *Gypsy.*] And so Jerry sat through a couple of performances and came to us afterward. We were hanging on his words, believe me. He said, "You need an opening number." We were astonished. "You're not telling the audience it's OK to laugh. They don't know what's in store. And they don't know it's supposed to be funny. You have to give them permission to laugh."

Mr. Abbott mentioned a song that was not being used, which Stephen Sondheim [this was the first show for which he wrote both the music and lyrics] didn't want in the show. Jerry said, "Let me hear it. If it won't do, I'll tell you." So they went up to the balcony where there was a piano. Steve played the song, and they stayed up there for several hours. Finally they came back down to the stage, and Jerry said, "Here's your opening number." It was "Comedy Tonight."

Well, Robbins was right, of course—that made all the difference! We were a hit.

As writer-producer Lynda Obst observed on *The Charlie Rose Show:* "No one ever really knows what is going to go. Which is why you have to believe in your guts." Which may account for this credo from almost every one of the experts who contributed to this book:

If there is anything else in the whole world that you can imagine yourself doing, that will give you even the smallest degree of pleasure, DO IT!

In this business the door is always open for volunteers. And it's not a nine-to-five existence by any means. If you're curious rather than cautious; if you want to be where there's excitement, energy, talent and creativity, the possibility of enormous personal satisfaction, and an absence of rote; if meeting new people, working in different places, in unexpected situations, appeals to you; if adventure is more attractive than security; if the expanding worldwide aspect of show business calls to you, then welcome! The operative words are *passion, determination, collaboration.* And *guts.*

> I really wanted to be in the theater. But when I tried to audition, I felt I just couldn't do it. Somebody saw me hanging around and asked if I'd help out with the costumes. It turned out that I was really good at it. So I realized that's what I could do! I studied, I got jobs. I've been doing Broadway shows now for fourteen years. And I still love it.
>
> JAN KASTENDEICK, costume designer

Theater

N 1996, BROADWAY THEATER CELEBRATED its one-hundredth year. The Great White Way, as it has been known since the beginning of this century—when New York boasted more theaters than any other city in the world. and the electric brilliance of their marquees effectively turned night into day—surely symbolizes the glamour of theatrical entertainment in America, and anyone aspiring to a career in the business may define "making it" as working on Broadway.

Professional theater has been a vital part of America's cultural scene since Colonial times; the earliest European settlers brought theatrical traditions from their homelands to the New World. We know that President George Washington enjoyed theater—Richard Brinsley Sheridan's *The School for Scandal* was reportedly his favorite play—and, in the late eighteenth century, his frequent attendance helped to further popularize playgoing.

By the middle of the nineteenth century, there were functioning theaters in most cities across the nation. Vaudeville troupes and touring companies, headed by actor–managers renowned for performing a particular showy role in a well-known play, were regular attractions. And eager audiences were in the habit of returning to enjoy the same stars performing in the same play more than once: James O'Neill (father of Eugene O'Neill) was noted for his performance in *The Count of Monte Cristo*; Joseph Jefferson played Rip Van Winkle for most of his career. Audiences for whom a night at the theater was the only real entertainment further celebrated the occasion by wearing elegant clothes, fine jewelry, and furs. Some ladies went so far as to crown their elaborate hairdos with hats adorned with flowing ostrich plumes. "Madam, will you please remove your hat?" is a request that predates motion pictures by decades.

Of course, the performer's search for roles with long-running potential and the public's desire to see them again and again continues to this day. Yul Brynner, who toured in this country and abroad for many years in *The King and I*, gave more than 5,000 performances as the King of Siam, the role he originated in 1951; Richard Kiley long played Don Quixote in *Man of La Mancha*; and Carol Channing has by now completed ten national tours as Dolly Levi in *Hello, Dolly!* Just as young audiences will see movies or rent cassettes over and over again, *Sunset Boulevard* fans were determined to see the performance of each new Norma Desmond, happily traveling to every city where a new company opened. There are show clubs whose members boast of having seen *My Fair Lady*, *Cats*, or *Grease!* more than a dozen times. Terrence McNally's hit play *Master Class* had its devotees—amazed by Zoe Caldwell's Tony-winning performance as Maria Callas, they also went to see Patti LuPone and Dixie Carter in the same role, to compare performances and interpretations. Repeat attendance translates into dollars not only for the performers, but for the writer, the producer, and all the other people connected with the show.

Throughout the United States today there are various kinds of theater: There is the Broadway stage and there is "the road"—the touring circuit—characterized by big houses where plays are presented prior to or after a New York opening; "resident," or regional, nonprofit theater companies in cities around the nation; dinner theaters; summer stock companies; and theaters (a few) whose productions are for children. University theaters are good places to workshop a new show, affording students the benefit of working with top professionals. Theater even exists in unconventional spaces—basements, restaurants, abandoned buildings—but where audiences nonetheless respond to what a playwright has to say or exult in the sheer imagination of a presentation. Several seasons ago, Manhattan's 67th Street Armory became the site of an unusual production, *Tamara*: The audience followed characters from room to room, upstairs and down, crowding into corners and sitting on the furniture to watch each scene. Whatever the show's size or degree of opulence (or lack of it), the process of mounting each new production is the same.

THE PLAYWRIGHT

"In the beginning was the word." Everything starts with the play. Somebody has to have an *idea*, an irresistible idea that demands expression in dramatic form. That person is usually the playwright.

Pulitzer Prize–winning playwright August Wilson, at the tenth anniversary celebration of the Kennedy Center's Fund for New American Plays, in Washington, D.C., said:

> Until the playwright works, no one in the theater works. Not the actors, not the director, not the designers, not the stagehands, not the ushers, not the agents. . . .

And Peter Stone, president of the Dramatists Guild, said: "Authors have always seen themselves as the providers of the work everyone is hired to perform."

THE ORIGINS OF STAGE WORKS

New work that is based on characters, incidents, and ideas imagined by the writer (though the events and people may be real) is original material. The plays of Sam Shepard—*Buried Child, True West,* and *A Lie of the Mind*—fit that definition. *Fiorello!* and *The Rothschilds,* by Sheldon Harnick and Jerry Bock, are original musicals based on real people and actual events.

If the idea is to write a play based on characters and a story from already existing material—a book, magazine article, opera, film—that work will be an adaptation. The Bible, or classics such as Homer's *The Odyssey* or the writings of Jane Austen and Charles Dickens, are in the public domain; anyone is free to make use of them. To adapt work that is protected by a current copyright, the playwright will need to get permission—that is, secure the rights—from the original author to use the source material. This may also be true in the case of a deceased author whose estate retains the rights to all works not in the public domain.

The Heiress is Ruth and Augustus Goetz's stage adaptation of Henry James's novel, *Washington Square. Rent* is a musical which Jonathan Larson derived from Giacomo Puccini's opera *La Bohème*. Both of the sources of these plays are in the public domain.

The Most Happy Fella is Frank Loesser's musical adaptation of Sidney Howard's original nonmusical play, *They Knew What They Wanted*, so Loesser had to secure the rights to use Howard's material before writing the musical. Both *Sunset Boulevard* and *Applause* were great movies before talented writers had the irresistible idea of bringing those characters in those situations to new life on the stage and set about getting the rights to do so. (*Applause* was derived from the film *All About Eve.*) Rights to John Steinbeck's novel *The Grapes of Wrath* also were secured before the classic movie and the exciting stage adaptation were scripted.

While a revival—a new production of a well-known play—may not seem an issue for novice playwrights, new productions of already established work are not limited to classics such as the works of Euripedes, Shakespeare, Ibsen, Shaw, and others. A significant number of productions worldwide are re-examinations of modern works that have not been seen for many years, but seem suddenly relevant to the present day. The 1996 Tony award-winning production of Edward Albee's *A Delicate Balance,* which won the Pulitzer Prize for drama in 1966–7, is a stunning example of a revival that attracted a new generation of theatergoers and sparked greater audience response than did the original production, to the immense gratification of Mr. Albee. David Ives, a writer with an impressive ability to dramatize quirky ideas in very short plays, is already seeing revivals of his early work *All in the Timing* while his newest, *Mere Mortals and Others,* plays on Manhattan's Theater Row.

If the material is significantly altered—scenes or characters cut, material added, scenes arranged in different sequence—the vogue word for the resulting work is *revisal.* Tommy Tune's production of *Grease!,* with new songs and an updated script, is a hit revisal.

Ideas need not necessarily originate with the playwright. For example, the impetus for the original production of *The King and I* came from Gertrude Lawrence, who was a major star when she saw the 1946 film *Anna and the King of Siam,* based on Margaret Landon's book about Anna Leonowens and starring Irene Dunne and Rex Harrison. Lawrence thought it would be an ideal musical-comedy vehicle for her. She approached Cole Porter, who declined to work on the project, and later persuaded Rodgers and Hammerstein to get the rights and create the show.

Inspiration for the stage musical version of *The Secret Garden* came from designer and producer Heidi Landesman, who had heard the recording of a British regional theater's musical based on the 1911 novel by Frances Hodgson Burnett. Landesman then called upon playwright Marsha Norman to write a new script and song lyrics. Their collaborator on the music was composer Lucy Simon.

Once a play is successfully produced, the original idea can seem obvious and commonplace, even to the writer. It's as if the subject matter had been in plain sight, just waiting to be noticed. For instance, Alfred Uhry's *Driving Miss Daisy,* which was produced off-Broadway by Playwrights Horizons, won the Pulitzer Prize for drama in 1987 and ran for 1,195 performances. (The 1989 film version won four Academy Awards, including Best Picture and Best Actress.) Uhry's play, detailing the long-term relationship between a cantankerous Southern Jewish woman and her black chauffeur, was based on the dramatist's recollections of his grandmother and her driver.

He recalled how he felt after *The Robber Bridegroom,* his well-received musical adaptation of a story by Eudora Welty (in the title role, Barry Bostwick won the season's Tony for best performer in a musical), and his script for the movie *Mystic Pizza* had failed to repay him sufficiently for his long years of effort:

> I thought: Well, maybe I'm not going to be a great writer, not a playwright. Maybe I really don't have any talent, or not enough talent. I'll just do this one last thing. And I went down to see the family and wrote this . . . and look what has happened. But if I hadn't been successful, I was ready to stop, give it up, and remain an English teacher for the rest of my life.

He was subsequently commissioned to write a play for the arts festival connected with the 1996 Olympics in Atlanta, Georgia. *The Last Night of Ballyhoo,* which also deals with a Jewish family in Atlanta, came to Broadway in March of 1997 and won Uhry a Tony Award. He then went to work on a new musical with director Harold Prince.

A DEMANDING CRAFT

Playwriting has been termed the most demanding of all forms because the words have to propel the idea, as well as character and action. Suzan-Lori Parks, author of *The America Play* and other works, said:

> Theater writing is the most difficult because it has to work perfectly. You can't drop the dialogue to cut to a description of the landscape.

The struggling writer, working for extended periods in isolation, needs a supportive environment where his or her work can get a reading or workshop production, which offers the chance to hear actors deliver the lines out loud. Dialogue that looks right on the page may not necessarily sound like real people talking to one another. The writer needs to know what works, and what doesn't.

As you might expect, the New York area is home to several play development groups and to theaters dedicated to producing works by new writers. The oldest of these is New Dramatists, a nonprofit organization founded in 1949 by playwright Michaela O'Harra to encourage and develop American playwriting talent. During the seven-year membership period, writers receive "the time, the space, and the tools to develop their craft," plus unlimited readings and workshops,

FOR INFORMATION, CONTACT:

New Dramatists
424 West 44 Street
New York, NY 10036

Chicago Alliance
for Playwrights
Theater Building
1225 West Belmont
Chicago, IL 60657.

The Actors Theatre
of Louisville
316-320 West Main Street
Louisville, KY 40202.

access to a national script-distribution service, a comprehensive theater library, and a valuable membership in a community of gifted peers. August Wilson, Maria Irene Fornes, and Arthur Miller are among the more than 500 playwrights who have benefitted from the program.

In the Midwest, the Chicago Alliance for Playwrights brings together writers and development groups, providing services and educational programs to encourage production of new plays by local writers. The organization co-sponsors meetings with the Dramatists Guild and the Society for Stage Directors and Choreographers, in New York City, and maintains an author/script directory.

The Actors Theatre of Louisville, in addition to the Humana Festival of short plays they have produced each year for the past two decades (earning them international attention), also produces showcases of ten-minute plays. What do they look for in addition to good writing? Originality, some sense of theatrical impact, and an idea that may be developed into a full-length work. Will the audience care enough about the characters to want to know what happens next?

Doubtless because of the acknowledged need to nurture good writers, there are numerous opportunities for playwrights—in the form of play festivals, grant programs, contests, internships, residencies, and scholarships. Information about them is not hard to come by. Judy Boals, a literary agent at Berman Boals & Flynn, advised:

> *The Dramatists' Sourcebook* is the bible for most of my writers. Just recently, one of my writers got in the mail an invitation to a very prestigious foundation conference out in California. So that is going to do wonders for her. She had slipped into a really serious block and she found out about the foundation through *The Dramatists' Sourcebook*. We also tell people to try out for the Eugene O'Neill Theater Center's National Playwrights Conference and the more auspicious festivals.

Like *The Dramatists' Sourcebook, The Playwright's Companion* (Feedback Theatrebooks) is another "bible" for playwrights—an annual listing of opportunities for writers to get their plays produced or to gain income or knowledge for the pursuit of their craft.

For example, these works list festivals and workshops that are invaluable opportunities for the writer to develop a new play. Such activities serve the extremely important function of bringing material to the attention of potential producers and directors. Workshops may alert the theatrical community to the fact that a talented newcomer has arrived on the scene, deserving attention. Favorable reaction—even to a ten-minute piece—can be like the click of a switch, turning on the buzz of interest in what this or that writer is up to.

My partner dragged me to a workshop of *Rent.* He had heard Jonathan Larson's music before and had been enthusiastic. I was blown away. We knew they needed to work on the show and gave them some seed money.

KEVIN MCCOLLUM, producer

ATTRIBUTES OF A PLAYWRIGHT

How would you answer these questions:

- Are you a storyteller?
- Do other people's lives and motivations interest you?
- Do you find yourself making up stories about people you see on a bus or train, or a woman in a painting?
- When asked what you did on your vacation, do you describe incidents in vivid detail, or just say where you went, with whom, and what the weather was like?
- Do you like to read? Are you curious about the ways people lived in other times, other countries? Do you enjoy doing research on other cultures?
- Do you enjoy going to the theater?
- Can you take criticism without becoming angry and frustrated?
- Do you like to write? Are you content to go on writing for hours at a time?

Not all playwrights necessarily answer yes to every question, but they certainly should recognize some aspects of themselves in the profile.

A writer's age and sex are irrelevant. While many well-known playwrights, such as Wendy Wasserstein (1989 Pulitzer Prize for *The Heidi Chronicles*), Jon Robin Baitz (*The Substance of Fire*), and Tony Kushner (1993 Pulitzer Prize for *Angels in America*), found success in the theater at a young age, there are others, such as Marsha Norman (1983 Pulitzer Prize for *'night, Mother*) and Jerry Sterner (*Other People's Money*), who had already established careers outside the theater. She worked on a newspaper; he was in the investment business. *The Kentucky Cycle,* which was awarded the 1992 Pulitzer Prize, is the work of an actor, Robert Schenkkan.

RECOMMENDED TRAINING

Courses in dramatic writing and play analysis are essential. A liberal arts education, with emphasis on comparative literature and creative writing, and familiarity with works by noted playwrights in all genres, is strongly advised. Playwrights should read plays to see how good writers solve problems.

Writers should also become involved in production and performing, to understand the physical limitations and emotional elements of theater. Anyone who expects to write for actors will do well to learn how it feels to play a scene.

Where to study may depend upon one's location and finances. Information on writing programs is available in annual publications and on the Internet. Where did the writers whose work you admire study? Who were their teachers? Suzan-Lori Parks and Wendy Wasserstein followed similar paths— both were undergraduates at Mt. Holyoke College and went on to graduate study in playwriting at Yale Drama School. University programs—such as those at Yale and Carnegie Mellon—offer opportunities for networking with aspiring directors, designers, and performers. However, finding the perceptive instructor who nurtures your talent at your stage of development may be more valuable than attending a chic school before you are ready. Investigate. New programs are always coming into prominence, as theater departments look for good teachers as well as the most promising students. Find out who the instructors are, what classes are taught, and who the graduates are.

Adult extension classes or a short-term playwriting course at the local Y could be ideal starting places.

JOB CONDITIONS

Even with a collaborator, writing is solitary, isolating work. Developing a play for production can take an agonizingly long time. Three years is not unusual. Once a play is in production, however, the situation is reversed; the author must be on hand at rehearsals, is under intense pressure from many people, and must be able to make changes quickly and furnish rewrites between performances, if necessary. Travel to regional theaters is a frequent necessity.

ANTICIPATED INCOME

Playwrights are self-employed and therefore do not receive a salary. They are paid only when someone wants to use their work. An interested producer will offer an option fee, to reserve the rights to stage the material for a specified period, during which the producer tries to raise the funds for a production. If a production materializes, producer and playwright (through their agents and lawyers, see pages 29–34) negotiate a contract for the production.

While the show is in rehearsal and tryouts, the playwright may receive a weekly stipend, which is an advance against royalties. Once the show opens, the playwright receives the agreed-upon royalty—a percentage of theater gross receipts (also negotiated)—during the run of the play. Additional royalties are earned each time the show is performed, by any company, anywhere.

Some playwrights earn very little money during their career. Others, such as A. R. Gurney, Jr., Beth Henley, David Mamet, Marsha Norman, and Neil Simon, win prestigious awards and achieve enormous satisfaction as well as great financial success.

As an example of how much can accrue from a seemingly innocuous idea—excellently produced, directed, and performed by a brilliant acting ensemble—consider Neil Simon's 1965 comedy *The Odd Couple,* which originally starred Walter Matthau and Art Carney as the incompatible bachelor-husbands. The show won three Tony Awards: best director (Mike Nichols), best play, and best actor (Matthau). That it would make a terrific movie was obvious; the film, with a screenplay by Simon, starred Walter Matthau and Jack Lemmon and reportedly broke all records when it opened at New York's Radio City Music Hall in 1968. Following that huge success, the title, situation, and characters—the leads now played by Jack Klugman and Tony Randall—became the basis for a long-running TV series. Later, it thrived as one of the most widely syndicated programs: Reruns are still being shown, Monday through Friday, on independent stations and on cable TV. Coming full circle, *The Odd Couple* was presented on Broadway again in 1985, when Neil Simon wrote a "female version." Rita Moreno and Sally Struthers played the ill-matched roommates. The TV series was later reprised with actors Ron Glass and Demond Wilson, and an animated cartoon version, *The Oddball Couple,* cast a fussy cat and a slobbering dog as the leading characters.

Neil Simon told an interviewer that the idea for the play came to him at a party in California. He realized that all twenty-four guests were divorced, and the men were all sharing apartments because it was the only way they could afford to pay alimony. In his memoir, *Rewrites,* he bemoaned the fact that he naively sold the rights to *The Odd Couple* to Paramount Pictures, and so has earned nothing from its television afterlife.

PROFESSIONAL AFFILIATIONS

Playwrights do not belong to a union, per se. But they can join the Dramatists Guild, a professional association of playwrights, composers, and lyricists that works to improve conditions, protect authors' rights, and formulate contracts. Associate membership is open to anyone who has written a play. Student membership is available to anyone enrolled in an accredited writing degree program. The Dramatists Guild publishes a quarterly journal, a monthly newsletter, and an annual theater directory.

FOR INFORMATION, CONTACT:

The Dramatists Guild
1501 Broadway
New York, NY 10036

Theatre Communications Group, Inc.
355 Lexington Avenue
New York, NY 10017

Anyone looking to become a member of the theater community is advised to join Theater Communications Group, or TCG, the national organization for the American theater since 1961. TCG publishes *The Dramatists' Sourcebook, American Theater* magazine (which includes scripts, interviews, and relevant information about theatrical activity across the country), and *Playsource,* a quarterly bulletin with information about new American plays. Their *Theater Directory* is an annual reference guide to the theaters, artists, and arts organizations that form the theatrical community. It's a fine networking primer.

CAREER SIDELINES, WITH PAY

While their work is being circulated for consideration at theaters, festivals, and production offices, playwrights can earn money writing monologues and scenes for actors who need original audition material. One playwright paid the rent by creating audition scenes out of what happened between the scenes in well-known plays, much as Tom Stoppard's *Rosencrantz and Guildenstern Are Dead* reveals the courtiers' behind-the-scenes experiences at Hamlet's Elsinore.

Local politicians and other office-holders who need to speak in public need good writers to help them sound charming and intelligent. They are likely paying clients, as are corporate executives. And independent production companies employ freelance scriptwriters for documentary and industrial films.

GETTING STARTED

Between rewrites for the new production of his play, *Teddy and Alice*, Jerome Alden took time out to discuss the playwright's life. His writing career began at the University of Oregon radio station, where undergraduates were required to produce, direct, and adapt material for broadcasting as well as perform it. Married to a sought-after ballet and Broadway show dancer, he enjoyed a busy acting career in New York. "I quit acting when my wife got pregnant and couldn't support me any more," he declared.

Writing documentaries and one-person shows—such as *Bully!*, which actor James Whitmore played on Broadway and on tour—provided the ample, steady income needed to send their four children to private school and college. Alden said:

> The way to get started is to write. Write something and submit it. And then write something else. Use what you have written to try to get an agent. It is very hard. Write and submit, write and submit. And say *yes* to everything! Because of the ten things that people will talk to you about, maybe one will come to fruition.
>
> You just have to keep doing it. If you're going to be in this business you have to have a positive attitude, because you are going to be rejected seven times a day. I've had wonderful things said about my work, and I've had terrible things said about it. I've had some plays optioned five times— they can't find a theater, or the right actor. Things happen that take the material out of your control. You have to be very secure. Maintain a sense of humor about yourself as well as your work.

SIMPLE RECOMMENDATIONS

One script reader was offended by the shoddy condition of several manuscripts piled on her desk. Here was material submitted in expectation that her company would spend hundreds of thousands of dollars to turn it into prime entertainment, yet one writer was content to send a bundle of loose pages, in varying colors and sizes, stuffed into a brown paper shopping bag tied with heavy string; another indicated corrections with red arrows and the words, "This goes after the next page." Some manuscripts were handwritten, with crossed-out phrases and inserted speeches that were almost impossible to read. She suggested to her employer that writers be made aware of basic submission standards. "We can't demand that people write well," she said, "but what they send us should at least be readable."

Anything going out with your name on it should attest to your professionalism. That means it is neatly typed (or computer-printed) on 8½ × 11 inch sheets of white paper (one side only). If you feel the need of a little color in your communication, confine it to your personal stationery, for cover letters—and keep it pastel. Day-glo orange does not exactly inspire optimism in a harried reader.

For each listing in *The Dramatists' Sourcebook* and *The Playwright's Companion* information is provided on what sort of material is wanted and how each contact prefers to be approached. Follow that advice. When sending a query to a producing organization or agent, include a polite cover letter telling the recipient what you are seeking. Give a brief overview of the work—how many characters, scenes, or set changes, as well as a concise summary of the action. If the script has been performed at all, include that information (the script history) and how it was received. Your own résumé should be included.

Never send out your original manuscript—only copies. Pages should be properly formatted and fitted into a sturdy cover bearing the title, the name of the author, and the author's representative, if any. A very good playwriting manual, *The Playwright's Process,* by award-winning dramatist Buzz McLaughlin (Back Stage Books) will answer all your questions about formatting, as well as the entire play-development process.

Your submission package should always include a brief cover letter; your synopsis of the action; the script history, if any; copies of any favorable reviews; your own résumé. Any original music that is part of the show should be represented by a professionally recorded audiotape.

What most people tend to omit is a self-addressed, stamped envelope (SASE) for the reader's response; a stamped, self-addressed postcard to be mailed when the material is received, and a SASE large enough for the manuscript to be returned to you. The cost of answering thousands of queries and returning hundreds of plays submitted to a nonprofit theater would quickly bankrupt the company.

THE PRODUCER

Everything that happens in a theatrical production is, ultimately, the producer's responsibility. Or, to put it another way, without a producer who is willing to accept the invigorating artistic and financial challenge, the best play will remain merely a script.

Veteran producer Barry Weissler said:

> I choose a project because it speaks to me. And I believe it works in a universal manner. Or it's just something so wonderful I feel I have to do it. *Falsettos* was a very esoteric piece. I felt I had to do it, since it was a very important piece of American theater. I did it because I wanted to. Luckily, it became a success.

To find material with dramatic potential, the producer cultivates relationships throughout the theatrical community. It's his or her business to attend play festivals, meet promising writers, talk to agents, read scripts, and scout college and regional theaters. He is also alert to what local talent is offering wherever he happens to be.

> In Miami, visiting my family, one evening I was alone, looking for something to do, some place to go, and I went to the theater. Someone had recommended *Family Secrets*. I felt that it would work in New York, so I made arrangements to get the rights. It took a year to get it all together. And I was right: It came to New York and was a smash.
>
> DAVID STONE, producer

Having identified a property and become convinced that it will captivate an audience, the producer's first step is to acquire production rights to the material. (At this point, the lawyer steps in—see page 29). Prior to officially seeking investors—angels, as they're fondly called—a producer will invest considerable time and money in developing the project—helping the writer discover and improve character development, plot construction, or dialogue, if necessary. Preliminary discussions with a director who is sensitive to the material will provide additional insight.

The producer will arrange staged readings, perhaps with an invited audience in attendance; following that, the property may be developed in a workshop production. Each showing is an opportunity to sharpen the material and gauge audience response. Together, producer, playwright, and director will consider a likely team of artists to fulfill their vision of the play.

> You fall in love with a project. You make it happen, whatever it is.
>
> James Freydberg, producer

As will become increasingly evident, personal relationships are of tremendous importance in show business. Unlike businesses that last for generations, each production has its own life—period. There's no time for someone to eventually catch on to the routine or be transferred to another department. Once agreements are signed, the clock starts ticking. Therefore, creative people working together for many months under tremendous pressure—after all, careers and money are at stake—need to do more than get along politely. People want to work with others whom they trust and whose work they know. Respect, admiration, plus the ability to spark each other's creativity—good chemistry—are required.

Doing the preliminary work leads to a clearer idea of the play's requirements: how many actors must be cast, how many sets and costumes must be built, what special effects, lighting, and sound are needed. The size, or scope, of the show will dictate the size of the theater needed to house the production. Those expenses, plus the cost of selling tickets and paying the company each week of performance, add up to what it will cost to produce and run the show. For specific line-by-line production cost analysis and operating budget, the producer engages another professional—the general manager (see page 35).

FINDING INVESTORS

Once he or she knows how much money it will cost to produce the play, the producer's job is to persuade investors to put up the money.

> People wanting to produce say to me, "I know raising money is important, but what about the rest?" I say: "Without the money, there is no 'rest'."
>
> Mitchell Maxwell, producer

> Raising money is one of the most cumbersome, least favorite parts of the job. Don't be shy. Tell people you are raising money. It's time-consuming, it's mean, it's bitter, but you must go after it with tenacity. Raising money is what separates the men from the boys and the women from the girls.
>
> Dorothy Olim, producer, general manager and former executive secretary of the Association of Theatrical Press Agents and Managers

In the hilarious Mel Brooks film *The Producers,* Zero Mostel and Gene Wilder oversell shares in their production of *Springtime For Hitler,* a musical they expect will never get beyond its opening night performance. Their plan is to get rich on the failure, because "No one cares what happens to the money in a flop!" To their consternation, the show is a smash hit, their double-dealing is exposed, and the rascal producers are sent to prison—where they soon have their fellow inmates lining up to buy shares in the upcoming jailhouse variety show.

Entertaining, certainly. Realistic? No.

Soliciting investors for a theatrical production is a legal transaction subject to carefully monitored securities regulations. In addition, New York is the only state which expressly regulates theatrical syndications. Theatrical productions are most commonly financed through the creation of a *limited partnership*. Other forms, called *subchapter S corporations* and *joint ventures*, are sometimes used as well.

The tax codes in effect when productions are organized may be a factor in determining the form of business. In any event, regulations spell out the number of people who may be solicited, how the money is to be spent and—most important to everyone anticipating a hit show—how the profits will be distributed.

Opportunities to invest in a show, called *offerings,* are described in a formal prospectus, each copy of which is numbered and registered with the office of the state's attorney general.

Potential investors attend backers' auditions, which may be held any place from the living room of a townhouse to a sparsely furnished rehearsal hall. The producer attempts to communicate enthusiasm about the play and its great potential to people who know little or nothing about the material. Supporting him or her will be the writer, the director, and possibly some of the leading players. If a star is interested in the show, that news will be imparted. The producer outlines the plot and may introduce the reading of a short scene. For a musical, the composer and lyricist perform their favorite parts of the score.

When the presentation is finished, interested individuals request a prospectus. Everyone on the team hopes that a slew of people will insist on writing a check. Otherwise, backer's auditions continue until all the shares have been sold, and the checks have been received.

INVESTORS WITH TITLES

Many shows' programs nowadays list a string of producers, associate producers, "produced in association with"s, and so on. Those titles usually indicate people who have been major participants in financing, or in locating investors for, a production. They rarely participate in production decisions.

> In 1960, my friend Shelly heard about a show that was looking for its last money. They needed $4,000. I said, "Are you crazy? We don't have that kind of money. Certainly not money to lose." But, if we liked the show, he said, we might be able to find people to invest, and we'd be associate producers.
>
> We went to someone's apartment to hear the backers' audition of this musical, and the composer, who couldn't play the piano very well, was plunking out the melodies. It seemed sort of simple, but I thought we

might find people who would be interested. And just think, we could be associate producers. So, we signed on.

That show was *The Fantasticks.* It is still running! And we're still listed as associate producers.

DOROTHY OLIM

STARTING PRODUCTION

Once financing is obtained, the producer engages the creative team. To the director will be added the choreographer and music director, if the show is a musical. The set, costume, and lighting designers, whom the producer has been talking to from the start, will be hired. And, perhaps, the leading actors will be signed, or a casting director will be engaged to assist in the talent search.

To trigger audience interest, the producer hires a press agent, an advertising agency and, possibly, a marketing specialist to dream up a dynamite sales campaign that will entice people to buy as many tickets as possible in advance. A healthy advance sale can be crucial, allowing a show to last until positive word of mouth begins to draw the anticipated crowds.

After consultation with the director and the playwright, the producer approves the set and costume designs; these are then exhibited and explained to the cast. The race to opening night is on.

IN PRODUCTION

The play is now in the hands of the director, the actors, and all the other experts involved with the physical production and interpretation of the script. Producers are less involved in day-to-day rehearsals than you might expect.

> I don't go to rehearsals, only to run-throughs. When you go to the rehearsal, you start to believe the stage stuff that goes on, and you believe it's happening. When you go to the run-through, you see the result of those rehearsals, and, if necessary, you are able to say, "Somehow, it's not happening."

JAMES FREYDBERG

What the producer has to focus on is increasing "the dollar possibility" of the project, Freydberg added. How is this done when the number of theater seats and weekly performances is limited and ticket prices are established? See to it that every seat gets sold for every performance.

The indefatigable producer also initiates plans for additional outlets—thereby widening distribution—for the product. For what is *not* limited is the possibility of playing in several theaters in cities across the country, in Canada, and overseas. At the beginning of 1997, there were several companies of Disney's *Beauty and the Beast,* and four of Andrew Lloyd Webber's *Sunset Boulevard*; A. R. Gurney's *Love Letters* was being performed in a small regional venue; and the national touring company of *How to Succeed in Business Without Really Trying* was playing in Los Angeles.

Producers thus get busy thinking ahead, arranging for all those kinds of subsequent presentations. They also seek to extend the initial run of the play by maintaining audience interest through innovative cast changes and attention-getting events.

> What made us survive, as opposed to those that fail? Taste, experience, an understanding of what it takes to make a theatrical piece live. A sense of how to sell a theatrical piece. Have you seen the campaign we did on *Grease!*?
>
> BARRY WEISSLER

No one who walked across 49th Street could miss it: The exterior of Broadway's Eugene O'Neill Theater, where the long-running revival of the musical *Grease!* is playing, is painted hot pink and covered with 1950s teenage lingo. The Weisslers have made the show a destination to be visited again and again by casting in leading roles for short engagements a series of highly visible performers the target audience will want to see: Rosie O'Donnell, Joe Piscopo, and Brooke Shields are among those who have played to packed houses. Between performances on summer weekends, outdoor celebrations featuring the cast encourage audience participation; one can only guess how many curious passersby became ticket buyers as a result.

ANTICIPATED INCOME

The producer does not get a salary. Until the show earns back its initial investment, he or she receives a weekly office fee for his or her activity and that of the producer's staff. After production expenses are recouped—recoupment is the point from which profits flow—the producer usually receives 50 percent of the profits. The investors share the remainder, apportioned according to the percentage of their investment.

Royalties due the writer, director, star, and any other participants who may have negotiated them, come from the producer's share.

To speed up the possibility of recoupment in what are now multimillion-dollar productions, the concept of a *royalty pool* has been put in place. When a show's weekly receipts exceed its weekly costs, 40 percent of the surplus is set aside to be distributed to the investors. In this way, investors see some return on their money before the entire cost of mounting the show has been recouped.

A show that fails to earn any surplus is just breaking even—paying its weekly operating expenses to the company and the theater management. If expenses exceed income the production operates at a loss and closes.

While costs must be recouped for each additional company, the possibility of substantial additional income exists there also, for producer and investors alike.

ATTRIBUTES OF A PRODUCER

Consider which aspects of the producer's role appeal to you—besides reaping half the profits, of course:

- Is it reading scripts? Approaching investors? Being part of the theatrical world?
- Do you have an entrepreneurial bent?
- Do you like organizing the endless details so that everything goes smoothly according to your plan? Do you think of yourself as well organized? A good manager?
- Do you have a talent for putting people and projects together?
- Can you deal persuasively with all sorts of people—even people who may disagree with you—and explain why your idea will surely achieve the desired result?
- Do you see yourself working with a writer to improve a script?
- Do you care about bringing new ideas to a larger audience?
- Do you believe you can tell what audiences will like?

Also consider your ability to stick with an assignment for a long period of time. Do you tend to lose patience? A capable producer has to stay the course while doing all of the above—and do them well.

Many of today's producers got their start as performers. Some of them shared their insights:

> I was an actor, and then I became a director and was partners with a fellow with whom I produced a company called the National Shakespeare Company. In 1964, my wife and I set out to produce theater on all levels for the school systems of the United States. We had plays and musicals that fit the Catholic parochial school system; we had Shakespearean productions; plays that were classics in the American theater, by Arthur Miller or Tennessee Williams, that fit the high school or college curriculum; and we had a series that played for elementary schools that included such children's classics as *Tom Sawyer, Swiss Family Robinson, Oliver Twist,* and so on.
>
> We began to take on other companies—some of these contained the stars of their medium, be it dance, or opera, or theater. James Earl Jones was one of the gentlemen working for us, doing a one-man play on Paul Robeson. We had eighteen productions going at the same time—nine companies did two each.
>
> My wife and I were untrained. We trained ourselves. But then we had the entire United States to tour for so many years, learning our craft. I wanted to be in the theater business. Doing plays for schools seemed to be a less risky way to go about it.
>
> BARRY WEISSLER

The Weisslers' first Broadway production was *Othello,* in 1982 and starred none other than James Earl Jones in the title role, Christopher Plummer as Iago, and Dianne Wiest as Desdemona.

> I was a working actress, although not an obvious ingenue heroine. I had a definite musical sound and a sense of comedy, so I found more work in nightclubs. Julius Monk [producer of an acclaimed series of cabaret revues] called me a *diseuse*—a singer who talked.
>
> When my daughter was born, I no longer wanted to work at night, come home in time for her 5 A.M. bottle, and then go to sleep. I got together with another performer, Lee Reynolds, and we decided the thing to do was to put on our own revue. We knew the performers and all the writers. We put the talent and the material together and called it *Wet Paint.* Linda Lavin was in the cast. We managed a respectable run because it was good. It was a great experience, and I was on my way.
>
> ISOBEL ROBINS

Her 1972 production of *The Changing Room* earned the New York Drama Critics Circle Award for best play (and a best actor Tony for John Lithgow).

For the past several years, she has been developing *Jack,* a musical about President Kennedy and his father by Will Holt, the composer and lyricist. She mounted a workshop and then sought a way to develop it further with a different audience:

> Max Weisenhofer [a fellow producer] introduced me to the musical theater department at the University of Oklahoma. Out of that production, we found that we need a different set and that the piece needs a more defined focus. Working in colleges is great, because they have such excellent facilities, and this way the students learn what theater really is. They learn discipline. Now, the University of Oklahoma offers a master's degree in Musical Theater, thanks to *Jack*!

David Richenthal, producer of *The Kentucky Cycle* and *Mrs. Klein,* in New York, is a lawyer. So are Bruce Lazarus, Donald I. Farber, and the legendary David Merrick, whose more than ninety productions include *Hello, Dolly!,* *42nd Street,* and *Oliver!* James Freydberg was in the brokerage business. Actress Carole Rothman teamed up with Robyn Goodman to bring back plays they had seen and loved; they founded a theater for this purpose, refurbished a space on Manhattan's West Side, and called it Second Stage.

Like Elizabeth McCann, who was a top Broadway stage manager before she and Nelle Nugent teamed up as producers, Debbie Falb spent several years as a stage manager, particularly for the plays of Athol Fugard in San Diego and in South Africa. She later founded the Synergos Theater Project in Providence, Rhode Island. Also from the ranks of stage managers comes Michael David, of Dodger Productions.

Casey Childs, founder of the off-Broadway company Primary Stages, in Manhattan, is a director. He recalled:

> By the time I got here, I had done every job in the theater. And that is what I think all people interested in this business should do. Learn how to be a person of the theater. Do it all to get the training. Then you will respect it. You should paint scenery, sew costumes. The whole thing.

As Dorothy Olim told it, she was "saved from acting" by the director of the acting course she took after her second year of college:

> When he took me aside and said he thought I should be doing something else, I was devastated. I thought I was doing really good work. He said, "You are very talented. But you are also very tall. You are a character actress, not an ingenue. You won't work until you're 35."
>
> He suggested doing something else in the theater. "Why not be a producer? You say your parents are business people, you probably know about budgets and things like that."
>
> I admitted that I could add and subtract, but, I added, "Being a producer isn't artistic."
>
> "Oh, yes, it is," he said, and asked where I was going to school. I had just enrolled at Columbia University, which had an excellent theater program under the direction of Milton Smith, and a superb theater, the Brander Matthews. He said, "Excellent. Do the production work there. Do everything. You'll have plenty of opportunity. No one wants to be in production."
>
> I asked why, and he said, "Because everyone thinks it's no fun!"
>
> And it was! I did everything. It's smart to learn the crafts—painting, lighting, sewing. And I did the box office. And, with two friends I bought a theater, the Saranac Lake Summer Theater. Richard Edelman was the director, Shelly Baron was an actor, and I produced. We had a wonderful, awful time for five years. And then we sold it and made a profit!

PROFESSIONAL ORGANIZATIONS

The League of American Theaters and Producers is the professional trade organization of the commercial legitimate theater. Its members are producers, theater owners and operators, and local presenters across the country. The League handles labor relations and negotiations for the industry and does marketing, economic, and media research. Other programs include tourism promotion and presentation, with the Ameri-

FOR INFORMATION, CONTACT:

The League of American
Theaters and Producers
226 West 47th Street
New York, NY 10036-1487

A.R.T./New York
131 Varick Street,
Room 904
New York, NY 10013

Alternate ROOTS
1083 Austin Avenue
Atlanta, GA 30307

can Theater Wing, annual presenter of the Antoinette Perry, or Tony, Awards.

The Alliance of Resident Theatres/New York (A.R.T./New York) is the service organization for New York City's more than 250 nonprofit theater companies, and serves as an information resource and network.

A group called Alternate ROOTS (Regional Organization of Theatres South) serves Southern artists and arts organizations.

Theatre Communications Group (see page 15) serves nonprofit professional theater organizations, providing a national forum and communications network for 18,000 individual members and more than 300 theaters.

RECOMMENDED TRAINING

The simplest way to gain familiarity with the rudiments of producing for the theater—be it Broadway, off-Broadway, or touring ("road") productions—would be to attend the annual seminar of the Commercial Theater Institute. During the three-day intensive program, industry leaders—many of them CTI seminar graduates—conduct classes on the legal, financial, and marketing aspects of theatrical production. There's plenty of time for questions from the audience. A reception at the end of each day provides additional opportunities to talk with the speakers and to network with the rest of the group.

FOR INFORMATION, CONTACT:

The Commercial Theatre Institute
250 West 57th Street, Suite 1818
New York, NY 10107

A joint project of the Theatre Development Fund and the League of American Theaters and Producers, CTI was created in 1982 by Frederic B. Vogel, a former actor whose career had begun at the age of nine. After switching to the front office, he held administrative positions with theaters throughout the United States. This experience opened his eyes to the burgeoning regional theater movement. Vogel said: "There were all these people doing theater and they didn't know how. It was up to us to show them." He became head of FEDAPT—the Foundation for the Expansion and Development of American Professional Theatre—which offered developmental and technical assistance to more than 500 theaters, dance organizations, and performing arts centers throughout the country.

Each new season brings productions created and developed by CTI alumni. Teri Childs and her husband Tim have produced Patrick Stewart's version of Charles Dickens' *A Christmas Carol.* William Repicci and Linda Thorsen Bond, who had met at a CTI seminar, wrote and produced *Swingtime Canteen,* which played for ten months in New York prior to a London opening and a subsequent national tour.

In addition to the weekend seminar, the Commercial Theatre Institute offers a comprehensive fourteen-week course, "Producing for the Theatre."

GETTING STARTED

Just as beginning playwrights are encouraged to write original audition scenes for actors, novice producers can start by producing a showcase for actors who want agents and casting directors to get to know their work. The same producing skills will be necessary. (Instead of soliciting investors, the producer can ask the actors to share the cost of producing their show.) And many of the people a producer would like to know will probably be on the actors' invited guest list. If the program goes really well, it's conceivable that other performers might willingly pay a fee for such expertise.

The newcomer who seriously wants to go further may find that some producers are very willing to provide opportunities to learn:

Get in, like an immigrant in a new country. Pay attention. Contribute your savvy, your expertise, your resources. What are your tools? Volunteer to work in our office. Sit in and learn. The process is exciting.

MITCHELL MAXWELL

In my junior year at college, I was lucky: I got an internship at Jujamcyn. I was the literary intern. I got to see every play, read every script that was submitted and make a report.

In my last year of school, I wrote to everybody. I got an interview with the Weisslers. I was with them for four years, during which I worked seven days a week, fourteen hours a day. They were generous. They taught me everything, introduced me to everyone. And my age didn't matter.

To other people, I'd say, "Just do it!" I used the money I had saved to go to law school (I lasted there about a day). That kept me going a year and a half—and then I found my play.

DAVID STONE

We have an apprenticeship program here. We take young men and women—we must have four with us right now who are as bright and as hard-working as they can possibly be. They get a very small stipend each week, and they work and learn their craft by doing. We've had one young woman who's at Rutgers University. She started with us a year ago, went back to school, and now she's back for the summer. She's learning her way in the theater business. That's available for any young person who wants to work in the theater business. With each of the shows we do, there is always an apprentice program. They get into it by calling me, or writing. They work hard; they give a lot back to us.

BARRY WEISSLER

I sent out tons and tons of résumés to names I got from *Theatrical Index*. I am probably one of two people on Broadway who got there without knowing anyone. It has opened my eyes in so many ways. This has made me sure of my theater arts major.

To live a creative life—it is so much more interesting. I come home and actually have something to say about what I did at work. There is so much that goes on here. And we are such a part of it.

I have to give Barry Weissler credit. He wants to bring people into the field, which is probably the only reason I got this job.

Most of my friends think that theater is just acting. When I told them I was applying for a theater managerial job, they said, "Why do you want to do the business stuff?" But general managing, producing, it's not like being in a business—you deal with everything. I don't know whether I want to try company managing or think about going on the road with a show. . . . It has totally opened my eyes to how many different things there are to do behind the scenes. There are such opportunities that no one knows exist!

KATHRYN FINNEFROCK, apprentice in the Weissler office

In this business you need education, sure, but you really need street smarts. You need a little taste, and a lot of enthusiasm. The Oregon Shakespeare Festival is the most successful theater in the country—and that was started by a classics teacher in Oregon. And he even says that, really, they just didn't know when they were making mistakes or what they were. They just kept on.

CASEY CHILDS

ATTORNEYS AND TALENT REPRESENTATIVES

As soon as he or she has decided on a property, the producer consults an entertainment attorney—an expert in the particular terms and practices of theater law—to prepare the *option agreement*. This agreement grants the producer the right, for a certain length of time, to produce the play in exchange for a fee paid to the author. The author, in turn, may represent him- or herself or be represented by an attorney or agent. Essentially, writer and producer share the same goal—they want to increase the value of the property by achieving a long-running success; they differ in that the producer would like to pay as little as possible to try to do so, and have as much time as necessary to get the play securely on its feet and into a suitable theater. Lawyers are needed because the size of the payment, the length of the option, and the kind of production, are all negotiable.

If, as we mentioned earlier, the play is derived from other material, it is the attorney's job to secure the underlying rights from the original author.

Anticipating success, or at least favorable recognition, the producer will want to acquire the rights to produce the play in other areas—Colorado, Canada, England, or Japan, for example—and to create a touring company. The producer will also want to acquire the *subsidiary rights,* a share in the author's profits from a movie or television deal or fees paid by amateur or professional theater groups that lease the play for public performances.

> My play *Generation* is like an apartment. People who want to use it have to pay me rent.
>
> WILLIAM GOODHART, playwright

The author's billing in the ads and posters, the number of house seats, approval of director and cast, and most important, the amount of the author's royalty percentage, plus whatever additional relevant conditions the principals wish to arrange, are also part of their negotiations.

Preparation of the option agreement, contracts, and the financial prospectus to be offered to potential investors, represents but one facet of the work performed by an attorney in the field of entertainment.

> It goes beyond productions. I have clients who are industries in themselves. We do licensing deals, cosmetics—it's endless.
>
> LOREN PLOTKIN, attorney

The Bar Associations of New York City and New York State have separate sections for members specializing in entertainment, arts, and sports law (the fields are linked because sports nowadays is seen as entertainment). Legal developments are chronicled in a newsletter, *Entertainment Law and Finance.* This publication hosts an annual event, "Entertainment Law, the Year in Review," which is open to students and nonlawyers as well.

ATTRIBUTES OF ENTERTAINMENT ATTORNEYS

As entertainment attorney Loren Plotkin pointed out, most lawyers in this field have an affinity for the arts. One partner at his firm, he noted, is a long-time composer. Joyce Gordon, one of television's most successful spokes-women and former president of Screen Actors Guild, in New York, surprised her colleagues by stepping away from the microphones to study law. She now serves as a trustee of the union's health and retirement fund.

Certainly, the performance aspect of the legal profession is attractive to someone who is truly at ease communicating to any audience. Solomon Glushak, who was once a popular working actor, recalled: "The future, a life of role-playing, was not enough. What I wanted to do, I realized, was study law." Second in his class at New York University's Law School, he made Law Review, and on graduation Glushak became secretary to a justice on the U.S. Court of Appeals. Theater people were his first clients; recommendation from the owner of a summer theater led to a twenty-five-year assignment as coun-sel for the Council of Stock Theaters (COST). Subsequently, he represented the fledgling Society of Stage Designers and Choreographers.

On the other hand, Loren Plotkin already had a general law practice when a friend who was producing a show in London asked his advice. When he protested that he didn't know anything about the field, the friend pointed out that the information was available "if you pursue it." Plotkin explained:

I made it a point to learn something, went to London with him, and paid attention. I didn't like some of the things that were going on. I told him so. They were changed. I brought a new point of view. Then I really began to pur-sue it. And then some of his friends who were in the industry retained me.

I love it. Artists see, they create, and what they create has longevity. What they do causes evolution. And you stay young pursuing this avenue.

Pleasure in the energetic pursuit of information, attention to detail, and abil-ity to negotiate are necessary personality ingredients for anyone considering this career. Add to that the ability to think creatively:

We are involved in rethinking things. What is fair for the relationship? What are the historical antecedents? We want to do better for our client, but we are not trying to kill the other side. *Too* good a deal is not really good.

LOREN PLOTKIN

In this chaotic business, you try to make peace for both sides.

SOLOMON GLUSHAK

RECOMMENDED TRAINING

"Get the best education you can afford" is everyone's recommendation, and Loren Plotkin advised, "Learn about the business aspects of the profession."

> For theatrical law you must know something about the theater. You have to know your clients' needs . . . budgets, reserves, anything within the arena. You must be conversant with the industry. And you must network. Dealing with creative people in the arts, you are dealing with very thinly coated egos.
>
> You must know the territory, and with the new technologies, the law is being written almost as we speak. A few years ago, there was one volume to refer to. Now there are six, and more on the way.

SOLOMON GLUSHAK

At the moment there are no "feeder" schools for this specialty. However, an undergraduate major in communications, theater, or film production would provide excellent support for the law degree. As increasing numbers of productions are adaptations of books and movies and revivals (and revisals) of plays or musicals, it should be evident that the aspiring entertainment attorney cannot design his or her practice specifically for theater, or film, or television, but needs to know the ins and outs of all areas of show business, plus the wider worlds of art, fashion, and sports. There's a lot that comes under the general heading of entertainment these days.

Loren Plotkin has also observed that this is becoming "a great field for women."

ANTICIPATED INCOME

In our society, people are willing to pay well for advice from a qualified source. How much is difficult to say, because of the nature of the industry. Small shows can go from having legal matters arranged as a favor by an attorney friend to an expense of many thousands of dollars.

Getting some productions together can be difficult, but everyone seems to agree that it is rarely impossible.

> A producer may want to do a theatrical production based on a well-known movie. Well, the answer to that will probably be "No." A studio is not about to license the use of its blockbuster film. But rights can be assembled.

LOREN PLOTKIN

As you might imagine, the intricate task of assembling rights will include protecting the original creators while assuring that everyone involved in the resulting production is properly compensated for his or her contribution. It's a process that can easily consume many hours of an attorney's week, month, or possibly years. Legal services are billed by the hour. A ten-minute phone conversation will be charged at one-sixth of the attorney's billable rate. Ninety dollars may buy the hourly services of a recent graduate; expert guidance—on the phone or in person—will cost hundreds and, eventually, thousands of dollars per sixty-minute segment. The attorney's clock starts ticking with "Hello."

GETTING STARTED

The business in New York is characterized by medium-size firms whose clients' interests include fashion, sports, and books as well as theater. Los Angeles, as might be expected, is studded with huge corporations, guiding hundreds of clients whose affairs demand the service of a cadre of attorneys. Ideally, someone aspiring to the L.A. style will get experience with a New York entertainment law firm. Having learned the business, that attorney will head west.

> In Los Angeles, litigation is considered a form of negotiation.
>
> STAN SOOCHER, editor-in-chief, *Entertainment Law and Finance*

The attorney's career may begin in a producer's office, a general manager's office, or an agent's office. The legal departments of any of the unions and professional associations serving the industry would be appropriate places to look for an opening.

Go to the theater and see plays. Every theater program will include the names of those law firms in any way connected with the production. If you see that the same firms appear to handle several plays, the chances are that those are busy offices that might be seeking to enlarge the staff.

Volunteer Lawyers for the Arts would seem a good place for networking.

PROFESSIONAL ORGANIZATIONS

Volunteer Lawyers for the Arts (VLA) has been providing free legal assistance to artists and arts organizations since 1969. In the New York area, more than 800 attorneys donate their time to artists and arts organizations from all creative disciplines —not only the theater, but also the worlds of dance, visual arts, film, video, and music. They give counsel and representation on arts-related legal matters to those whose problems would otherwise remain unsolved or whose interests would be unrepresented.

> FOR INFORMATION, CONTACT:
>
> Volunteer Lawyers for the Arts
> 1 East 53rd Street
> New York, NY 10022
>
> Entertainment Law and Finance
> 345 Park Avenue South
> New York, NY 10016

In addition, VLA offers clinics and workshops which provide instruction on arts-related legal issues, organizes conferences and produces publications on topics concerning the creative community, and serves as a clearinghouse for arts organizations throughout the country. VLA also publishes a directory of other volunteer lawyers for arts organizations, runs a Speakers Bureau, and maintains a VLA ArtLaw Hotline for quick answers to emerging legal questions.

The American Bar Association, and your local county, city, and state Bar Associations, have divisions on entertainment and sports law. Specific information will be available at the local level; similar matters may be treated differently from one area to the next.

As mentioned above, *Entertainment Law and Finance* is a newsletter available to lawyers, law students, and other interested parties. This resource also publishes an annual review of cases in the field.

TALENT REPRESENTATIVES

In their negotiations with producers, artists such as playwrights, directors, performers, and even some designers are customarily represented by agents. In a sense, agents act as a buffer between the client and the producer, so their relationship can be solely about the project. The agent haggles for the money; the client creates the art.

Franchised by the talent unions or guilds, agents collect a commission, usually 10 percent, on the work their clients do. Some agents work exclusively with signed clients (agreements can be for a year). Others may handle talent on a freelance basis.

Agents have access: Presumably they have established relationships with all the producers and casting directors who are in the business of buying the talent they hope to sell. They also are présuméd to know everything that's going on in the business, so as to wrest the best terms for the client from any negotiation.

There are agents who choose to work as independents, handling only a few clients. The service they provide is almost like personal career management. This presupposes that the client has a thriving career to manage and the agent has the experience and imagination to further realize the client's potential.

Others may prefer to be part of a large agency, representing clients in all areas of the business. There is always the possibility, say, of a writer client and a director client collaborating on a project that employs the agency's performing clients.

Because they work on commission, agents will naturally tend to expend their greatest energies on the highest-earning of their established clients. They expect that lesser-known talents will be energetic in finding ways to showcase their own work: There is little to negotiate, or be realized, on a writer's first play or an actor's debut appearance.

The agent's challenge is to be able to recognize talent when it appears and to nurture it, until the anticipated success is achieved. In the early stages, both client and agent are gambling on their expectations for the client's future.

The late Marie Stroud, who represented writers as well as performers, was revered because of her willingness to devote time to unknowns:

You stick with them because you believe in them. Sometimes it just takes a while. You hope that your high earners will make enough for you to hold on until those slow ones hit their stride.

When the client of a small agency makes a breakthrough, the big offices pay attention. From her office in London, long-time agent Patricia Marmont reported:

One of my dear clients was doing a film in California. There was a concerted effort to persuade my client to leave me and join them. They were like sharks! I wondered if I should have been there with my umbrella, to fend them off.

ATTRIBUTES OF AN AGENT

Talent representatives do seem to share personality traits: They are energetic, perceptive, and confident, as dedicated to the business as any of the artists they represent. Many have worked as performers, directors, or writers. Some are highly educated; others gravitated to the business right out of high school. They all appear to have a knack for establishing relationships.

I love actors, I love the process of rehearsal, I love backstage, hanging lights, all of it. I love theater, and it never really mattered to me what I did.

I was an assistant in the business affairs office at the Dramatists Guild. Lois Berman's office was right next door to the Guild, and I'd walk over to hand her the royalty checks for her clients, so we got to know each other really well. She called me when *A Walk in the Woods* was on Broadway (Berman's client was the play's author, Lee Blessing) and asked if I wanted to work one day a week doing her books. And I was able to do that. Then, when she wanted a full time assistant she offered the job to me, and that was that.

I really began to notice that it was much more comfortable for me to promote other people, versus myself. And I enjoyed putting people together—that seems very creative to me, and satisfying.

JUDY BOALS, Berman Boals & Flynn

JOB REALITIES

The business of representing talent is highly competitive. Success, failure, or anything in between are almost totally unpredictable. Signed clients may be lured away by powerful rivals—who may promise more than they can realistically deliver.

The way to get started is, as always, to begin at the very bottom—perhaps as a gofer in an agent's office. Educate yourself. Be alert—keep your eyes and ears open and see if you like the action. Learn the business and learn the history.

Anticipated income? Ten percent.

THE GENERAL MANAGER

To raise money to finance the production, the producer needs to know how much it will cost. There is no seeking of funds without papers of solicitation —that is, a formal offering. You need an attorney, preferably one experienced in theatrical law, and a general manager, who creates a financial analysis.

The *capitalization budget* lists the amounts needed to open the show. These will include the cost of the physical production—sets, costumes, lights, and sound–rehearsal costs; salaries and rentals; advertising, publicity, and general administrative costs; actors' and musicians' salaries; and director's and designers' fees—plus all the deposits, advances, and bonds needed to comply with the requirements of the theatrical unions. There is also a healthy amount set aside as a contingency reserve.

Another budget, the *operating budget* shows how much it will cost to run the show each week. Included are:

- Salaries
- Equipment rental
- Departmental expenses: items used in the production, such as props, costumes, wigs, and their maintenance
- Advertising and publicity
- General and administrative expenses
- Theater rental
- Fixed royalties

The general manager also computes a *break-even schedule*—the number of tickets that will have to be sold, and at what prices, for the show to meet its weekly operating costs. Included in this also are recoupment schedules which give the number of weeks it will take for the show to pay back its original investment—the costs shown in the capitalization budget.

"Civilians" do not understand. When I describe my work as a professional general manager, I try to explain that this particular occupation in the theater is so exclusive that there are perhaps only a hundred people in the world who do it. That's not an exaggeration: Where there are theater people—the United States, England, France, Italy, Australia—there are only a hundred of us. And in all these countries we find the problems are the same, and the jokes are the same. When I visited Australia, I met a general manager there and we spoke the same language, except for a bit of local jargon. It was uncanny. Like being part of a very large world.

DOROTHY OLIM

Until the 1960s, a relatively small group of producers dominated the theatrical business—such legendary names as Max Gordon, Kermit Bloomgarden, David Merrick, Harold Prince, Roger L. Stevens, Rodgers & Hammerstein, Robert Whitehead—and they knew perfectly well how to produce by themselves. With lengthy lists of investors they could rely on for backing, they were multishow producers, always busy year in and year out. General managers in those days were full-time salaried employees who managed a single producer's shows, and they really knew the territory. Their heads were full of nuggets of information such as the rental cost and capacity—including the number of partial-view seats—of every theater in the district and out of town, which enabled them to read a script and suggest the two or three most suitable houses for the show. They knew the heads of all the theatrical unions, clauses of all the labor agreements, and could pretty much guess the total weekly salaries of cast and crew. Added to their store of knowledge were industry-wide relationships that had been built up over many years and innumerable productions. Thus qualified, they effectively ran the producer's business, freeing the producer to pay attention to the aesthetics of the show. A general manager was equivalent to a chief financial officer in the corporate world.

And then the theatrical world began to change:

Financing of shows became so much more complex, a lot of the older producers couldn't deal with it the way they did before. And new people came in. Financial people got involved. People of no experience other than investing.

RICHARD SEADER, general manager

Along came all these new people with no skills, and they were looking to produce off-Broadway. And these new people needed help with budgets, unions, technical stuff, financial details. By 1963, Gerald Krone and I, as partners, had produced five shows, and someone asked us to manage their show. We became working managers with a steady income. We never got back to producing, and we found we got great pleasure out of general managing.

DOROTHY OLIM

The job has not changed. However, the general manager is now an independent entrepreneur, employed by any number of producers. For the preliminary work—"getting out the papers"—the general manager charges a fee. When a show goes into production, the general manager is in charge of all operating costs and negotiates contracts with everyone, from leading players, designers, directors, and theater owners to scenery and costume shops and hairstylists.

Contract negotiations cover not just salaries, fees, and royalties, but such details as billing in the program, the relative size of an artist's name in all advertising and on the billboards outside the theater, size and decoration of the star's dressing room, and a car and driver for the star.

When rehearsals begin, the general manager assigns a company manager to be present at all times and serve as the production's representative in any matters concerning the actors, stage managers, and theater personnel (see pages 89–91).

After opening night, the general manager is in charge of all finances; he or she keeps costs under control and approves every bill for every penny spent. For this work the general manager is paid a weekly fee for the run of the show; some managers may also receive a percentage of the show's weekly receipts and/or a small participation in net profits.

> If they [the producers] have succeeding companies, the general manager makes all the arrangements. All those contracts are your job, your responsibility. It's a very exciting job. Of course, you do it 24 hours a day, seven days a week. The most I ever handled at the same time was six, and it was tough.
>
> RICHARD SEADER

Implicit in the general manager's effective handling of every detail is the ability to discuss all matters with the producer as an equal. Otherwise, the project will necessarily suffer.

> The general manager has to be able to talk to the producer and say: "Why spend on this and not on that?" The first question theater owners ask is: "Who's the general manager?"
>
> ROGER GINDI, general manager

BECOMING A GENERAL MANAGER

Roger Gindi was a theater business major, and started as a gofer in a manager's office. Richard Seader had been a cellist with the Dallas Symphony Orchestra and went into concert management. With those skills, he was able to transfer to theatrical management, starting as a company manager and moving up to general manager.

Among the many successful women in the profession, Maria DiDia apprenticed with a producer; since establishing her own office, she has functioned as both a producer and general manager.

> From the ranks of company managers, who carry union cards, up floats a possible general manager. Or, from the ranks of producers, down drifts a general manager. It's a demanding job. They have to run it all. And they have to have done it all, so they understand it.
>
> DOROTHY OLIM

What, then, does the aspiring general manager need to know? Everyone agrees that hands-on knowledge of the ins and outs of theater is essential. This sort of awareness can be acquired, early on, at no cost other than the investment of time in volunteering to work with a local school or community theater group. Be willing to assist in any and every area of management or production.

Excellent *formal* preparation for this career is the theater business major. One could also choose a liberal arts theater major, with a graduate degree in either business or arts administration.

ATTRIBUTES OF A GENERAL MANAGER

Handling full responsibility for a costly production demands a person of enormous skill who is able to interact with a wide range of temperaments—from explosive stars to meticulous craftspeople. To do well, that person must care about the theater, understand the artistic process *and* the business, keep their demands in proper perspective, and be able to act decisively.

ANTICIPATED INCOME

General managers belong to no union, although those who have risen from the ranks of company managers will be members of the Association of Theatrical Press Agents and Managers (ATPAM). Their fees, weekly salaries, and percentages are negotiated with the producer and will be in proportion to the scale and complexity of the production.

PROFESSIONAL AFFILIATIONS

The already mentioned (see page 25) League of American Theaters and Producers—the professional trade organization of the commercial legitimate theater—is a useful contact. (A similar group, the League of Off-Broadway Theaters and Producers is a loosely knit, floating aggregation.) The Alliance of Resident Theatres/New York (A.R.T./New York) is the trade and service organization for the city's not-for-profit theaters.

The League of Professional Theater Women/New York is a not-for-profit organization of women representing a variety of disciplines in the industry. The League was created in 1979 as an advocacy group to promote visibility and increase opportunities for women in professional theater. Through seminars, educational programs, social events, and festivals, the League provides an ongoing forum for ideas, methods, and issues of concern to the theatrical community and its audiences.

> **FOR INFORMATION, CONTACT:**
>
> League of American Theaters and Producers
> 226 West 47th Street
> New York, NY 10036
>
> A.R.T./New York
> 131 Varick Street, Suite 904
> New York, NY 10013
>
> League of Professional Theater Women/NY
> c/o Shari Upbin Productions
> 300 East 56th Street
> New York, NY 10022

THE DIRECTOR

It is the director's job to take the playwright's words from the printed page and bring them to thrilling life onstage. Well, yes, of course—but it's not as easy as it sounds, otherwise there would be legions of first-rate theatrical directors. But as Jon Jory, producing director of Actors Theatre of Louisville, wrote (in *American Theatre* magazine), there are barely ten directors to whom he would entrust a script.

What we need are good directors! Where are they?

UTA HAGEN, actress

The director's work can be divided into three major phases, and a good director is expected to be proficient at all of them.

In Phase 1, he or she studies the script to identify the play's theme, or spine, or center; works with the playwright to be certain that they are in agreement as to the theme and the director's visualization of it; meets with set, costume, lighting, and sound designers to generate ideas for the physical environment; makes a list of possible performers and, in most cases, consults with a casting director who will have additional suggestions. All this work begins long before rehearsals.

You can't fix the spine in rehearsals. So don't start until you have it.

LLOYD RICHARDS, director

If you don't know what the center of the play is, you won't know where to set it!

TINA PACKER, director, Shakespeare and Co.

I look for the spine, what all the characters want, all the time.

GERALD GUTIERREZ, director

Phase 2 concerns the director in relation to the actors. The common wisdom has it that good directing is 85 percent casting. When actors audition, the director has to imagine, or guess, what the finished performance will be like, and how it will serve the play. The director not only must choose the right actor for each role, but also gather actors who work well together within the demands of the script. They must belong to the same emotional family and appear to inhabit the same time period. Therefore, during the audition process, a director will frequently suggest that performers try different approaches to the material—to get an inkling of how they take direction and witness their improvisation skills.

Having selected the most impressive performers, the director has but a few weeks in a rehearsal hall to bring them up to the emotional levels the script demands. At the start of rehearsals, the director's first task is to create an emotional environment, an atmosphere, in which everyone can feel secure; actors need freedom to be dreadful while trying to find their way into their characters. The director's understanding that people work at different speeds is crucial. At the same time, the director is alert to the pace and rhythm of every moment, placing the characters within the space and deciding when they move, stand, or sit, so that punch lines and plot lines are properly punctuated. By focusing the audience's attention, the director ensures that the dynamics of the play are clear.

> Once you start rehearsals, it's like a toboggan slide: You pass a point where you have to go all the way. You can't get off.
>
> LLOYD RICHARDS

In Phase 3, the production moves into the theater. Actors, sets, and costumes finally come together, and the director can see how it all works and what needs to be changed. Timing the speeches and adjusting actions to fit the realities of opening doors on the set and sitting in real armchairs is simple and to be expected. But revamping sets, clothing, or props can be very costly. (Here is where the general manager's contingency allowance becomes useful.) These are long, difficult days for the director, who must give actors' notes as well as production cues, often simultaneously.

> The director's job is lonely. You are in charge of the production.
>
> JULIANNE BOYD, director and president,
> Society of Stage Directors and Choreographers

The technical rehearsals accomplished, the play goes into previews, where additional fine-tuning continues. And then the clock ticks to opening night. After that, the director delivers the play to the actors and the audience. The job is done. The director may look in on the show periodically to see that the level of performance is maintained and eliminate "improvements" that may have crept into the performance. He or she may rehearse cast replacements—particularly in the case of a new star—and additional companies, although the production stage manager is more often the one to handle those responsibilities.

WHAT DIRECTORS NEED TO KNOW

Since the 1940s, our best directors have been former actors. Elia Kazan, Robert Lewis, Gene Saks, Mike Nichols, Jerry Zaks, and Gerald Gutierrez are Tony Award winners whose names top the list. Bob Fosse and Michael Bennett were both superb performers in musicals before they directed them. In

Tommy Tune's impressive collection of Tony Awards is one for his performance in *Seesaw*. This is not to say that only performers can be fine directors, but that, certainly, a director should know what it is like to be a performer.

Acting breaks down inhibitions, liberates talent.

GERALD GUTIERREZ

Act! Then you know where they're coming from.

JERRY ZAKS

I was acting, and I realized the so-called director had not a clue. He had not prepared. He didn't know what each scene was about. And I decided then and there that directing was what I wanted to do.

JULIANNE BOYD

You must act. Actors are the director's tools. You must know how to use them.

ROBERT MOSS, director

Directors also need to know plays. Aspiring directors may not be able to ally themselves with playwrights who are willing to entrust their precious new works to a novice, but there is a wealth of opportunity in the public domain; as mentioned earlier, no one needs to acquire the rights to present the works of Shakespeare, Marlowe, Sheridan, Goldsmith, and many others.

Emily Mann and Marshall Mason, artistic directors of theater companies that have earned great acclaim, both offer the same advice: Know the classics. Do the classics. That's where the great minds and spirits are.

College training—a theater arts major—is helpful insofar as it presents the

DIRECTORS' PROPERTY RIGHTS

Equal in importance to the SSDC's establishing of directors' and choreographers' minimum pay rates has been the securing of a property rights clause, which declares that directors and choreographers own their stage directions and choreography. In 1994, SSDC filed a suit on behalf of Gerald Gutierrez, who had staged the 1992 Broadway production of *The Most Happy Fella,* against a theater company in Illinois which had used his stage directions and script changes, had purchased the same scenery, and cast the same star without attempting to secure performance rights or give Gutierrez credit or compensation. That suit was settled out of court.

A similar suit was brought in 1996, on behalf of director Joe Mantello, whose staging of *Love! Valour! Compassion!,* the Terrence McNally play which won the 1995 Tony Award, was reportedly reproduced by a theater in Florida without his knowledge or permission.

opportunity to study the riches of the world's dramatic literature and the development of theatrical forms through the ages, and to learn how to analyze plays, to gain at least some familiarity with the basics of moving people on a stage. And it is a place to meet other people like yourself, who passionately share the same interests.

Of my class at Carnegie Mellon, half of us came to New York and half of us went to Los Angeles. We all did well. By the time I got here, I had done every job in the theater. And that is what I think all people interested in this business should do.

CASEY CHILDS

PROFESSIONAL AFFILIATION

Theatrical directors and choreographers are represented by the Society of Stage Directors and Choreographers (SSDC), a national union organized in 1959 by Shepard Traube, a renowned director and producer. Even the most successful directors of the day suffered the experience of contracts that were breached, fees that were not paid, and royalties that were cut without their notice or consent. Their only recourse was through costly legal action, which took years to reach any conclusion.

FOR INFORMATION,
CONTACT:

The Society of Stage
Directors and
Choreographers
1501 Broadway, 31st Floor
New York, NY 10036

SDC Foundation
1501 Broadway, Suite 1701
New York, NY 10036

The Drama League
Directors Project
165 West 46th Street,
Suite 601
New York, NY 10036

The Directors Company
311 West 43rd Street,
Suite 206
New York, NY 10036

Lincoln Center Theater
Directors' Lab
Lincoln Center Theater
150 West 65th Street
New York, NY 10023

Not until 1962—when the leading Broadway directors and choreographers signed a strike pledge, and Bob Fosse refused to begin rehearsals for *Little Me* without union recognition—was an agreement reached between the League of American Theaters and Producers and SSDC. The union has since expanded its jurisdiction, signing agreements with the League of Off-Broadway Theaters and Producers and the League of Resident Theaters (LORT) and winning the right to represent directors and choreographers in stock theaters as well as choreographers in film, television and music video.

SSDC invites emerging stage directors and choreographers to apply for associate membership. Associates enjoy the benefits of full member status. They receive the membership directory, monthly newsletter, and biannual journal. Associates have access to professional advice and information on basic agreements, and the opportunity to interact with and learn from veterans at SSDC's seminars and roundtables.

Several theatrical organizations have recognized the need to uncover and develop a new generation of directorial talent. Here are some current ones:

The Stage Directors and Choreographers Foundation offers a number of programs—nationally and in New York City—designed to enhance the creativity of early-career directors and provide the opportunity to meet playwrights with whom they might collaborate. Among these are a director–dramatist exchange program, a professional guest director–choreographer program, and observerships that afford the chance to sit alongside another artist throughout the rehearsal process.

The Drama League has been helping young professionals through its Directors Project. Participants attend seminars with renowned theater professionals and then assist working directors at theaters in New York or out of state. At the end of the program, the young directors present a program of one-act plays with professional casts at an off-Broadway theater.

Among its several projects, the Directors Company runs an "Adapting for the Stage" workshop wherein directors find materials from nondramatic sources and adapt them into plays, which they cast and rehearse. The works are then shown to the public. No admission is charged.

The Lincoln Center Theater Directors' Lab is designed for young professionals with a few years' experience. Over a three-week period they participate in an intense round of workshops, readings of new plays and classics, and discussions with several of the theater's leading professional directors. Some participants direct plays for workshop production. The program, devised by André Bishop, artistic director of Lincoln Center Theater, and Anne Cattaneo, Lincoln Center's dramaturge, was begun in 1995 and is still developing.

ANTICIPATED INCOME

The Society of Stage Directors and Choreographers currently has ten basic rate schedules—that is, the union has established minimum pay scales. Higher rates are always negotiable, and minimums will change when contracts expire and are renegotiated. Here are current examples:

- For Broadway theater, the director's fee is $16,000, plus an advance of $24,000, which totals $40,000.
- The director of a bus-and-truck touring company is paid $10,000.
- The director of an off-Broadway production is paid according to the size of the theater. Theater capacity ranges from 100 seats (for a fee of $5,414) to 499 seats (for a fee of $9,625).
- Off-Broadway not-for-profit rates, for the same theater sizes as above: $4,389 to $7,860.
- League of Resident Theaters (LORT) rates are based on different lengths of rehearsal time and theater category: from $3,485 (for three weeks' rehearsal at a small "Category D" house) to $14,005 (for five weeks' rehearsal at a large "Category A" theater).
- Council of Stock Theaters (COST) rates are based on theater category:

$1,725 to $2,620, plus royalties that range from $308 to $471.

- Outdoor musical stock rates are based on an eight-day rehearsal period, with extra days payable at one seventh of the minimum salary of $2,605, plus $652 royalty.
- Council of Resident Stock Theaters (CORST) rates are based on theater category and an eight-day rehearsal period, with extra days payable at one seventh of a salary of $805 to $1,205, plus royalties that range from $303 to $436.
- Dinner-theater rates are based on theater capacity and eight-day rehearsal: from $617 to $1,273, plus royalties from $171 to $234.
- Association of Nonprofit Theater Companies (ANTC) salaries are based on the production cost and the theater's weekly gross. Directors' fees range from $1,210 to $2,800.

In addition, the agreements call for employer contributions to the member's SSDC health insurance and pension plan. The amounts vary with each contract. Always consult SSDC for the latest facts and figures.

The union has special form contracts to protect members who may wish to work for theaters that are not covered by any of the contracts mentioned above. Such agreements are designed to reflect (and respect) the resources and needs of the given theater.

FUTURE PROSPECTS

The first choices for high-budget commercial productions have long been male directors with a couple of hits to their credit. It is, after all, the theater *business*; a track record invites investor confidence. Nonetheless, women have been making undeniable headway: Emily Mann and Susan H. Schulman have not only made it to Broadway; their shows have been successful. Julie Taymor, with a well-received show at Lincoln Center, was named director of the Walt Disney Company's Broadway-musical version of *The Lion King* at the New Amsterdam theater in Times Square.

Regional theater is fertile territory for directors. Plays that open in New Brunswick, New Jersey, and Seattle, Washington, are transported to New York, bringing the director along. Robert Falls, Daniel Sullivan, and Garland Wright took time to hone their skills and build reputations far from New York.

In regional theaters there is less pressure to come up with a big hit, and one has the opportunity to lavish attention on challenging work. The number of theaters with SSDC agreements is an indication of the scores of places where plays are currently being produced. And there are new ones each season.

GETTING STARTED

Years ago, director Julianne Boyd began her career at an off-Broadway classical repertory company, the Classic Stage Company:

I really had no idea how to begin, but I knew I had to start somewhere. I went to CSC, and [artistic director] Christopher Martin gave me the chance to direct scenes, and I worked with actors. He let me do an evening of scenes, and they turned out well.

And that really is how directors begin. With or without role models, you simply have to start. Find a play, a book, a piece of material that engages you, and get it on its feet. In the beginning, you have to hire yourself.

Get five friends together and direct a play.

GREG MOSHER, director

Aspiring actors learn early on the importance of finding a vehicle to showcase their talent. And, since actors are continually looking to showcase their talent, directing their showcase scenes also serves an emerging director's purpose: It gets the director's name and work in front of people who are in the business of finding talent.

As in all other areas, you do whatever takes you closer to where the jobs are. Wherever there is a theater, there is a need for volunteers. Offer to assist. And pay attention. Sitting at any director's side is a golden opportunity to absorb the process, to match your (silent) judgment with another's. Are those the decisions you would have made? Do you discover meaningful moments in the play that no one else notices? If you prove to be a disciplined, reliable assistant, you may be given the chance to do what you want to do—direct.

I learned that Manhattan Theater Club needed a script reader, and I got that job. While there, I was able to direct a production of *The Voice of the Turtle*. MTC's Cabaret Series led me to the work of Eubie Blake and to him, and he said *yes* when I asked if, in time for his 96th birthday, I could produce *Shuffle Along: The Eubie Blake Musical*, at Theater Off Park. It was February, and there were sixty seats, and twelve producers came to see it! Somebody wanted to bring it to Broadway, and we opened at the Ambassador Theater in September. A full-scale production, with gorgeous costumes!

JULIANNE BOYD

THE DRAMATURGE

In the first phase of a production, the director may reach out to a relatively new member of the theatrical community. With the flowering of regional theater in the 1960s, many enthusiastic young people decided to open new theaters in new places. The playwrights who emerged at the same time were busily sending their manuscripts off to the new theater operators to consider for production. Who had the time to read all those plays? Who could really tell if they were worth doing at all?

Enter the dramaturge.

The *dramaturge* (often spelled *dramaturg*) serves to get new playwrights' scripts read, catalogued, and circulated and then assists the director in analyzing scripts.

> With new plays, the dramaturge is the director's aide. You want someone to talk to who knows as much about the play as you do, who has theatrical sense, and knows and understands what you and the writer are trying to do—someone who speaks the same language.
>
> CASEY CHILDS, director

The mission of many of the new theater companies was to present the classic plays. They were spared the avalanche of new scripts—anthologies of the world's best plays are plentiful. But great literature demands great understanding, and many of them soon realized that their knowledge and experience were not always equal to the challenge of the material. What were those great writers really talking about? And how deeply should today's audiences care?

Enter the dramaturge.

As these two theatrical needs suggest, there are two types of dramaturgy—play development, which has to do with new works, and production dramaturgy, which is concerned with existing works that are newly mounted.

> The position is to make oneself as knowledgeable as possible about the playwright, the period, the literature, the genre, the production history of the play, essentially to know everything you can about the production itself and the roots of the production. If the director has a particular concept, to help the director research that concept. And if the director hasn't a concept, perhaps to provide one. Or to provide a context for discussion.
>
> You're someone who asks the difficult questions: Why are we doing this play at this time? Not necessarily to provide the answer, but to ask the

question so compellingly that the director and the design team factor it into their decisions.

ALLEN KENNEDY, dramaturge

The director and I meet regularly, analyzing the structure of the play in terms of the action, to root out the author's intentions. It's a method of studying the plot, the action, the structure. It is most valuable to the director, who is then better prepared to go into rehearsal. Otherwise a director can get enmeshed in details, emotions, and personalities. This way he or she has the analysis to return to.

DALE RAMSEY, production dramaturge, Pearl Theater Company, New York

Historical research is part of my contribution. When Robert Falls was to direct *A Midsummer Night's Dream* at the New York Shakespeare Festival, we met for two months to read the play and found the way through the play. I would talk to him about the era that Shakespeare wrote in—the fact that writers like Shakespeare and Jonson were really members of the working class. We don't think about that because that's not the status of our writers today. It made such a difference.

ANNE CATTANEO, dramaturge, Lincoln Center Theater

While production dramaturgy has been a mainstay of European theater since the eighteenth century—the time of the great German dramatist Friedrich von Schiller—prior to the founding of Yale Drama School's dramaturgy program, in 1976, there were perhaps a dozen dramaturges working in the United States. In effect, the program recognized—and gave a name to—the work that these people had been doing; their pioneer experiences were now encompassed in a course of study. Now, nearly every theater in this country has a dramaturge on staff.

Most of the successful, ongoing institutional theaters have a literary department, which includes literary managers, dramaturges, and literary associates who work in this vein.

ALLEN KENNEDY

An on-staff dramaturge, or literary manager, will read, evaluate, and catalog scripts—solicited or unsolicited—that are submitted to the theater. Information about outstanding scripts deemed worthy of attention is circulated to literary departments around the country through professional channels and by way of an LMDA newsletter called *Script Exchange.*

Dramaturges also play a major role in play development—arranging for staged readings or workshop productions of new material, with the playwright present, to investigate the possibilities of the script. Being able to hear and see the work makes it easier to discover any places where the writer is not clearly communicating the ideas of the play.

In this the dramaturge functions like an editor at a publishing house: The editor assists the writer by tightening or editing the text. But the dramaturge must be mindful of a crucial point: the play remains the writer's property; he or she does not become a co-owner of the work, as a collaborator would.

At some classical theaters, dramaturgy workshops prior to the start of rehearsal help performers to gain perspective on their individual roles in relation to the entire action of the play. Through scene-by-scene analysis of the writer's intention, actors and director arrive at a shared understanding of the play they are doing. Performers supplement this with their personal work on character motivation. While remaining available to the actors, dramaturges must be careful never to intrude on the actor–director relationship.

> As a production dramaturge, I also write for the company's newsletter to subscribers, providing whatever program notes may serve as a background piece. I engage in discussions with the artistic director regarding next season's choices. I read old plays and pitch them. I always hope to unearth a forgotten classic.
>
> DALE RAMSEY

GETTING STARTED

People are drawn to this position from different avenues.

> There are two kinds of people who love the theater—those who want to be onstage and those who really want to be offstage. I never wanted to act, but I was passionately intent on a theater career. I had done a lot of work as a translator, I knew that in theaters abroad there was a history of dramaturgy, and I knew theater history. For me this was the perfect job. I was an intern with American Conservatory Theater, in San Francisco. I also worked as a drama critic for an underground newspaper in the sixties. I was passionate, I can tell you.
>
> ANNE CATTANEO

Assignments frequently grow out of relationships—working closely with a director is an obvious route. Then, when the director gets a job, he or she hires the dramaturge. Serving as a freelance script evaluator in a production office is also a way to get in the door.

> My first job was with the Broadway producers McCann and Nugent. I was an actor, my "between shows" job was reading scripts at their office for possible production. And when they did something, they asked my opinion; they respected my knowledge and my background. I wasn't called a dramaturge—that was in the early 1980s, and there weren't many at that time. But I functioned as a dramaturge. Play reading was a small part of it.
>
> ALLEN KENNEDY

For many years, designers have been the best dramaturges, because they are trained researchers. They know production history, they know period and style, and they are happy doing exhaustive research. They also know how to look at a production as a whole. Frequently the dramaturge's research will influence or illuminate the concept and that translates into a design approach.

There are dramaturges who take enormous pleasure in the research end of the work. Those who come from acting or directing usually have lots of ideas; in the pre-rehearsal process they are able to offer perspective on the work from that viewpoint.

ANTICIPATED INCOME

The dramaturge is a collaborator on the design team level and expects to be paid on a par with the designers. The on-staff salary is on a par with that of the department heads.

PROFESSIONAL AFFILIATION

Literary Managers and Dramaturgs of the Americas, founded in 1985, is the membership organization for the 400 or so members of the profession. LMDA seeks to expand the roles that dramaturges and literary managers play in the theater and to elevate their standing through exchange of information about the function, practice, and value of literary management and dramaturgy; their target audience in this effort is other theater professionals, scholars, and the general public as well as their own membership. The organization seeks also to enlarge the field to include literary and performance media and institutions. Dramaturgy is, tentatively, being applied to screenplays.

FOR INFORMATION, CONTACT:

Literary Managers and Dramaturgs of the Americas Box 355-CASTA CUNY Graduate Center 33 West 42nd Street New York, NY 10036

LMDA holds an annual conference; local branches conduct regional meetings and symposia. Members receive a newsletter, production notebooks, script critiques, and information about job openings through a job hotline.

PROFESSIONAL TRAINING

The LMDA *Guide to Dramaturgy Programs* lists college and university programs in dramaturgy and related fields in the United States and abroad. Updated annually, the guide describes each school's faculty, requirements, degrees, and production opportunities. Copies may be purchased through LMDA.

Just as many noted writers teach their craft at colleges and universities, a majority of freelance dramaturges also teach at schools that offer dramaturgy, performing arts, or dramatic literature programs. For instance, Allen Kennedy heads the theater program at New York City's Dalton School.

Staff dramaturges or literary managers at resident companies are frequently called upon to conduct community theater arts-education and outreach programs in addition to fulfilling their regular artistic function. By so doing, they show the public at large what dramaturges do and demonstrate their valuable contribution to the production process.

André Bishop, who currently heads New York City's Lincoln Center Theater, was earlier the literary manager at Playwrights Horizons. Former dramaturge Tim Sanford is now at the helm of Playwrights Horizons. Within recent seasons dramaturges have been installed as artistic directors of companies in Chicago, Providence, and San Francisco. This may signal an emerging career path for dramaturges, or may simply be the inspired casting of artistic staff in a management role.

RECOGNITION OF ACHIEVEMENT

Anne Cattaneo is widely credited with transforming LMDA during the four years she served as its president from a New York–based bunch who met and swapped theater stories at a restaurant in the theater district to a national presence. Under her leadership, regional networks were established, encouraging the exchange of ideas and information among dramaturges from coast to coast, script exchanges, the job hotline, and even the commissioning of dramaturges' production notebooks for publication. (She gives the credit for the latter idea to dramaturge Mark Bly, of the Yale Drama School.)

Cattaneo has taught theater, theater history, acting, and directing. She has also worked as a director. For two years she was literary manager at New York's Phoenix theater. During the 1970s she ran the writers' development program at Playworks, where she was instrumental in developing scripts submitted by then-emergent writers Wendy Wasserstein, Christopher Durang, and others.

While she was a freelancer with The Acting Company, Cattaneo recalled:

> They wanted to do Chekhov, but not the same old Chekhov—something more contemporary. I created a project we called *Orchards*. Stories from Chekhov were dramatized into seven short plays by the writers David Mamet, John Guare, Michael Weller, Maria Irene Fornes, Wendy Wasserstein, Samm-Art Williams, and Spalding Gray. These plays were created for the company, and they toured widely.

"Those plays are still being done and," she added, ever respectful of the position of the writer in the theater, "the writers own the plays."

THE VISUAL DESIGN TEAM

Everything you see and hear onstage has been designed. Sets, costumes, lights, sound—the entire physical environment in which the action takes place—are the designers' translation of the playwright's and director's vision. Designers customarily speak of their work as a collaboration.

> It is ideal to have all the key creative personnel together as soon as possible so we are all speaking the same language technically, visually.
>
> The director serves the collaboration by getting everyone together, with lots of food. We sit around, tell jokes. We talk. It's truly scary early on. We read the script. It's the ability to take the time to feed each other, and avoid "flashes of insight."
>
> TONY WALTON, award-winning set and costume designer

> We are all directors at that point, really. I tell the story through costumes . . . . The set designer is the team leader, the initial energy, the idea.
>
> I love the process. It is thrilling to work constantly and collaboratively in that kind of newness and fresh discovery.
>
> PATRICIA ZIPPRODT, costume designer

What is the mood of the play? The period? The country? Are the characters young? Old? Wealthy or poor, sophisticated or rural? Answers to those important design questions will be in the script.

> I need to know history, sociology, something about why it is these people are behaving in the way that they do, and how I can help explain that to the audience with what I am doing.
>
> MARC WEISS, lighting designer

To arrive at imaginative designs which not only fulfill but somehow illuminate those conditions, designers need training. They must have, in addition to the intangible ingredient that is their talent, a knowledge of history. They must do painstaking research through books and study the sculpture, paintings, and drawings of the period of any given play. They accumulate copious scrapbooks for reference. Frequently, the designers' interpretation will affect the structure of the work. As award-winning lighting designer Paul Gallo remarked: "The set designer plants the seed."

The quintessential example of a scenic design that became the icon for a play is Jo Mielziner's set for Arthur Miller's *Death of a Salesman*, produced in 1949. Mielziner told an interviewer that the idea for the multilevel unit set came to him because there were so many short scenes in the original script that it would take forever to change the sets—the dramatic tension would be lost. He suggested that they consider a basic set, based on the idea of the salesman's castle—his home—and then suggest the other locations. They would eliminate or pare down the physical props to the smallest possible number, even have the actors bring them onstage with them. This would allow freedom of movement from one scene to the next. He allotted space for a small forestage for the final graveyard scene. Time transformations would be accomplished by lighting. Using projections, he would show the changes in the neighborhood by having the other houses gradually encroach on the Lomans' territory.

Accepting Mielziner's idea meant that rehearsals would have to be postponed because much of the script would have to be rewritten. And yet, his reasoning was so persuasive that everyone—playwright Arthur Miller, producer Kermit Bloomgarden, and director Elia Kazan—agreed. Kazan later told him that simplifying the physical needs of the play proved to be a godsend. *Death of a Salesman* won the Pulitzer Prize, the Tony Award, and the Drama Critics Circle Award for best play.

BASIC REQUIREMENTS

In addition to their talent, creativity, imagination, and discipline, designers need technical skills. Scenic designers are expected to construct scale models of their designs, supply working drawings and ground plans for the construction carpenters, and color schemes or color sketches for the scenic artists. They supervise the building and painting of all sets.

> You design a set for its use. If there's going to be door slams, you don't want the walls to shake. And you have to think of the wear and tear.
>
> Tony Walton

SCENIC DESIGNERS also design, select, or approve the props—including furniture and draperies—needed for the show. They attend the dress rehearsals and conduct the scenic rehearsals for the production.

Every performer is costumed from head to toe, and a designer's supervision is needed even if the play is contemporary and all the outfits can be pulled from the performers' closets or scrounged from a flea market. The COSTUME DESIGNER is responsible for a costume plot and color sketches, color schemes, and samples of the materials to be used for each costume, as well as all ornaments and accessories. Designers need to understand how movement affects fit, how to accommodate a lightning-quick change, how to flatter a variety of body shapes and sizes. They supervise the building, or making, of each costume, as well as any necessary painting of fabric or accessories. Hairstyles, wigs, mustaches, beards, and any special makeup must meet with their approval. Of course, costume designers are present at all dress rehearsals.

> You are creating a visual image for the audience to look at that says in a heartbeat, before the actor moves, sings, dances, or speaks, just who that person is.
>
> JANE GREENWOOD, costume designer

LIGHTING DESIGNERS provide full equipment lists, color plots, and light plots drawn to scale. They provide a control plot, showing the allocation of all instruments for lighting control. They design and plot special effects and supervise their execution.

> When I read a script, I look for the visually memorable moments. Once I figure out what those are and get the director's approval, that's my storyboard of the show. The rest is figuring out how I get it to look that way. A streak of light comes through the blinds and hits the gun on the floor. If that's the picture I want, then this is the equipment I need, and this is where I need it placed. Scene by scene, I build up the list.
>
> MARC WEISS

Lighting designers supervise hanging and focusing of all equipment and the setting of all lighting cues. They attend the dress rehearsals and conduct all necessary lighting rehearsals. During the run of the play, the lighting designer checks the show periodically to make sure that the focus, color, intensity, and cues are all as originally set.

All the designers are required to get pre-production price estimates from at least three companies. At the "bid sessions," the general manager will almost invariably declare that the estimates are too high. Everyone will then look for ways to achieve the desired effects and still stay within the budget.

Designers' contracts specify that, subject to their availability, they will render the same services on any future productions of the show.

RECOMMENDED TRAINING

Marc Weiss was a chemistry major who had been headed for a career in research biology ever since junior high school. But it was not to be:

> As things went along I spent more and more time at the theater, and I decided *that's* what I ought to do for a living. Then I needed some sort of formal education. I was winging it, and I needed some background.

Swift advances in technology have made a degree in design essential. With the premiere of *A Chorus Line* in 1975, award-winning designer Tharon Musser brought computerized lighting to Broadway. Her contribution to the extraordinary success of that show has been termed equal to that of writers James Kirkwood and Nicholas Dante and director Michael Bennett. Musser is credited with transforming theater lighting into an art form and changing forever the way lighting would be done.

Indeed, with the rapid development of computers, transistors, plastics, and microfibers, changes are coming at an ever faster pace in sound, scenery, costuming, and lighting.

Working professionals recommend going to schools where working professionals are doing the teaching. For many years, the schools best known for the professionalism of their faculty have been Yale Drama School; Carnegie Mellon University; North Carolina School of the Arts; and the University of California at Los Angeles. Columbia University has recently energized its theater and film department; New York University's Tisch School of the Arts is attracting a great deal of favorable attention, with students working in the neighborhood's many off-Broadway theaters; and the University of California at San Diego has established a working relationship with that city's Globe Theater.

Acceptance at a school with a work-study program can help to pay for the degree and provide valuable on-the-job training. Master classes with top professionals, workshops, summer intensive courses, and internships wherever there are theaters offering them, are opportunities to do the all-important networking.

> I would hang out at any theater where anything was "loading in" to watch what was going on. I'd see if I could talk them into letting me stay for the tech rehearsals. Just to see how they'd do it. I considered it part of my job.
>
> MARC WEISS

Just as colleges with acting programs showcase their students' work in New York each spring, professionals who teach at design schools invite senior students to present their projects and/or portfolios at gatherings to which the professional design community is invited. New York University's Tisch School of the Arts exhibits students' work in its art gallery on Washington Square. The New York City chapter of Carnegie Mellon University's Alumni Association invites the graduating class of design majors to New York to meet successful Carnegie alumni and tour the studios and theaters where they work. The students' portfolios and models are evaluated by a jury of industry professionals, and everyone gets to exchange cards and résumés at a farewell party.

> The best way for a person to get a job in this business is to know a lot of people. When you go through a college program, you meet the directors, the choreographers, and the actors—all the other people who will eventually be your peers and hire you in the theater. You *can* do it as a fine artist and freelancer and meet people that way, but it is very difficult to hook up the network that you need.
>
> DON PADGETT, assistant business representative, United Scenic Artists

AUDITIONING A SCHOOL

For high school juniors who are keenly interested in a theatrical career but really don't know what such a course will entail, Carnegie Mellon University offers a six-week precollege summer program. Several recent Carnegie graduates, who had originally thought of themselves as acting majors, enrolled in the program and were elated to discover that their far greater talent was in the realm of crafts and set design.

Northwestern University's Cherubs Program is reportedly similar (in fact, some prospective theater majors have been known to take both programs). The success of these introductory programs may encourage other schools to emulate their example. It may even be sensible for a student to write, fax, or e-mail a likely school (other than these two) and ask whether the theater department offers such a program, or is considering doing so.

PROFESSIONAL AFFILIATION

Scenic, costume, and lighting designers in theater, film, and television are represented by United Scenic Artists (USA), Local 829—an autonomous local office of the International Brotherhood of Painters and Allied Trades. This organization was originally chartered in 1918, when all entertainment was performed live in front of hand-painted scenery and lit by gaslight. In those days, actors provided their own costumes.

The union has broadened its scope as the entertainment industry has grown. USA's collective bargaining agreements currently cover opera and ballet as well as stage, film, and television. In addition to lighting, costume, and scenic designers and art directors, there is a membership category for SCENIC ARTISTS, who may be classically trained, with fine-arts skills, and are responsible to the scenic designer for painting floors and floor cloths as well as the scenery, surfaces, and cycloramas that will be used onstage or in front of a camera. There are additonal

> FOR INFORMATION, CONTACT:
>
> United Scenic Artists
> 16 West 61st Street
> New York, NY 10023

categories for sculptors and people with specialized skills working in the *allied crafts*—for example, multimedia specialists, specialty prop makers, commercials stylists, storyboard artists, and certain theme-park employees.

Membership in USA is open to professionals who have secured a job in any of the covered areas, or by application, which is followed by an interview and, in the case of the four major categories, by an examination. People in the allied crafts are not required to take an exam but must show suitable samples of their work. There are application forms, filing fees, exam fees, initiation fees, and annual dues for each category.

> If a person is interested in coming into the theater, there are a great many skills that on the surface don't seem to be connected to theater or film or TV but are very much needed. — DON PADGETT

ANTICIPATED INCOME

USA's collective bargaining agreements establish minimum salaries and royalty payments. Experienced artists negotiate higher fees. In 1996, the Broadway minimums were:

- Scenic designers: $6,237 for a single-set play; $9,080 for a multi-unit play; $6,237 for a single-set musical; $11,348 for a unit-set musical; $20,441 for a multi-set musical.
- Lighting designers: $4,677 for a single-set play; $6,810 for a multi-set play; $8,510 for a unit-set play; $4,677 for a single-set musical; $8,510 for a unit-set musical; $15,331 for a multi-set musical.
- Costume designer: Fees are based upon the *number of characters*.

    Ranges for dramatic shows:

1–3: $3,406	4–7: $295 each
8–15: $5,674	16–20: $295 each
21–30: $7,940	31–35: $295 each
36 and more: $10,208	

    Ranges for musicals:

1–15 persons: $6,814	16–20 persons: $335 each
21–30: $13,614	31–35: $335 each
36 and more: $20,441.	

The contract also provides for contributions to the union's pension and health funds.

GETTING STARTED

Doug Hustie, a freelance designer, does a lot of drafting and builds models for other designers. "When I want to work, I make a lot of phone calls," he said.

> Never be shy about talking to people. Write to them, go to see their shows! The more times your name comes up, the better your chances. When they say, "Let me know what you're doing," they mean it!
>
> Jason Kantrowitz, lighting design consultant

> Cutters, stitchers, props people, craftspeople are *needed.* If you are into crafts in any form, there is work!
>
> Arnold Levine, craftsperson

Designers always need assistants. When they are working, they need shoppers, people to do the leg work, locating props, furniture, and swatches. In addition to listings in the *Theatrical Index,* the unions issue lists of incoming productions. It is always smart to volunteer, particularly during vacation times that would otherwise be frittered away. This can put you in contact with the people you will want to work with.

One winter, I was in Boston setting up a show for an award-winning director, and I called the university theater department asking if any of the lighting students would like to come over. This is an opportunity you cannot buy—to work with such professionals. The professor asked, "What do you pay?" Not one of those students showed up. They lost the chance of a lifetime.

MARC WEISS

A valuable source of information and an introduction to industry professionals is the United States Institute for Theater Technology, the American Association of Design and Production Professionals in the Performing Arts (USITT). Their members include set, costume, sound, and lighting designers and technicians; technical directors; production managers; prop, makeup, and special effects craftspersons; stagehands and stage managers; manufacturers, suppliers, and distributors; and educators. To keep these professionals in touch with the rapidly changing scene in design and production, USITT sponsors projects, programs, and symposia on innovation and creativity in the performing arts.

> FOR INFORMATION, CONTACT:
>
> United States Institute for Theater Technology
> 6443 Ridings Road
> Syracuse, NY 13206

The organization disseminates information through a newsletter, *Sightlines,* a quarterly magazine; *TD&T: Theater Design & Technology;* and an annual Conference and Stage Expo, which is held in a different North American city each year. Each year thousands of attendees from all over the world learn about the latest opportunities and innovations in design and technology and take advantage of the more than 150 seminars, workshops, and roundtables conducted by industry leaders.

Through OISTAT, an international theater organization with centers in Europe, Asia, and the Americas, USITT maintains worldwide access to leaders in theater and design. Students can receive these and the many other benefits of USITT membership at a reduced rate.

OUTLOOK FOR THE FUTURE

Designers today work everywhere—ballet, opera, concerts, pageants, festivals, award presentations, and political campaigns. Special events, global conventions, and industrial shows for multinational corporations now take designers not only to New Orleans and Denver, but to Europe, Australia, and Singapore as well.

It has been a great joy to have worked all over the world, on five continents. Fabulous! In Japan I learned to cue a show in Japanese.

MARC WEISS

I do the costumes for [the Las Vegas act] Siegfried and Roy. I have created

the most incredible inflatable dragon costume! They have their own theater! And you get royalties.

WILLIAM IVEY LONG, award-winning costume designer

I went from lighting to production manager to producing events. Now I am
working at Sea World, the only theme park with an indoor theater. We are
using technology you don't even see on Broadway—lasers, dancing water!

JASON KANTROWITZ

VISIT TO A SCENE SHOP

THE ELEGANT MANSION that John Lee Beatty designed for the 1996 revival of Edward Albee's *A Delicate Balance* told the audience everything they needed to know about its privileged inhabitants before a word was spoken.The walls, which appeared to have absorbed genera-tions of family secrets, were actually can-vas flats that had been cut, assembled, and painted with stunning attention to detail at Variety Scenic Studios, in Long Island City, one of New York's premier scene shops.

"The set was 40 feet wide, 30 feet deep, and built for a raked stage with exaggerated perspective so you were able to see way into the back of the house," recalled Herb Lager. Lager, his partner Bob Hutchinson, and business manager Phyllis Restaino (who also happens to be Lager's wife) have been running Variety Scenic for almost thirty years.

At Variety Scenic, they don't just do walls and windows, they make skies too, with hundreds of twinkling stars, like the one they've sewn for *Beauty and the Beast*. "It looks seamless, doesn't it?," said Lager as he lifts the hem to show how many widths of fabric have been invisi-bly seamed together to create the incred-ible expanse. A full-service shop, offering construction in fabric, wood, steel, and aluminum, Variety is the only shop that

sews its own draperies. "We know the fabric, how it hangs, how it reacts to light. . . . And"—Lager gestures toward the large sample room—"we have it all on hand. The designer can choose from what is available. This is not like deco-rating an apartment, where you can wait months until the material arrives from overseas. We are always working under the gun. We have less than six weeks to do a musical."

The company is particularly noted for the quality of their painted work on almost any material. "The designer draws blueprints, makes a paint sketch, and usually a model. However, designers rely upon the scene shop people for advice about materials, because we know how to fabricate and what works on a stage with people, lights, and the stress of performance," Lager explained. "The designer must be confident that the scenic artist, or *chargeperson,* understands what he or she wants and doesn't go off in a different direction."

Scenic artists are artists in their own right, he went on: "They have their own talent; yet they have to follow and exe-cute another artist's rough sketch of what's wanted. The scenic artist can often improve on it and surprise the designer by adding things he or she did-n't even think of. To translate that sketch

High-definition, computers, virtual reality—this is the dawn of that age. People who are learning that skill now are the people who will be doing a vast amount of work in the future. And the painting skills will remain. They have to have a model image to work with. We are not talking about a loss of jobs, but an expanded horizon.

DON PADGETT

into the real thing is a creative task. It's always a guess, because you have never done this before. No one has done *this show* before. For Tony Walton [designer of *A Fair Country*], we had to attach foliage to a painted backdrop, and it had to be secure, because there were a great many scene changes. What adhesive do you use? You have to experiment."

Heidi Landesman's Tony-winning designs for the 1991 musical *The Secret Garden* were the most complicated of any show ever done at Variety, and possibly in the industry. "We broke new ground in computer painting, how to use it, how to apply it. We helped to develop an entirely new process, painting on clear plastic—so that the light could shine through those incredible flowers Heidi designed. We used sheets of Lexan 50 feet high and 28 feet wide. Computers can now read a picture and tell the paint spray heads which colors to spit out. We used a combination of computer and hand-painting. Some of the work was so complicated that hand-painting exclusively would have been prohibitively expensive."

Lager once worked at NBC, in the busy days of live TV, when the networks produced their own shows and ran their own scene shops. As assistant to the scenery supervisor at the network's huge Brooklyn studio, he estimated the costs of constructing and moving sets. His

skill at reading blueprints provided a basis for estimating costs. When the networks switched from creating to purchasing shows from independent packagers, he and several colleagues opened their own scene shop. Though that effort failed, he was able by 1970 to open Variety Scenic Studio. "We are now one of the oldest established shops."

Chargeperson Jane Snow, responsible for painting, decorating, and sculpting, returns after overseeing the work of five scenic artists doing touchups on a set that was just loaded into a theater. Jane describes herself as someone who's "been painting and building stuff" since she was fourteen. At the University of Tennessee, she majored in art and theater "and in designing shows." Originally hired as a scenic artist, within a few years she became the on-staff chargeperson.

Many of the company's crew come from the building trades, "They have the basic skills, and after they learn to build scenery our way, they work here when our shop is busy and they're not."

Young designers who are between shows are frequent members of the flexible crew. "They love to see what we're doing, because we are always finding new materials, new ways to do things. And now," Lager observed, "we're getting new people in the business, like computer people who can draft, estimate, and do the art."

VISIT TO A COSTUME SHOP

OF THE MANY LEVELS of collaboration in the theater, one of the most important is that between the people who design the costumes and those who make them. Translating the designer's two-dimensional sketch into a three-dimensional costume that a particular performer will wear is the business of the theatrical costume shop, most of which are centered in and around New York and Los Angeles.

One of New York's busiest costume shops, Parsons Meares, Ltd., occupies several floors of an old brick factory building near Manhattan's Greenwich Village. Following draper Jan Kastendeick through the high-ceilinged, maze-like space, a visitor collides with a camel ("He's been sent up here from Disney World to be repaired. See how he leans?"), then swerves to avoid a trio of freshly painted bodysuits dangling over a sink ("We're testing new dyes on this stretch fabric. Sally Parsons designed the original unitards for *Cats,* but we're way beyond that now.")

Passing a deserted alcove, Jan pointed to a long-sleeved lace gown of white satin and silver suspended in front of a three-way mirror. "This wedding dress had to be washable; the bride gets blood on it in the last scene," she said, fluffing the multilayered skirt with her fingers. "What's great is that it needs no ironing!"

Colorful pants, skirts, and gowns in opulent fabrics hang above the sewing machines from pipes that span the length of the huge workroom. At an oak table in the far corner, Jim Meares and a stitcher compare samples of trim. By an open window, two women apply feathery plumes to silk hats; a young man nearby sews sequins on long satin gloves. In an adjacent office, Sally Ann Parsons and her assistants check their "bibles": the industry term for enormous looseleaf books which contain the swatches and sources of every item used for every garment in a show. And they answer the constantly ringing phones.

"We are known for doing difficult and innovative costumes," Kastendeick explained. "For *Starlight Express* I developed a way of decorating costume armor without a metal backing. Otherwise a costume could weigh 75 pounds. They use the technique for those things Norma Desmond wears in *Sunset Boulevard.*

"Most drapers and first hands [drapers' assistants] have college degrees and design degrees. And some of us are designing projects periodically. The draper looks at the sketches and has to make them work both for the actors, who must move in them, and for the designers, so that the costumes say what they want them to say. You could give five different drapers the same sketch, and the garments would all come out looking different, because each draper has his or her own approach. Sometimes it's the choice of fabric, or how you actually cut and sew something.

"A sketch just has a front view. You have to decide what the back is. You ask, 'What do you want this to do?' The designer can say, 'I don't know. What do you think it should do?' And you might say, 'Well, I think it would look really nice to have it sweep up and cascade into a train.'

"A costume is a work in progress between the designer, the actor, and the draper. You start out draping it on a mannequin, so you have the general shape. You may have a sketch that looks like it should be on a 6-foot-tall person, but you have a 5-foot, 4-inch actress. You have to change the proportions, the way the whole thing works together. You do all that on the mannequin, using muslin or crepe. Then you have a fitting on the performer. That's your base. Then you make a paper pattern. In following fittings, things may change again. It's easier to change the paper than the expensive fabric you will really be using.

"We have two to three weeks for the whole show. This company has eight drapers on staff. If a show has fifty costumes, each draper will get to do seven or eight costumes. When a show has 300 costumes, you hire more people.

"It can take hundreds of hours to build a costume. It's *construction,* not just sewing seams, so $3,000 is not unusual for a simple dress. Some can cost $15,000."

Jan has a regular team of two or three assistants, which can grow to as many as seven or eight, plus operators and finishers. "I have to be in control of what they're doing—always keep the work moving. There are always deadlines, which are very important.

"When you are working on a new show, you go out of town with the show. There may be fifty or sixty extra local people there, just to set it up and get it going. Think of how long it takes to sew in dress shields, organize underwear for women and men, labels, T-shirts, bras, socks, pantyhose, everything they need specifically for each costume.

"Technology in costumes is at its highest ever. We can do more. And this is where the experimental work is being done. People expect more because of the movies and TV. Well, there you use a costume once. In theater, you have to use it eight times a week, again and again. A lot of our costumes come back for repair or to be remade after they've been used for four or five years. They've been maintained at the theater by wardrobe, but the base is there, your inner structure. All you have to do is cover it."

Jan earned her M.F.A. at Penn State and then worked in regional theater—at Actors Theatre of Louisville and at Long Wharf Theatre, in Connecticut—before joining the in-house costume staff (now closed) at the New York Shakespeare Festival.

Jan prefers to do unusual clothes. She described a costume for *Beauty and the Beast,* at Disney World: an ice cream sundae that turns into a dancer. "The whipped cream on the sundae becomes the ruffle on her skirt. When it's well done, you don't notice any of it.

"You're always experimenting. Even if you've done the show before, you're always looking for ways to make it better. And then you adapt that technique to new things. For the *Aladdin* ice show, we had to figure out how forty genies can grab onto each other and still skate. We'll use that technique with *The Hunchback of Notre Dame.*"

Theatrical costumes are considered garments until they go into the theater, which is why theatrical costume workers belong to the garment workers union. There is no entry exam. Each costume shop does the testing, which boils down to: If your work meets the shop's standards, you're hired.

In a smaller workroom, where pots of paste and paint cover the work surface and dazzlingly decorated turbans sit on the shelves, Joe Stephen experiments with a quick-change gargoyle outfit. The face, which looks like stone, is actually carved foam covered with gray stretch fabric painted to look like a Gothic cathedral carving. He is a head draper, and his wizardry as a master of masks, headdresses, and other unusual items is known throughout the industry.

"I stumbled into this. I have a fine arts and costume-design background, but whenever there was a prop to be made, I'd be the one who could figure out how to do it. I discovered the world of special props. As a mask maker, I used my sculpting skills. I moved on to head-dresses.

"This is about problem-solving and invention. You're dealing with the human body. We work with plastic, foam, rubber, wire, stretch fabrics, rib-bons, whatever works for the project. I recently made a robot out of foam and latex; it looked terrific, and it was com-fortable for the actor to move in, but it didn't work—until I figured out how to ventilate it so he could breathe. Other-wise that would have been a very toxic costume.

"My shoppers are invaluable. They're so good they can often make choices for me. We are all flexible people who can do lots of things. You do need training for this work—we all have studied—but you also need to be open to ideas. We know the names of the periods, and their political and religious history and styles. We know about costume and adornment, but we also know how to interpret those old forms with new materials. The Indian feather headdresses I made for *The Will Rogers Follies* were authentic, spectacular, but I had to add sculpted calves' heads, so they would stay on when those beautiful girls danced up and down the narrow stairs.

"I do a lot of note-taking and research. You learn by doing. It's very unpre-dictable, and very challenging. There are people here who have discovered their own talent for innovation in fabric lami-nating or construction. There are pup-peteers. There are sculptors—not in mar-ble, but in foam, epoxy, papier-maché, or some other material no one has yet seen. I tell people, if you believe you have an affinity for any of this, look up the prop houses in the *New York Theatrical Source Book*. In this little world people with tal-ent become known. And they are respect-ed, because talent is very rare.

"Those headdresses you see on the shelves are for the [Radio City Music Hall] Rockettes. For them you need forty of everything!"

THE SOUND DESIGNER

For a long time, sound in the theater was concerned solely with special effects—sounds of barking dogs, offstage music, thunder, screeching brakes, or gunshots. The advent of rock concerts and discos, bolstered by increasingly affordable, elaborate home-stereo systems and inexpensive portable cassette players changed all that. We became consumers of sound. In 1971 the term *sound designer* was first used on Broadway: a credit for Abe Jacob, and his work on *Jesus Christ Superstar.*

Today's aurally sophisticated audiences are comfortable being blanketed by sound. As a result, the emotional properties of sound and silence—their ability to evoke place, time, and mood—are more and more an integral element in the director's concept of the play. At the same time, today's Broadway performers are usually expected to wear wireless microphones so their voices can be heard in the last row of the balcony and appropriately blended into the overall ambiance. Stephen Sondheim told an audience at a recent Show Business Expo that, to his surprise, veteran performers seemed more comfortable hearing their own voices amplified, even in a small theater. They'd become accustomed to the "big" sound.

> Sound design in the Broadway theater is comparable to the other elements in that the sound designer is hired by the producer by the start of rehearsals, if not sooner, and works with the director in creating the sound design for the specific production. Part of the designer's responsibility is to prepare a shop order detailing the list of equipment required and drawings indicating the hookup and use of the equipment. This order is sent to the various union sound shops for bidding, like lighting equipment. The equipment is installed by the union crew.
>
> ABE JACOB, sound designer and business representative of Local #922

With the approval of the designer, the producer hires the necessary stagehands to run the show; the minimum for a dramatic production would be a sound engineer, or mixer, who operates the control console. For large musicals, there can be two or three engineers, plus two or more assistants who take care of wireless microphones and other cues onstage.

PROFESSIONAL AFFILIATION

On Broadway, members of the operating sound crew are considered electricians, and are members of the International Alliance of Theatrical Stage Employees (IATSE). The Theatrical Sound Designers Association is Local

FOR INFORMATION,
CONTACT:

Theatrical Sound
Designers Association
Local #922
130 East 63 Street,
Suite 4E
New York, NY 10021

#922 of IATSE. The local office accepts any applicant who has a Broadway design credit and satisfies general requirements for IATSE membership. Sound designers who are not working on Broadway can become Allied Crafts Members, with all the benefits of membership, but for a lower initiation fee. Dues are the same for all members.

According to the current contract, the minimum fee for a sound designer on a musical is $2,500; on a dramatic show, $500. Designers may negotiate fees above the minimum. In addition, the producer pays the designer's health and retirement benefits.

On a musical, sound designers receive an additional fee of $125 per week (also with benefits paid) once the show is open. (Electricians are hired by the producer to work the sound once the show is running.)

Salaries for assistants are negotiated by the producer and the designer.

TRAINING

Several of the new cadre of theatrical sound designers were formerly production electricians. They know theater, and they became experienced with the equipment by working as sound operators on a show.

There are now resident sound designers at repertory theaters across the country. Finding a way to assist any of them would be an opportunity to participate in the design of new productions and gain expertise working with the newest equipment.

> I want to capture everything that sounds right for this scene. I hear a very specific river in the background. In the river, I hear very specific frogs.
>
> JAMES LEBRECHT, sound designer

Other sound experts are on staff at recording studios. Assistants here are exposed to a wide range of work, with the possibility of meeting performers, directors, composers, and conductors from every avenue of the industry.

Two noted sound designers—David Buddries and Jon Gottlieb—are on the faculty at Yale Drama School and UCLA, respectively. Studying with them means doing graduate work at a highly visible school, whose alumni are known throughout the industry.

A library of Macintosh and Powerbook software already exists to fill sound designers' needs. More is surely on the way, as working designers and educators participate in the development of the tools they need for quality, speed, and flexibility. To read five experts' views on equipment, and an evaluation of (what was then) the newest sound software, see the August–September 1996 issue of *Theatre Crafts International*. You can request reprints from:

Ms. Chris Lotesto
Intertec Publishing
1 IBM Plaza
Chicago, IL 60611

OTHER REQUIREMENTS

One needs more than a keen ear, manual dexterity, and familiarity with computer and electronic equipment for this career. The sound designer must have an understanding of period and style, coupled with the capacity to study a script and to imagine what every aspect of that universe sounds like. The ability to handle a host of tiny details simultaneously is essential.

As one designer told an interviewer, "With lights, they call the cue, and all you need to do is make the change, and then wait for the next cue. But with sound cues, the tape has to be stopped, the levels have to be balanced, and the next cue has to be set up, and you don't always have a lot of time to do all that. And, then, if something blows—well, you have to be alert at all times."

Like the other members of the creative team, sound designers find employment working on live concerts, radio, recordings, and multimedia publishing as well as in theater, TV, and film, This is a career that can be practiced around the world.

THE CASTING DIRECTOR

Simply put, the success of any show depends on good casting. The only argument among theater professionals of long standing is whether casting accounts for 85 or 90 percent of a show's success. While playwright, producer, and director undoubtedly have wish lists of the stars they'd love to see playing the parts, they nonetheless rely on a creative casting director with a knowledge of the talent pool to suggest capable performers whose work may be new to them.

It has been said that the best casting directors are those who have acted, because they understand what actors do and the problems they have. Ideally, casting directors go to see everything they possibly can, remember all the good performances they have seen, and are willing to believe that mediocre work is not necessarily the actor's fault, but may be due to poor direction or unfortunate casting.

WHAT CASTING DIRECTORS DO

Casting directors study the script and then synthesize their impressions of the characters with ideas they get from the director, producer, and playwright. They then make recommendations and after further discussion contact actors' agents to arrange interviews.

According to Actors Equity Association rules, casting directors are required to set aside dates for open calls, so that all eligible performers may have an opportunity to be seen for the play; placing casting call announcements in the trade papers is also the casting director's responsibility.

Having confirmed dates with director, producer, and playwright, the casting director schedules audition appointments, arranges for the space—usually in a rehearsal hall, theater, or production office—and has copies of scripts or audition scenes sent to, or picked up by, the actors. With the help of one or more assistants, the casting director conducts the auditions: Each performer is introduced and reads, and the director's comments on the reading are noted on the backs of the performer's photo–résumé. Auditions continue until the play is cast.

> Ideally, you would like to audition many people for the role, but there isn't time. Directors who don't know the talent pool are the most difficult because they want to see all the available talent. Directors who know the talent pool will trust us.
>
> MEG SIMON, casting director

Should the show settle in for a lengthy run, the casting director will usually be in charge of cast replacements and touring companies. Here is where the notes taken at original auditions come in handy. An excellent actor who was second choice (or wasn't enough of a name to open the show) may get a second chance to play the part.

With their days spent looking at photos and résumés—as many as a hundred may arrive in the morning's mail; that number quadruples after a casting notice appears—and talking to agents, and listening to actors read, casting directors' evenings, which constitute other people's relaxation time, consist of going to plays, showcases, comedy clubs, and cabarets, or watching movies and television, in a continual search for talent no one else has yet discovered. To do this they are also in contact with talent agents and managers, acting teachers, coaches at professional schools, and directors of college theater programs. They often travel to see promising students in leading roles. Legend has it that casting directors and agents flocked to New Haven to see Meryl Streep's work before the end of her first year at Yale Drama School. And they regularly attend the scene showcases presented each spring by a consortium of colleges and universities.

Casting directors may be on-staff at a resident company or busy producer's office, but nowadays the majority of casting directors work on a freelance basis. In addition to theater, they cast for films and television, where they handle commercials as well as dramatic shows. (For casting directors in film and TV, see pages 131–133)

PROFESSIONAL AFFILIATIONS

Casting directors are not represented by a union. In New York, Chicago, and Los Angeles, freelance and staff people join the Casting Society of America (CSA). Casting directors consider themselves in a curious position:

> We are seen by the talent unions as being part of management, while management sees us as related to talent.
>
> DAWN STEINBERG, casting director

CSA is trying to set standards and gain recognition for what their members do—which is know talent and the range of work that individual performers can do, seek out the right talent for the current openings, and make imaginative choices. Casting credit is included in theater programs.

> When I was casting *Biloxi Blues* I saw well over two thousand people. In Chicago I found an actor, and I told him to get to New York—I couldn't afford to fly him in. He found a way. He got cast.
>
> MEG SIMON

CAREER TRAINING

Casting is a career that demands attention to details and a highly developed frame of reference. When directors, playwrights or producers say they want a younger so-and-so, or someone just like what's her-name but maybe not so frail, the casting director is expected to know who they're talking about and come up with a recommendation.

Dealing at all times with sensitive egos in emotional situations, courtesy and tact are essential. Here, acting training or experience should develop one's ability to communicate with performers and the people who hire them. Mari Lyn Henry, former casting director for ABC, put it simply:

> You must love actors. And respect them. Too many people in this business don't do that. You have to be willing to go and see them. You have to have an open door. You have to remember their names and what they've done. And you have to know the plays. I think you should know something about the theater, know who the great actors have been. And the great plays and playwrights. Otherwise you're in a foreign country.

While there is no course of study especially designated for casting directors, a college theater degree provides the necessary background.

Remember that casting directors are *not* talent agents. The frequently heard term "casting agent" is incorrect, a contradiction in terms. Agents represent (or sell) talent and receive 10 percent of a client's salary, when the client works. Casting directors are intermediaries; they sell their knowledge of talent to producers (and directors and writers) who are the talent buyers.

ANTICIPATED INCOME

Casting directors are employed by producers. Reliable, creative casting directors have a roster of loyal clients and do very well.

There are no set fees. They are paid according to their experience, the size of a given production, the amount of time it has taken them to find the right performers, and the work they will be engaged to do after the show opens.

GETTING STARTED

The best place to start is in an internship with a casting director, a talent agent, or a producer. You can get more general experience by assisting at a production house, a theater company, an advertising agency, or even with a press agent.

> I came to New York to be an actress. I had taken a typing course, and that enabled me to get a survival job at an ad agency. When there was an opening in the commercials casting department, I asked to be considered. The casting director was Maxine Marx, daughter of Chico, of the Marx brothers. She was glad to know I was an actress, and she hired me.
>
> MARI LYN HENRY

THE STAGE MANAGERS

Just as the general manager heads the production's business team and the director is head of the creative team, the stage manager is in charge of the production team. A frequently heard job description is that the stage manager is present from the start of rehearsals and, after opening night, runs the show as a stand-in for the director. But that is an oversimplification.

More accurately, the stage manager is the one person who knows the entire show and is in charge of everything that happens from the curtain to the back wall of the theater.

Peter Lawrence, the production stage manager for the Broadway company of the Andrew Lloyd Webber musical *Sunset Boulevard,* summed it up this way: "The stage manager is the only one who knows what the actor has to do and what the set must do."

And Steve Adler, head of stage management in the graduate theater school at the University of California at San Diego, said:

> This is an under-recognized job outside the business, but inside we all know how important a good stage manager is, and we know how a not-good stage manager can make it miserable for all.

PREPRODUCTION

The stage manager's job actually begins with the preproduction planning.

> To my way of thinking, as early as possible you need the stage manager, who is the nucleus of the operation. The director is the boss, but the stage manager must effectively put the team all together.
>
> TONY WALTON, designer

The stage manager's preliminary goal is to have discussions with the director to gain a very clear understanding of his or her interpretation of the show, how the director expects their relationship to function, and the director's routine. If they have not worked together before, the rapport they establish between them is vital; they will be working side by side until the opening night curtain has gone down.

Having earned the director's approval, the stage manager is then interviewed by the producer, who does the hiring.

The stage manager does a careful read-through and analysis of the script and prepares a page-by-page production breakdown, identifying scenes, actors, costumes, sets, lights, props, furniture, technical requirements, sound and special effects, and any unusual items—such as any permits that may be required if the script calls for firearms, flames, or fog. The stage manager prepares an estimate of how many dressers, makeup people, and wig and hair stylists will be needed.

The information in this comprehensive breakdown provides the basis for the production budget. It is also the source for preliminary lists drawn up by each of the production departments:

- The costume plot—what character wears what outfit, when, and with what accessories
- The initial prop list—everything mentioned in the script, who handles it, and what happens to it (is the spaghetti eaten, thrown, spilled?)
- Set changes
- Rehearsal schedules, with breakdowns of scenes
- Technical schedules

It is also the stage manager's responsibility to devise a production schedule. This will encompass a great many activities, including the time and place of auditions, delivery deadlines for every item required for the production, the allotment of time for loading-in of the scenery, lighting, and sound equipment, and scheduling of technical setups and rehearsals.

REHEARSING THE SHOW

When rehearsals are to begin, the stage manager readies the rehearsal space, taping the exact ground plan of the set on the floor, indicating the position of all doors, windows, and stairs, and arranging rehearsal chairs and tables to represent the furniture (and then explaining it all to the cast). Because the rehearsal space will be used all day every day for several weeks, the stage manager checks to be sure there are adequate toilet, closet, and rest facilities, as well as working telephones, coffee machines, water coolers, and places for the company to sit and run lines privately.

For the first day of rehearsal, the stage manager assembles an information packet for every cast member. Each one contains the cast list, contact sheet, everyone's phone number (including that of the stage manager and the rehearsal hall), the director's rehearsal schedule, copies of all the forms that actors need to fill out before the work begins—including their employment contracts—and a numbered copy of the script.

The stage manager will need two copies of the script. In the first, he or she records the director's blocking, notes, and rehearsal comments. Any of the director's and writer's words to the actors, explaining motivation or meaning, will be useful later on when the stage manager has to run understudy rehearsals. In the second script, referred to as the prompt book, are written all technical cues and notes—light, sound, scene shifts, entrances, and exits.

Augmented with stage directions, character notes, and all of the designers' lists and instructions, the prompt book becomes the basis for the publication of the *acting edition* of the play. This is the copy that actors buy when they're working on scenes for acting classes or auditioning for subsequent productions. It is also the version sold to organizations presenting the play in local community theaters.

Daily rehearsal reports—a complete log of the rehearsal period—are kept by the stage manager, who also has to schedule time for performers' costume fittings, photo sessions, and interviews. The stage manager stays in touch with the production departments, relaying to designers and crew any script or blocking changes that may necessitate changes in sets or costumes. In turn, the stage manager receives all notes from the departments, so as to be on top of any possible problem which might conceivably derail the schedule.

Despite the fact that the clock is always ticking, the tone and atmosphere at the rehearsal hall must present a delicate balance of trust and adventure: a calm but busy place where actors can feel secure as they inch their way toward performance. Just as the stage manager receives notes from the director and relays them to each actor, so, too, the stage manager is the one the actors can turn to when they have a problem or questions about the way their work is going. And, if the director gets bogged down on a scene and begins to fall behind the rehearsal schedule, it's the stage manager's job to deftly point that out.

> You are father confessor and company psychologist. There are many egos to juggle, and you must make them work together. You create the environment to encourage good artistic work.
>
> STEVE ADLER

Having people and props ready so that there are no stops and starts in the rehearsal day is part of the stage manager's responsibility. During everyone else's rest period, the stage manager is at work preparing for the next scene, so that when it's time for the cast to work, they can start immediately.

> I was following the trail of each prop—when it starts, where it goes, where it stops. The show's other stage manager was at the dance rehearsals, and we relayed all the changes.
>
> BRIAN MEISTER, stage manager, *Once Upon a Mattress*

AT THE THEATER

Transferring all the elements of production—sets, lights, costumes, speakers—from the various shops into the theater is a lengthy process called the *load-in.* Anyone who has ever moved, even from a bedroom to a studio, knows what a nightmare packing and unpacking just a few dozen cartons can be. Imagine the potential turmoil if truckloads of scenery and an avalanche of electrical equipment were simply to be deposited on the stage, along with trunks, racks, and boxes full of costumes and accessories. Establishing order amid chaos, the stage manager schedules the times when certain materials are brought into the theater and where they are to be deposited, while still leaving space for the work of hanging lights and erecting scenery to be accomplished. The stage manager also must ensure that offstage areas permit movement: there must be crossover spaces behind the set for people to get from one side of the stage to the other; quick-change booths; prop tables; and the stage manager's console, from which all the cues will be called.

As the load-in progresses, the stage manager's knowledge of the director's blocking and furniture arrangement helps the lighting designer and production electrician to focus lights. The stage manager makes a separate cue sheet for each department, wherein each cue is numbered according to *when* in the show it happens, and *what* it does, including the level and/or speed of desired change. Copies of cue sheets go to the person who will be taking the cue from the stage manager and to the head of the department getting the cue—it could be lights, props, costume, or any of the production crew. The stage manager also prepares a cueing script which contains all of the cues in numerical order: curtain, lights, sound, warnings for actors' entrances, warnings for moving a set on- or offstage, and so forth.

The stage manager schedules every technical rehearsal, or "tech." The show is run with the cues; then just the cues are run, so that everyone—actors included—can learn how long it takes to do them and how much, or how little, time they have between cues.

> Communication is the key. Often five, six, seven people need your attention at the same time.
>
> ANDREA NAIER, stage manager

In this era of two-story sets, revolving stages, and frequent blackouts, stage managers are also concerned with company safety.

> There are five of us on wireless headsets. No one but the stage manager calls the cues. The others give "clears" or "stops." I am not in this business to do a speed record. My job is to watch safety, and safety takes time.
>
> PETER LAWRENCE

Everyone in the company enters and leaves the theater through the stage door, so that's where the stage manager sets up the company call board. This is the message center, where official company notices, dressing-room assignments (deciding where to put the actors is also the stage manager's task), performance schedules, and sign-in sheets are posted.

SHOW TIME

Eventually the tight little family group that every company becomes has to let in strangers—the audience. The stage manager gets the director's thoughts on how he or she wants the show to start, then accordingly coordinates with the house manager the routine for opening the house (letting the audience into the theater), lowering the lights, and raising the curtain.

During this period of rampant anxiety and exhilaration, the stage manager, pleasantly calling "half-hour," "fifteen minutes," "five minutes," "places," and finally "curtain," is virtually the captain for a voyage into the unknown. First previews can be technical nightmares. Cues that were set without taking audience reaction into account can be late, early, or not happen at all because they were drowned out by wild applause. Actors' timing can be thrown beyond belief by audience laughter, or the lack of it, and by last-minute rewrites or directorial changes. Imperturbable, the stage manager notes all the changes and is available to quell hysteria in any of its forms.

> On opening night, after weeks of tech rehearsals, where there have been pieces of the show all over the place, you are ready. You call it. You keep everyone going toward the goal with a maximum of élan and flair.
>
> STEVE ADLER

RUNNING THE SHOW

After opening night, the writer, director, and designers are free to go on vacation or to other assignments. But the stage manager now takes charge of the show, seeing to it that every performance flows as smoothly as possible. He or she checks all the production elements before each performance and files a report, or performance log, for every performance—giving curtain times up and down for each scene and noting any deviations from the norm in any department. Acting as the director's representative in the theater, the stage manager may give notes to the actors to correct the "improvements" that can drift into performances over an extended period.

The stage manager runs weekly understudy rehearsals and even trains a replacement for him- or herself.

> We will take turns watching the show, so that any one of us can call the show, and we can replace each other when someone is on vacation.
>
> BRIAN MEISTER

ENDING THE SHOW

News that the producer and the general manager have decided to close the show is given to the stage manager and the crew. The load-out needs planning, too. Arrangements will depend on whether the set and costumes are to be used on tour, stored, or disposed of. Borrowed and rented items have to be returned and the production's property must be safeguarded. After the last performance, the load-out begins as planned.

ATTRIBUTES OF A STAGE MANAGER

Clearly, the ideal stage manager is someone who can successfully handle an enormous number of production details as well as the diverse egos and temperaments of the artists and craftspeople who collaborate to make a live show happen eight times a week.

> This is a great career for someone with a lot of interests who wants to be in production. I feel that the stage manager is not only the most disciplined person in the company but also the most well-rounded. You have to know *structure*—of plays as well as scenery. You have to have a knowledge of directing, acting, design, and administration. You have to know it all and be turned on!
>
> STEVE ADLER

PROFESSIONAL AFFILIATIONS

Stage managers in the professional theater are members of Actors Equity Association (AEA) because, historically, the stage manager was an acting company member who was not playing in that day's performance and stood in the wings holding the script, ready to prompt any actor who forgot a line. As theatrical production became more sophisticated, one person was assigned the job as a full-time responsibility.

According to AEA's agreements with the League of American Theatres and Producers, minimum weekly pay rates on Broadway for stage managers working on a musical are $1,643; on a straight play, $1,413.

There are other agreements covering theaters outside the New York City area, covering touring companies, and so forth. For example, the stage manager working on a bus-and-truck tour of a musical would earn $1,380; of a straight play, $1,265.

Producers also contribute a percentage of the stage managers' salary to the union's pension and health funds.

The Stage Managers' Association (SMA) is a professional organization created by and for stage managers. The organization grew out of a get-together that New York stage managers held in 1981 to meet their British counterparts in the Royal Shakespeare Company's production of *Nicholas Nickleby* on Broadway. Both groups realized that their worlds were essentially the same, while some of the terms were different. They were inspired to start regular meetings on a social and then on a business basis.

A network through which stage managers share ideas, stories, and problems, educating each other and eliminating the isolated feeling which strikes from time

FOR INFORMATION, CONTACT:

Actors Equity Association
165 West 46th Street
New York, NY 10036

Stage Managers' Association
Box 2234
Times Square Station
New York, NY 10108-2020

to time, SMA holds forums on relevant subjects such as contracts, benefits, new technology, theater architecture, and design. Their program, Operation Observation, allows members—and SMA has three membership categories, including novices—to go backstage in theaters around the country and observe other stage managers at work during performances. Their annual publication, *The Stage Managers' Directory*, contains résumés for stage managers nationwide and is distributed to more than 500 potential employers across the country. Meetings, held every five or six weeks in midtown Manhattan, are open to all stage managers. Information on meetings and employment opportunities can be accessed via the member hotline.

SMA also has space on the *Playbill On-Line* web site, at America Online.

RECOMMENDED TRAINING

Every production of every play needs a stage manager. That stage manager needs one, and possibly, two assistants. An ideal way to get an introduction to stage managing is by working in a community theater. However, to go on to a professional career nowadays demands professional training. "You have to keep abreast of the new stuff," advised Karen Carpenter, head of the stage management program at Yale Drama School. "Courses in stage mechanics are necessary."

There are numerous colleges and universities offering total theater training; the big programs include those at Yale Drama School, Carnegie Mellon, and New York University, but, as noted earlier, over time other schools invariably begin to attract recognition. One of these is the University of California at San Diego (UCSD), whose M.F.A. program in Theater, created in 1974, offers a stage management concentration. The faculty are working professionals, many with high-level international credits. In 1983, La Jolla Playhouse, under the artistic direction of Des McAnuff, began producing at UCSD, providing opportunities for students to work with visiting professionals of the finest caliber. Several of their productions—among them *Big River*, The Who's *Tommy*, and *How to Succeed in Business Without Really Trying*—have moved successfully to Broadway and won numerous awards.

In 1994, Michael Greif, a UCSD alumnus, was appointed La Jolla's artistic director. Greif directed the original production of Jonathan Larson's Pulitzer Prize–winning *Rent*.

> Every one of our graduates is or has been working in the business, as stage managers, company managers, or starting their own companies, directing—lately, in TV and film. We have two assistant stage managers on *How to Succeed*.
>
> STEVE ADLER

The latest news about colleges with programs in stage management is available through Theatre Communications Group (TCG), and should also be accessible on the Internet.

GETTING STARTED

Any work you do backstage on a show is a way to learn more about the theater and meet people who will be working on other projects. If you're good, they'll want you to come back, and then you may be on salary.

> Jobs come via network, the grapevine. Show up. Volunteer.
>
> LOREN SCHNEIDER, stage manager

> Read a lot. See as much live performance as you can, as much as possible, no matter what it is—dance, speech, everything. Volunteer at any level— local, community—people always want free labor. Any job will help you. Do the props, box office . . . everything, anything.
>
> DEBBIE FALB

> I had studied stagecraft as part of my acting major in college. When I realized how much organizational work I had done, I put together a résumé and started going after work as a stage manager. I've been working almost continuously for more than ten years.
>
> SANDRA BLOOM, stage manager

A newcomer with no networking possibilities can learn about job opportunities by reading "the trades"—for example, the weekly publication *Theatrical Index,* which purports to list every show, plus those that are in the planning stages; *Back Stage,* which concentrates on New York production; and *Back Stage West,* which does the same thing for West Coast production. TCG's biweekly *Art-Search,* the national employment bulletin for the arts, lists openings in academic institutions, resident theaters, and offices around the country.

The Alliance of Resident Theaters in New York (A.R.T./New York) serves that region's not-for-profit theater and maintains a file of job openings as well as a résumé book for stage managers (and other technical people). One can also obtain a list of their member theaters.

FOR INFORMATION, CONTACT:

A.R.T./New York
131 Varick Street
New York, NY 10013

Actors Equity Association
165 West 46th Street
New York, NY 10036

ASSISTANT STAGE MANAGERS

One way to become a production stage manager is to earn a reputation as a very good assistant stage manager (often referred to as an ASM). The Actors Equity agreements with producers call for an assistant stage manager on a dramatic show and a first and second assistant stage manager on a musical. Large-cast dramatic shows may also need a second assistant stage manager.

Assistant stage managers—who are also members of Actors Equity—are employed at least a week before rehearsals begin. The stage manager assigns the ASM's responsibilities, many of which will depend upon the complexity of the show, the ground plan, the cues, and the performers. At the theater, the assistant stage manager, serving as the stage manager's eyes and ears on the side of the stage opposite that of the stage manager's podium, is ready to relay signals for entrances, exits, and scene changes.

According to the present-day contract, minimum weekly salaries for Broadway ASMs are:

- First assistant stage manager on a musical: $1,300
- First assistant stage manager on a straight play: $1,154
- Second assistant stage manager: $1,086

To give you an idea of the salary range in other venues, the weekly bus-and-truck tour minimums are:

- First assistant stage manager on a musical: $1,150
- First assistant stage manager on a straight play: $1,035
- Second assistant stage manager: $673

These amounts are supplemented by various benefits. Contracts are negotiated at three-year intervals. You should contact Actors Equity Association for information on eligibility requirements and salaries.

JOB OUTLOOK

The future looks fairly bright for stage managers willing to work in regional theater, to travel with a touring company, to work off- or off-off-Broadway, or to apply those same skills working with dance or opera companies. Once you've acquired the requisite experience, chances are you'll be calling cues on Broadway or at the Metropolitan Opera.

Because they are so knowledgeable about every aspect of theater production, experienced stage managers have been able to move into other areas, notably producing and directing. Former stage manager Harold Prince is the stellar example of one who has succeeded at both careers. Lauded as the producer of the original productions of *A Funny Thing Happened on the Way to the Forum* (1962) and *Fiddler on the Roof* (1964), he directed *Cabaret, Company, A Little Night Music, Evita, Phantom of the Opera,* the 1996 revival of *Showboat,* and other hits as well.

THE PROPERTY DEPARTMENT

Everything on the stage, except the walls, the floor, and the actors, is considered a *property*, or prop—furniture, lamps, carpets, curtains, accessories, and any items the actors touch, bring on- or offstage, eat, drink, and cook. The person who knows how to locate, buy, borrow, rent, or make any and everything called for, do it quickly, and meet the designers' specifications, is the property master.

The property master is employed by the production before rehearsals begin. How far in advance will depend upon the size and complexity of the show.

The property master works with the director, designers, stage manager, and the actors to get a sense of the tone and style of the production. Collecting all the items on the prop lists demands creative choices that not only fulfill, but can enhance the designer's vision. A living room set may specify a wall of bookshelves—but what sorts of books? leather-bound classics or used paperbacks? A fancy telephone can serve as a showoff's status symbol or become a comic nuisance (the actor using the prop will doubtless have something to say about that decision). A property master may have to *create* a phone that the actor can handle comfortably, that telegraphs the right information to the audience, and makes designer and director happy.

Property masters who have an extensive list of reliable prop sources, or who have demonstrated a talent for making unusual items that are important to the play, will be the designers' first recommendation to the producer and director.

Depending upon the needs of the show, the property master will require one or more assistants—the prop crew for the run of the play. For unlike the design team, which departs after opening night, the prop department stays on the job, setting up at the theater for every performance. Items that are used up must be replenished, furniture must be placed on its marks, hand props must be ready in the order in which they are used, food and drink must be freshly prepared to the performers' taste.

Between scenes some props may be moved, or struck (removed), and others set in place. If an actress carries in a sack of groceries, a prop man hands it to her before she enters. Prepacking the groceries in the order the actress wants to set them out on the kitchen counter is also the prop department's job. And, of course, all properties must be kept clean and in good condition.

If the show goes on the road, the property master duplicates the props for each touring company. In the case of rare, unique pieces, this will mean making copies. Each company will need its own prop crew. Sometimes the original property master will assemble the props—much as a designer will oversee the second version of the original set—and then assign an assistant to handle the daily running of the show.

BASIC TRAINING

There is no school per se for aspiring prop masters. In fact, this is one career that does not require more than a high school diploma. Props people have come into the job from various directions. Several young designers and scenic artists have settled into this niche. Others began as "gofers" on the backstage crew, working in regional or community theater. Many have worked in department store display departments, as shoppers at interior design firms, as crafts instructors, and as stylists for magazines and commercials.

ATTRIBUTES OF THE PROP PERSON

A keen theatrical sense, an awareness of the principles of staging, and familiarity with furniture design and construction are necessary. The property master should be able to understand designers' blueprints and technical drawings, and will need to be adept at handling tools, strong enough to move and lift furniture, and able, on occasion, to drive a truck.

Creativity is essential, as is the knack of coming up with great substitute solutions when the exact item proves unobtainable.

Props people should be outgoing, tireless, and enjoy poking around in flea markets and antique shops. They need excellent visual memory and a careful notetaking system, so as to be able to recall in what window of what little boutique, on what side street, they spied the Biedermeier desk that would be perfect for the sitting room they are "propping" now. This job requires keen attention to details coupled with flexibility—as when that sitting-room scene is cut and the elegant Biedermeier desk has to go right back to the boutique.

GETTING STARTED

Young people can get a taste of the experience scouting props for school or college productions. Any community theater group will need props of some kind. Even if someone on the production crew is already the assigned prop master, a bright volunteer whose assistance will make the job a little easier is sure to be welcomed.

If there's a film school in the vicinity, student productions will need props. Offer to find them.

Touring companies—opera and dance as well as theatrical—may expect to hire local people for the working prop crew, to handle those items that are replenished for each performance. Consult the theater manager for this information. Do not be shy.

PROFESSIONAL AFFILIATION

While the property master works closely with the scene designer (and may even have design training) and sits with the design team for preproduction meetings, this field is organized by the International Alliance of Theatrical and Stage Employees (IATSE)—not United Scenic Artists. One reason for the separation is that the design team leaves once the show opens, whereas the property master, working with the prop crew, remains with the show for the length of the run.

New York City members belong to Local #1. There are other local offices throughout the country, a fact which may be to the advantage of aspiring property people in the regional markets. Working as the extra—that is, nonunion—person on a local crew, one may accumulate enough hours of experience to qualify as a replacement person and earn union membership more readily than in New York.

FOR INFORMATION, CONTACT:

International Alliance of Theatrical and StageEmployees
Local #1
320 West 46th Street, 3rd floor
New York, NY 10036

Minimum wages and working conditions for union members will differ according to the contract and the area. Contracts are usually negotiated every three years. Always contact the union for up-to-date information on wages and working conditions and news of incoming productions.

PUBLICITY AND ADVERTISING

"There is no 'shelf life' to a theater ticket," said Nancy Coyne, CEO and creative director at Serino Coyne, Inc., an ad agency. In other words, an empty seat represents lost dollars. Therefore, as soon as the show definitely goes into production, the producer has to let the audience know about it. Audience awareness, interest, and expectation generate ticket sales. To accomplish this, the producer employs a PUBLICIST, or PRESS AGENT, and an ADVERTISING AGENCY. Because live theater is a unique market, both must be theater specialists who complement, or augment, each other's work. (Publicists and ad agencies are not supposed to compete.)

A healthy advance ticket sale is essential, so there's enough money for the show to last until the word of mouth clicks in.

RICHARD SEADER, producer and general manager

Advertising is targeted space or air time that is purchased in a number of selected media outlets (newspapers, magazines, radio and television spots, and so on), at specific times, for a specific purpose in a carefully planned overall marketing campaign.

Publicity is unpaid advertising. The late Tim Taylor, a publicist before he became an entertainment reviewer, referred to it as "the art of stealing space" in outlets that cover theatrical or entertainment news or in outlets that do not ordinarily cover theatrical topics but will write about your show because some aspect of it is interesting to their audience. That means you have not only found the space, you have found the hook that grabs audience attention.

In New York City not so long ago, there were seven daily and Sunday newspapers, each of which employed a daily theater or entertainment news columnist, in addition to a regular theater critic. Over three decades, Sam Zolotow's show business column on the entertainment page of *The New York Times* was eagerly read. These outlets have shrunk to three daily papers nowadays, and Zolotow's replacement, the *Times*'s Friday "On Stage and Off" column, goes on hiatus during the summer.

There used to be a great many magazines in which theater coverage was considered fundamental. Writers and press agents—buyers and sellers at the same agora—knew each other, regularly dined and swapped stories at the same taverns and respected each other's professionalism. Which is not to suggest that any one pal's mediocre efforts were more or less guaranteed publication in another's column. The challenge was always to come up with a great idea or story that a particular columnist, whose predilections the press agent had figured out over the years, would find irresistible. The reward was seeing the item in print and adding it to the client's coverage.

Veteran press agents agree that the 1957 Burt Lancaster-Tony Curtis film, *The Sweet Smell of Success,* with its superb screenplay by Ernest Lehman and Clifford Odets, presents a fairly accurate picture of the scene as it was around that time. (It's worth trying to find at the video store, or catch on one of the movie channels.)

WHAT A PRESS AGENT DOES

The theatrical press agent assembles press kits—these are packets of information that he or she writes, supplemented by photographs, about the show's newsworthy talent—and distributes them to the agent's list of media people and organizations. "Talent" refers not only to the star; it may include the director, designers, an unusual set—whatever may be considered newsworthy about the show.

The press agent writes a one-page *release,* telling a story about some element of the show that, it is hoped, will provoke interest. He or she sends these, often by fax, to appropriate outlets.

> A press release must have a good lead. In the first sentence you have to tell who, what, where, when, why. And make it interesting.
>
> SUSAN L. SCHULMAN, press agent

> Find out what's interesting about the elements of the project. The people. Other jobs they've done. Figure out what you are selling and who to get it to.
>
> DIANE JUDGE, press agent

The press agent arranges interviews with newspaper and magazine writers, sets up appearances on radio and TV news and talk shows. Three minutes on *Good Morning, America, Today, Charlie Rose,* or *Entertainment Tonight* is tantamount to striking gold. The press agent creates events, such as a fashion show or a cooking demonstration (is the star handy with a wok?) in a local department store, a visit to a neighborhood school, a benefit for a worthy organization, or a contest ("The first five people who call this station with the correct answer will each win four tickets to . . .").

The press agent has at his or her command all the facts about everyone and every outlet and is thus able to anticipate opportunities for coverage and take advantage of them. And never miss a deadline.

> If you're featuring your costumes, you can make it to the papers. The week-

end listing sections are great for photo placement. Make sure the costumes are photographed against a light background, so the details can be seen.

JONATHAN SLAFF, press agent

The press agent must have ideas for hooks and for gaining access and, most important, credibility. One Broadway story concerns Merle Debusky, a highly esteemed press agent for more than forty years. In 1962, he became the first press agent to be elected president of the Association of Theatrical Press Agents and Managers (ATPAM); he served in that position for more than twenty-five years.

> He was a press agent with a superior reputation. When he said, "This deserves your attention," people believed him.
>
> Merle was handling press for *For colored girls who have considered suicide/when the rainbow is enuf,* which was a great show that, for some reason, wasn't catching on. It was an unusual piece. He did something he had never, ever done. He called people directly. He said, "Come see this show. This is something special." And because of him doing that, putting himself on the line in that way, they went. And, of course, he was telling the truth. They raved about it in print, and then the audience started to come. And the show, rightfully, did very well.

PAUL LIBIN, producing manager, Jujamcyn Theaters

For colored girls . . . , by Ntozake Shange, opened at the Booth Theater on September 15, 1976, after an off-Broadway run at the Public Theater, and played 742 performances.

> Your credibility is all you have. You create expectation. Be true to the project, the material.

DAVID ROTHENBERG, press agent

The press agent invites the press to opening night, arranges for their seating (who needs to sit where), thanks them for coming, and then leaves the reviewers alone.

As press agents gain more experience and skill, they get to handle more prestigious shows. They also personally represent celebrity clients, publicize theater companies and also corporations in other venues. Some of them appear on radio and TV talk shows. Sometimes, they host their own talk shows.

PROFESSIONAL REQUIREMENTS

Theatrical press agents are members of ATPAM. To become eligible for membership, novices must apprentice to an ATPAM member for two years and then take a two-part (oral and written) exam. On being accepted, the press

FOR INFORMATION,
CONTACT:

Association of
Theatrical Press Agents
and Managers
165 West 46th Street
New York, NY 10036

agent pays the $1,000 initiation fee and joins the union. Annual dues are $140, plus working dues of 2 percent of their salary when employed.

The minimum payment for press agents is currently $1,504 per week, plus benefits. Contracts are renegotiated periodically.

Press agents may handle more than one show at a time, according to a formula devised by ATPAM. For the second show, an associate, also an ATPAM member, must be hired. The resulting pair of agents may then take on a third show. If they land a fourth show, the team must hire an additional ATPAM associate. This trio of agents is then able to accept a fifth show. If the head press agent gets a sixth show, the office must hire another ATPAM associate, and that is the maximum that any office can handle.

Regarding off-Broadway productions, a sliding scale is in effect. Fees are contingent upon the size of the theater housing the show and the potential gross. In theaters with a capacity of more than 200 people, a press agent is required.

Off-off-Broadway is not union-organized. ATPAM members cannot even work in that arena, but it's open to young people who want to get started.

TRAINING

Because the Broadway press agents of the past prided themselves on their persistence, talent, guts, and savvy, the notion of a college degree program for this particular career has not been strongly advocated. That attitude seems to be changing. Certainly, courses or degrees in journalism, public relations, advertising, communications, arts administration, arts management, and marketing are all relevant and useful. So is a knowledge of theater, of course—it's hard to know what's newsworthy about a project if you don't have a clue about what has been considered usual over any length of time.

New York University's School of Continuing Education offers a public relations series; usually taught by working professionals, the courses provide an ideal introduction to the field. ATPAM seminars that are given in conjunction with NYU's apprentice program should be very worthwhile.

There are more than a hundred chapters of the Public Relations Society of America (PRSA), in ten districts across the country, each of which schedules member activities. The PRSA catalog offers a range of professional tools and training materials, including several designed for those interested in exploring the career.

GETTING STARTED

An energetic idea person who writes well can begin by publicizing events in high school. If good results are evident, it's not hard to go on from there.

Community theaters and local fundraising organizations will welcome your efforts.

Local arts and business organizations are excellent places to network. Volunteer for any event that needs community attendance and support. If you manage to get local coverage for events that you publicize, you have the beginnings of an impressive portfolio.

Unions within the industry, such as Actors Equity Association, AFTRA, or UNITE, all need publicity. They don't have a lot of money, but their leaders know a lot of people, most of whom a press agent should know. So volunteer. If you're good, they may want to hire you.

Press agentry is all around you. Read the "entertainment press," and study newspaper Sunday supplements to see how events are being publicized. Try to recognize items that are a press agent's work. What story angle was given to each item? Would you have thought of the angle that is featured yourself? What other ideas might you have suggested?

ATTRIBUTES OF A PRESS AGENT

Unlike the many people who seem to talk and talk and never get to the point, press agents are able to formulate an idea and explain it quickly. One might say that they automatically talk in sound-bites or captions. Excellent at retaining information, they are born storytellers. They are persistent, observant, likable, and able to establish rapport quickly. And they work hard.

PAID ADVERTISING

Anyone reading *The New Yorker* magazine during the summer of 1996 would have noticed a full-page ad for *Titanic*, the Broadway musical that opened in the late spring of 1997 and, to many people's surprise, won that season's Tony Award. The show's logo was a sensational design in which the ocean liner's smokestacks and stateroom lights spell out the name. By Thanksgiving of 1996, the logo had also been spotted in other publications. The audience would have the better part of seven months to learn to recognize the logo, become curious, and decide to buy tickets. There was also an element of mystery to the campaign: No other news about the show, its cast, or director, appeared in any of the media.

February of 1997 brought full-page, full-color ads for another new musical, *Ragtime*. Previews of the show were to begin the following December!

There is such intense competition for audiences and for whatever media space is not given over to coverage of movies and TV that distinctive advertising has become essential to the existence of a theatrical production. From the start, the press agent and the advertising agency are involved in a campaign to achieve recognizable brand-name status for their show.

Consumers will not buy enough of a product if left alone. Therefore you need to sell. Entertainment is our product, and we have to get the audience. You need months to build awareness and demand.

Nancy Coyne

Producers are in love with their product and do not realize that the market is not as turned on as they are. The ad agency works with the producer to identify what they are selling and who their target audience is.

Linda Lehman, account executive, Serino Coyne, Inc.

Also on the team are a direct-mail expert—a specialist in charge of creating the flyers or brochures that will be mailed to potential ticket-buyers well in advance of the opening, with the aim of producing a healthy advance sale—and a mailing list consultant, who is able to define the ideal recipients of the mailed pieces.

As a founder of the Indiana Repertory Theater, in 1972, I discovered I had a talent for the managerial side of the business—generating income, selling tickets. Which is what I was asked to teach at Yale.

I'm now hired as a marketing consultant. The attempt is to identify the multiple-ticket buyers, because a mailing to them would be so much more productive.

Ben Mordecai, associate dean, Yale Drama School

Every commercial producer uses direct mail. Especially to fill the theater with an audience for those early previews.

Linda Lehman

Identifying the market and going after it may sound like standard advertising and marketing procedure. But in live theater, things change on a day-to-day basis, not according to 13- or 26-week cycles. When the reviews come out after the show's premiere, the advertising agency staff rushes not to the celebration party but to the office to compose a new ad that will be faxed in time for local TV stations' 6 A.M. news broadcast.

Good or bad, you're news. We work close to a 16-hour day.

Nancy Coyne

AN IDEAL CAMPAIGN

Of the five major agencies with the awareness and staff to handle a live-theater account, Serino Coyne, Inc. reportedly handles more than 80 percent of the current New York productions. Agencies do not charge the client a fee; they receive a 15-percent commission, or rebate, whenever they place an ad or purchase time on radio or TV. Nancy Coyne estimates the cost of the ideal advertising campaign at $200,000 per week. She said:

Advertising should be as entertaining as your show, a "free sample" on radio and TV. You need to be in the alphabetical listings (ABCs) of The New York Times nationally on Tuesday, Wednesday, and Thursday; you need a larger ad on Friday. On Sunday, a quarter-page, in color, so it jumps out. Then you need brochures; you need to be in the hotel magazines. You need to be visible outdoors, on buses, on train stations between Boston, New York, and Washington, on the Long Island Railroad, on highways. You need a great logo and great art in front of the theater. You need a great property. It can only be live. And you need a star or two. And you need a sense of urgency. When Ralph Fiennes was doing Hamlet, we said, "Only 85 performances left!"

But, she explained, most shows don't have a $200,000 advertising budget. "So we have to be creative." The agency conducts a great many focus groups for each show—little expense there—in order to understand how the play is perceived and to get a better picture of the audience attracted to it. To get the most response out of every dollar spent, the office has come up with some solutions to the problem of ad money, or the lack of it. Among these are sales promotion tie-ins, combination packages, corporate sponsorship—strategies for enlarging the potential audience by seeking a variety of marketing partners.

CHANGING TIMES

The need to optimize ticket sales through effective single-ticket and group sales techniques has attracted people with marketing training into the business. Realizing their community of interest, ATPAM has recently added a member category for marketing directors. To join ATPAM as a marketer, one needs to be working at a theater or on a show. No apprenticeship is necessary.

ATTRIBUTES OF AGENCY PEOPLE

So who belongs in this area of advertising, with its tight budgets, long hours, and unpredictable deadlines?

To be in show business, you have to be just a little bit crazy. The most you can do is sell out eight times a week. That is x number of seats times the amount you can charge for them.

NANCY COYNE

This career demands creative, articulate people for whom the excitement of show business is an added attraction. Majors in advertising, marketing, theater management, arts administration, or communications have the requisite background. Working alongside the publicity or marketing person at any local entertainment outlet, such as a theater or local cable station, is a good way to build a résumé.

CAREER EXPECTATIONS

The demand for live entertainment being what it is, this area of the business is certain to flourish. Using ATPAM's Broadway minimum as a base—$1,504, plus benefits, per week—press agent work, marketing, or advertising are promising careers whose skills are always transferable to larger venues.

THE COMPANY MANAGER

To represent management with the company—actors, stage managers, and crew—from the first day of rehearsal until the show closes, the general manager selects a company manager, who is officially employed by the producer. The company manager may work on only one show at a time, and is present at every rehearsal and every performance.

The company manager is in charge of setting up the weekly payroll. This includes negotiating standard, or non-star, contracts; seeing that everyone who is paid a salary files the appropriate income tax forms; and checking the accuracy of all payments, deductions, and contributions made on behalf of everyone in the company—who are members of fourteen or so theatrical unions, each of whose agreements are different.

During rehearsals, the company manager works with the production stage manager to ensure that whatever needs to be ready—from sets and costumes to specially designed props—is ready at the scheduled time. All day-to-day expenses incurred by the people doing work for the production are checked with the stage manager and paid by the company manager.

The company manager is also responsible for counting the amount of money taken in at each performance. This tabulation is of the utmost importance for such matters as recoupment, the royalty pool, and contracts that call for additional payments when the gross exceeds a certain amount. These matters depend upon:

- How many tickets were sold
- The prices at which they were sold
- Exactly how many discounts there were, if any
- Exactly how many giveaways there were, if any

Once the box office closes, and the audience is watching the show, the company manager and the house (theater) manager do these totals for every performance. They document the figures with a signed statement each time.

If the company goes on tour, the company manager travels with the show and is responsible for filing the same reports after every performance. When notice of the closing of the show is posted, the company manager checks with the stage manager as to the return of items that are rented, borrowed, or will be stored.

PROFESSIONAL REQUIREMENTS

In the commercial theater, company managers are members of the Associa-

FOR INFORMATION,
CONTACT:

Association of
Theatrical Press Agents
and Managers
165 West 46th Street
New York, NY 10036

tion of Theatrical Press Agents and Managers (ATPAM). Novices must first apprentice to a general manager or company manager. The two-year stint of on-the-job training requires participation in a series of seminars that the union presents in conjunction with the League of American Theaters and Producers. Apprentices must then take a written and an oral exam. If they pass, they are accepted into the union.

The initiation fee is $1,000; annual dues are $140, plus "working dues"— 2 percent of the salary you make while you are working. At the start, company managers usually get paid according to an established pay scale, which is currently $1,319 per week. As their experience and reputation grow, they are able to negotiate over-scale salaries. And once they are union members, they can work in theaters across the country.

At this time, ATPAM has no contract with off-Broadway producers. Company managers are customarily paid on a sliding scale, based on the potential gross of the show and the size of the theater. Some theaters seat only 99 people. When a theater seats 200 or more, the show must hire a company manager.

ATTRIBUTES OF A COMPANY MANAGER

This is a career for detail-oriented people. They need to understand the theatrical production process. As we have seen, they must also be totally familiar with all the other unions' contracts.

Accounting skills would be a definite plus. And, when not involved with the strictly financial task of totalling each day's receipts, company managers have to communicate effectively with the wide range of people who are all part of a show.

It is a difficult business, in that you are always looking for work from other people in the same business. I think you need an inherent love of theater, a love of words.

BERENICE WEILER, secretary–treasurer, ATPAM

RECOMMENDED TRAINING

In addition to well-publicized courses of study at Harvard, Yale, Columbia University, and the University of Miami, classes in theatrical business administration and/or arts management are offered by colleges and universities throughout the country. Theater Communications Group (TCG) is a source of current information.

Bookkeeping and/or accounting training, available at the high school level, are extremely useful.

GETTING STARTED

As Berenice Weiler pointed out, off-off-Broadway is not union-organized. Young people who want to get started as company managers are encouraged to look for entry-level work in those venues.

According to Berenice Weiler, "It's all networking—who you know, where you are, and using all your contacts." This is a position in which you may end up being both artistic and a very successful businessperson. Said Weiler: "A young man who started as an apprentice with my partner and me—we were general managers—just stopped by to say he is now managing a regional theater. That's nice."

THE BACKSTAGE CREW

Once the set is loaded into the theater, an army of technicians—the stage-hands—goes into action. Stagehands belong to one of three departments: carpenters, electricians, or props people. Their responsibilities, at least in the commercial theater, are discrete: Everyone understands that electricians don't hunt for props, carpenters don't focus lights, and so on. However, during the show, any scenery that moves on electrically powered platforms is run by the master electrician.

The stage manager, who has previously determined from the production analysis and from discussions with the designers how large a crew will be needed in each department, has planned the load-in and setup so that the PRODUCTION CARPENTER and CARPENTERS can begin to erect the set at the rear of the stage, while the PRODUCTION ELECTRICIAN and the LIGHTING CREW can work at hanging the lighting instruments at the front of the stage and in the house. Then the SOUND CREW ELECTRICIANS can place their equipment.

PRODUCTION CARPENTER

The production carpenter is responsible for everything concerning installation of a show's set and scenery—the rigging, hanging, and movement of all the pieces of the set. He or she also creates a *hanging plot*, which shows where on the overhead grid (the so-called *fly floor* high above the stage) everything that must be hung will be attached. If wagons, winches, or turntables are needed for scene shifts, the production carpenter is involved in building those—more or less creating a false floor with hidden grooves to accommodate the electric cables needed to pull, push, or turn the sets. The production carpenter also decides whether special crew members will be needed to handle them.

This is a job that demands a knowledge of engineering in addition to a proficiency with hammer and nails. Today's complicated sets are built of metal and plastic as well as canvas and wood; a kitchen used in Scene One may have to be flown out of sight, and safely anchored, until it appears again in Scene Five. All the rigging, anchoring, and split-second flying is the carpenter's responsibility. And the carpenter also sees to it that the sets, cables, and related equipment are maintained in perfect condition for each performance of the play.

PRODUCTION ELECTRICIAN

Everything concerning the lighting of the show is the responsibility of the production electrician.

The job begins in preproduction; the lighting designer and production electrician work together from the start. The lighting designer's plot is the basis for the production electrician's rental order for lighting equipment. (Lighting equipment is not purchased but rented from theatrical supply houses which offer many of the latest inventions.) The production electrician ensures that every instrument matches the designer's specifications and is in top working condition, and the order is delivered to the theater at load-in.

It is the production electrician's responsibility to make certain that the theater's power supply can handle the show's needs. In the case of a theater with insufficient power, the production electrician orders whatever additional equipment is necessary.

If the prop list calls for lamps that the actors switch on or off, if water really has to pour from the faucets of the kitchen sink, the production electrician is the one who must wire such practical props. He or she also cuts all the colored gels for the lights.

Working with the lighting designer, the production electrician supervises the ELECTRICAL CREW as they hang and focus every instrument on the equipment list. The complicated task of setting light cues and programming them in sequence—a job that is done nowadays using a computer—can involve more than 350 separate instruments and as many cues. This is accomplished during an arduous series of run-throughs and technical rehearsals.

During the show, the electrician "runs" the light cues from a console, or control board, as he or she receives them from the stage manager through a headset. There will also be FOLLOW-SPOT OPERATORS working spotlights that must be moved manually—as many as needed, depending upon the staging and size of the show.

GEARING FOR SOUND

The production electrician also oversees, in conjunction with the sound designer and the stage manager, the installation and wiring of sound equipment. Having studied the theater's size and layout and the production's ground plan, the sound designer creates an equipment list of cables, mixers, speakers, circuits, tape decks, power cords, performers' microphones, and any other items necessary to fulfill the show's sound design. Prior to load-in, the SOUND TECHNICIAN checks the condition of every piece of equipment. After that, the crew's major task will be to place equipment such as speakers so as to avoid interference with the lights or scenery.

For sound designer James Lebrecht, the first technical rehearsals are not run-throughs but "crawl-throughs"—merely the opportunity to go from one cue to the next, with the actors saying their lines. They are the first chance for the sound technician to hear how the cues sound in relation to the actors' voices, and to make necessary adjustments in timing, volume, and mix. During subsequent technical rehearsals, as all the elements fall into place, final readings are set. When opening night arrives, a backup or safety copy of the show tapes is made.

Actors' timing will vary with audience reaction. The sound technician operating the control console must be alert to nuances that will affect both the overall sound balance and the execution of sound effects.

Once the show is running, the sound technician should allow plenty of time to run a sound check on every piece of equipment before each performance. He or she creates a "top-of-show" list of all equipment settings and checks them off in order, then sees that the cue sheets are all in order. All controls should be preset for the opening curtain. Nothing about running the show should be left to memory.

Depending on the size of the show, there will be technicians assigned to handle the body mikes that most principals wear.

PROFESSIONAL REQUIREMENTS

Erecting sets, hanging backdrops, positioning speakers, and focusing lights is demanding work physically and technically. Carpenters and electricians climb ladders and scaffolding and attach ropes and cables to heavy, frequently cumbersome instruments that, once in place, must be absolutely secure. When a show is setting up, the work days are long. When the show is running, continual vigilance is essential. Despite the casual-seeming nature of the work—the odd hours, the idea of reporting to a theater rather than an office, and the lack of a dress code—the crew, like the cast, works the same eight performances a week.

Stagehands, therefore, must be depended on to work calmly under pressure and often in cramped quarters. The best of them are smart, observant, and skillful with tools and equipment. College degrees are not required, but familiarity with carpentry, electrical work, rigging, and hanging is necessary. Because they are welcome to hang around sets, watching for a chance to join the team, many stagehands learn on the job. However, plenty of excellent theater-related courses are offered at vocational schools and in community and junior colleges.

Carpenters and electricians in the commercial theater, like property masters, are among the more than 2,000 members of Local #1, the stagehands' union in New York City. There are other local branches of the union across the country.

> FOR INFORMATION, CONTACT:
>
> International Alliance of Theatrical and Stage Employees Local #1 320 West 46th Street, 3rd floor New York, NY 10036

Wherever there are lots of shows, and work for everyone, there are opportunities for nonmembers.

> You need three years of nonunion work to qualify as a replacement. You come in, you sign up; if they need people, you work. In this business, you learn as you go. The more you learn, the more you earn. We give classes for our members, and if there's room others can come in too—I guess it's like being a standby for tickets. You can earn about $20,000 a year as a replacement.
>
> FRANK MCCARTHY, Local #1

Local #1 is frequently accused of being a "father-and-son" closed union. People may tell you: "The only way to get in the union is to be born into it." Officers and members deny this. In many families whatever the father did for a living was good enough for the sons, and they were not only expected, but proud, to follow in their father's footsteps. Paul Dunn, of Local #1, reported: "I am the fifth generation of my family to be in this union."

Keep in mind that the house manager (see pages 106–107) oversees a separate crew employed by the theater owner which consists of the HOUSE CARPENTER and a HOUSE PROPERTY PERSON, who are responsible to the house manager for maintenance of the theater's furnishings. There is also a HOUSE ELECTRICIAN, who may work with the production electrician, but is basically responsible for the theater's lighting fixtures and other electrical equipment.

THE WARDROBE CREW

The wardrobe supervisor (if this person is female she is often referred to by the traditional title of WARDROBE MISTRESS) is hired by the producer before rehearsals begin. She or he confers with the costume designer, stage manager, and company manager to learn how many performers and costumes the show will have, and watches rehearsals to determine the number of costume changes, when they occur, how quickly they must be made, and whether quick-change booths will be necessary. Those conditions determine how large a crew of WARDROBE ASSISTANTS and DRESSERS the show will require. Taking into account the types of costumes—from tattered jeans to evening gowns—and whatever special care they will require, the supervisor selects her crew and assigns dressers to performers.

Everyone in the union (Theatrical Wardrobe Union) is a dresser. Wardrobe supervisors and assistants begin as dressers and accumulate lengthy résumés. A supervisor will notice dressers whose work is particularly efficient, who are well liked by performers and the other members of the department; the supervisor will ask such a dresser if he or she is interested as working as an assistant. If the show's current assistant goes on vacation, that dresser may move into the empty slot.

Assistants who have proven themselves over a long period and feel confident that they can supervise a show make themselves known to producers. When they learn that a show is coming in they request an interview with the producer and bid for the assignment. Presumably, they know the available, conscientious dressers and will be able to staff the production with an excellent crew.

One may also begin as a wardrobe supervisor with the road company of an established show.

The SHOP STEWARD is elected by the wardrobe team. He or she is the person to whom the others bring any problems related to getting the work done efficiently. There is no added compensation for this responsibility, but, as dresser Bob Branigan noted, "We can't have anything go wrong with our backstage choreography. We have to separate business from personality. Backstage it is also show *business*."

AT THE THEATER

At load-in, all the racks of costumes and cartons full of accessories are gathered up by the wardrobe supervisor and crew. Each costume is assembled in its entirety—garment, undergarments, hosiery, shoes, accessories, even handkerchiefs. Every item is labeled with the performer's name, and all the outfits are hung in the performers' dressing rooms. Dressers make their own lists—personal costume plots—of every costume piece to be handled in the course of the show: what goes where, who gets what, what the cue is, where the exits and entrances are, what must be preset, what has to be moved, and what changes when. If a costume change must be made behind the set, the dresser, in the quick-change booth, is ready to remove the first costume as soon as the performer exits the scene and replace it with the second. The dresser then takes the costume that's been worn and folds or hangs it for its next use.

One of Julie Andrews' costume changes in *Victor / Victoria* reportedly had to be made so quickly that one dresser removed parts of the star's outfit as they dashed from one side of the stage to the other, where her next costume was suspended from an overhead rod just behind the door she would walk through. At the moment she stood beneath the garment, arms raised, the costume was lowered over the actress' head by a second dresser, while a third, working with a tiny flashlight in her mouth, knelt to change her shoes. Zipped up, hair in place, she turned, opened the door and stepped onstage.

Dressers may be assigned to take care of more than one performer. During each performance they work solely with that performer, unless there is an emergency—such as someone's zipper getting stuck.

> Things go wrong plenty of times. This is live theater, after all. People can forget their lines. Actors get caught on things on stage. You have to do the actors' mike changes—you unsnap them and the microphone people have to be there to get them rewired into the microphone as fast as possible. Every night the show is different, onstage as well as backstage. People don't feel well, there's something in the air, buttons come off. We have our needles and thread ready.
>
> BOB BRANIGAN

Costume maintenance is an important function. The dressers' day call begins at 1 P.M.

> In addition to sewing, this job now requires some painting skill. We frequently have to paint shoes and tights. For *Crazy For You*, we applied rhinestones to the dancers' tights! That was such a success; it made a difference.
>
> E. SUSAN ERENBURG, business representative, Theatrical Wardrobe Union

> During the day you do laundry, cleaning, polish shoes, mend rips and tears. Buttons, beads, sequins, and feathers have to be replaced all the time. You iron or steam clothes. Once I spent the entire day polishing shoes for *Dreamgirls*. It's amazing how things start wearing out under the lights.
>
> BOB BRANIGAN

During the run of the play, the supervisor examines costumes for any tears and generally examines seams looking for weak spots. He or she notes when understudy costumes and replacement costumes are needed, when hosiery should be ordered, and when shoes need new taps or rubber soles.

GETTING STARTED

In the past, the greater number of wardrobe supervisors were ex-dancers—whose careers are short—or the wives of stagehands. Today's more elaborate shows are much more physically demanding, requiring younger people with plenty of stamina.

> For *Showboat* there were 500 costumes for seventy-one people. Luckily, it was in a new theater, so there was room for all those people. But *Crazy For You*, which was also a big show, was in the old Shubert Theater. There was much less space backstage and lots of running up and down flights of stairs, carrying heavy baskets full of costumes, accessories, tights, shoes, and headdresses. That's hard work.
>
> E. Susan Erenburg

New dressers get a chance to break in as swings when permanent dressers go on vacation. A so-called *swing* comes in and follows—or *trails*—the departing dresser for a number of performances to learn his or her responsibilities and practice making all the moves and changes.

> On my first job I trailed someone who was going on vacation at *La Cage Aux Folles*. My first task was to climb up to the catwalk over the stage to retrieve the costumes that were flown up to the ceiling in the opening number. I managed to do it.
>
> And then it was amazing to me, but working on Broadway was just like the backstage work I'd done in college and at a dinner theater in Pittsburgh. We had to make the same list of cues and *be ready*. I must have been good, because I started getting calls from other shows. Broadway is like a big fraternity: Once you're in, you're in.
>
> Bob Branigan

Many of the best dressers are experienced performers; they understand the actors' needs. Nowadays, many are working actors who happen to be "between shows." Branigan, who is also an actor and has done TV commercials and print ads, advanced to shop steward on *Cats*—"the middleman between management and dresser. I'm the one to whom the others bring their problems, and I try to iron them out." He explained how he became a dresser:

> I composed a dresser résumé, listing the shows I had worked on. I added a cover letter, explaining that I was new in New York City and looking for day work, or swing work. Then I went up to the union. When my application was

approved, I paid the initiation fee and went out and left a copy of my résumé with the backstage doorman of every show, saying I'd be back at half-hour. At 7:30 I was at the famed Palace Theater. I asked to see the wardrobe supervisor, and said, 'I'm here to put a face on the résumé I left this afternoon.' To my surprise I was asked, 'What are you doing now?' I said, "Nothing." 'Good, you're hired!' I was at the right place at the right time.

STAR DRESSERS

Dressers are ordinarily expected to be able to do everything but design the clothes. However, it's not necessary to excel at every facet of the work. The prime requisite for a dresser tending the wardrobe of a performer who is carrying the show is the ability to keep the star happy. This is a business relationship of a very personal sort that demands great skill, an intuitive personality, and theater wisdom. Some star dressers belong to "dresser families"—one young woman who is already doing "swing" for Broadway shows is the sister of a star dresser, and their mother dresses a well-known musical star whenever the actress comes to New York from Hollywood.

If you are asked to be a star dresser you can earn more. The job is different. Fifteen minutes after the curtain falls, we are all out of the theater except the star dresser, who stays as long as the star is in the dressing room. There are guests to greet and special meetings going on in the dressing-room foyer.

BOB BRANIGAN

GETTING JOBS

Wardrobe maintenance requires sewing skills, particularly the ability to make alterations. The necessary training can be acquired at any number of high schools, the YWCA, or through adult extension courses. Sewing machine and/or fabrics stores usually give classes to demonstrate how easy it is to make, or alter, one's own clothes. For someone whose interest goes a bit deeper, New York City's renowned Fashion Institute of Technology (FIT) offers professional quality instruction in every aspect of fashion, design, and execution. The classes are open to nonmatriculated students as well as those working toward a degree.

E. Susan Erenburg, of the Theatrical Wardrobe Union, recalled her beginning:

At college I spent almost all my time with the dramatic club, working backstage. That's where my talent for sewing was discovered. I decided a degree from FIT made sense. Pretty soon after that, I was working in the costume shop at the Metropolitan Opera [a shop also organized by the wardrobe union]. The costumes were constantly in need of alteration, as new casts came in to sing the operas in the repertory.

Erenburg is glad to see that costume technicians are getting lots of training and graduate degrees.

> It increases the respect for the training that our people need. It's not just the scenery that's complicated. And this work can lead to a design career if you pursue it. Several of our members hold cards in both unions.

Hands-on experience in wardrobe, as in any area of theater, begins with volunteering to work wherever there's a local community production. Summer theaters have historically provided opportunity for apprentices or interns to assist with costumes, particularly for movie or television stars touring in summer packages, who need personal attention.

> If you want to do this, get involved in theater. The more you know how to do, the more employable you will be. And have a good attitude.
>
> BOB BRANIGAN

PROFESSIONAL AFFILIATION

In New York, to work in the professional theater—or films or television—requires membership in the Theatrical Wardrobe Union, which is Local #764 of IATSE. As with props, scenery, and lighting, other locals may have jurisdiction outside the metropolitan area.

There is a $100 registration fee, which entitles the applicant to an interview and the chance to learn about the work, ask questions, and receive helpful pointers on finding jobs.

Upon acceptance into the union, there is an initiation fee of $1,000. Annual dues are $140 plus working dues of 2 percent of the salary earned while employed. According to the latest contract, weekly salaries are as follows:

- For wardrobe supervisors—$892.57
- For wardrobe assistants—$826.65
- For dressers—$519.84

These salaries are supplemented by benefits. Additional payment is required if a show gives more than eight performances in any week. (Wage scales for dressers in television and films are not the same as in theater. Contracts are negotiated every three years. As these negotiations tend to go on for many months, always check with the union for current information.)

> FOR INFORMATION, CONTACT:
>
> Theatrical Wardrobe Union Local #764 International Alliance of Theatrical and Stage Employees 151 West 46th Street, 8th floor New York, NY 10036

> What's nice about working backstage is that you can have a permanent place in the theater with a steady income. . . . I am in New York City and making more money as a dresser than I was after fourteen years of teaching, and with less stress.
>
> BOB BRANIGAN

HAIRSTYLISTS AND MAKEUP ARTISTS

To fully realize the costume designer's vision of each character, two additional experts are needed: the HAIRSTYLIST and the MAKEUP ARTIST. Unfortunately, most of the contributions these professionals make to shows are, like those of the stage managers, unrecognized outside business circles—no Tony Award calls attention to their work. Thus, few people realize what the stage would look like if hairstylists and makeup artists weren't working behind the scenes, performing their daily magic.

STYLING HAIR AND WIGS

The trend toward more elaborate productions and the near-universal use of body microphones has increased the need for hairstylists' services. The connection? Almost everyone onstage these days is wearing a wig, and a wig provides an invisible, secure hiding place for a performer's microphone and battery pack.

> *Show Boat* had nine hair people alone. There are 250 wigs in that show.
>
> JEAN BLOCK, hairstylist and wig designer

Because wig hair doesn't need to be cut or permed or colored every few weeks, the look is always consistent. Wigs also represent a kind of security for performers—against dreaded "bad hair days," rain, humidity, colds, or the simple fact that the performer's own hair color, quality, or length may not be anything like the character's. For her role as Norma Cassidy in *Victor/Victoria*, Rachel York had the short, marcelled auburn hair of a 1930s chorus girl. In real life, York wears her own long, pale blonde hair in an elegant chignon.

Designing each wig is a process that begins in preproduction under the supervision of the costume designer. As with garments, there are measurements and fittings.

> You have to know period, costume. For *Meet Me in St. Louis*, I designed eighty wigs. You style, color, and cut them. You work with the costume and set designers and, of course, the actors. Some people have very definite ideas about their hair—what styles they look well in, as well as what colors. Your job is to satisfy everyone and have it all come out looking great.
>
> JEAN BLOCK

The wig designer's sketches are turned over to the wigmaker. Depending on the type of hair used—yak is considered most practical—a wig can cost from

$1,500 to $5,000 and can take two to four days to complete. For a fantasy show such as *Beauty and the Beast,* creating the 274 wigs and hairpieces plus the Beast's hairy clothing was reportedly an eight-month project for a staff of six.

At the theater, the wigs are the responsibility of the hair supervisor who, like the wardrobe supervisor, oversees a crew of hairstylists and assistants. Stylists do their own wig-change plot, to pair the right wig with each costume and to be ready to make changes quickly. Wigs are shampooed and styled daily. Famed wigmaker and makeup artist Bob Kelly (he also manufactures a complete line of theatrical makeup and offers instruction in the application of the products) expects wigs made by his staff to last a year. Built upon lace bases, wigs used in theater and movies are not everyday wigs.

In the case of shows whose directors decide not to use wigs, hairstylists nevertheless work closely with the costume designer to achieve the desired unified look. Hairstylists on these shows set and style the performers' hair for each performance. They also wash, cut, and color as is necessary to keep the look consistent.

GETTING STARTED

Production hairstylists need to have graduated from a licensed school of hairstyling and cosmetology and hold a state license in hairstyling. The licensing exam usually consists of a written test and a practical demonstration of color and styling techniques. A college degree is not essential, but the understanding of lighting, color, costume design, and historical periods is a must. You also need a strong theatrical sensibility.

> In Rochester, I dreamed of doing the hair for a Broadway show. The only way to do that was to come to New York City. Once I got here, I realized I knew absolutely no one. I got a job at a neighborhood salon to pay expenses and started hanging out at Broadway shows, particularly *42nd Street,* which was such a terrific show that I think I would have given my eye teeth to work on it.
>
> JEAN BLOCK

On a Broadway show, hair supervisors usually engage stylists whose work and personality they know as they assemble the initial crew. For the newcomer, getting started means getting people to know you and be willing to trust you to do the work, which is often intense.

> When there was a temporary opening on the show *42nd Street,* I got the chance to fill in for someone on vacation. The procedure is, you "trail" the one you are going to substitute for—follow that person every moment—so you know the job. You learn that job, whose wig goes with which hat, which costume, and when, and how much time you have for each change.
>
> JEAN BLOCK

To work in the professional theater (as well as in television and films) licensed hairstylists join the Makeup Artists and Hairstylists Union, Local #798, of IATSE. Applicants take an exam to show their aptitude at theatrical and period styling and present their résumé of salon experience.

Because they do not actually handle performers' hair, wig designers need not be union members, nor are they necessarily trained hairstylists, per se. Many designers come from the crafts area or from costume design. David Lawrence, whose wig designs for *Beauty and the Beast* have been applauded as "a ground-breaking display of inventiveness," was working as a craftsman at Connecticut's Hartford Stage Company when someone asked him to shampoo a wig. Something in the way he cared for the piece prompted the resident wig designer to grab him for the hair department.

> I have been a hairdresser for sixteen years and in the union two years. I do wigs, too, for movies. I am a black woman and my opinion is that white hairdressers don't know how to do black hair.
>
> I also do makeup in my salon, but in the union you cannot do both—you cannot take another person's job away. That is good, because then we all respect each other.
>
> DAISY CARBEON

ADDITIONAL OPPORTUNITIES

A number of theatrical hairstylists, including Ms. Block and Ms. Carbeon, open their own salons, where the staff consists of other stylists in the business. Their clientele is predominantly theater, film, and TV people, plus a few editors and fashion consultants.

Because Local #798 also has agreements in film and television, the Broadway talent pool works on projects that are shooting in New York. When a change in the schedule meant that the head stylist on a Barbra Streisand film, *The Mirror Has Two Faces,* would be away on location for the first week of shooting, Jean Block was called to substitute for him. "That means doing the job quietly, asking few questions, being confident, and taking direction from the performer at the same time," Block explained. She was then asked to continue with the film, doing the day players and extras.

MAKEUP DESIGNERS AND ARTISTS

Like the wig designer and hairstylist, makeup artists and designers work in conjunction with the costume designer, taking into account the style of the play, the size of the theater, and the stage lighting.

The majority of stage performers apply their own makeup. In the show *Cats,* which has had many cast changes over its long run, the original makeup was designed to complement the individual cat costumes. Just as they are taught the choreography by the dance captain, replacement cats are taught how to do their makeup by the makeup artist. They are given face charts, showing where each color and line belongs. And they rehearse, with her assistance, for several performances. When they have learned their faces, the artist takes their photo, which they hang over the makeup mirror to use as a guide.

> At first they cry, because they think they'll never learn to do it in half an hour. But in a few weeks they're ready in ten minutes.
>
> Bob Branigan, dresser

Performers in a realistic play that takes place in another era may be taught by a makeup designer how to apply makeup in a particular way. But some makeup effects are far more complicated than any performer can manage, and they frequently must be accomplished within a very limited time. Flabby cheeks, bulbous noses, gnarled hands, claws, fangs, scars, or bruises which are extra pieces of molded foam or epoxy are called *prosthetics* and must be applied to the actor's face and body by a makeup artist. They are made to adhere and stay put despite the heat of the lights and vigorous actor movement. Makeup is then applied to the prosthetic pieces so that the audience sees them as real.

Characters who age—or grow younger—over the course of the play require the expertise of a makeup artist, so that the changes are visible in the balcony of the theater as well as the front orchestra. Actors who change character between the acts—a beautiful artist's model, say, who returns in Act II as her own grandmother—will need a makeup artist to create that dramatic difference.

TRAINING

College theater majors customarily take courses in theatrical makeup. Classes such as these are usually available to nonmatriculated students, too. Attendance at an accredited school of hairstyling and cosmetics provides basic training as well as the opportunity to become a licensed cosmetologist and hairstylist.

Makeup artists frequently give seminars on creating special effects. Information about these may usually be found in the trade papers, such as *Back Stage* or *Theatre Crafts International*.

Once you have training, there are many ways to gain experience. One can volunteer to do, or assist with, the makeup for a local theater company. Bridal salons might be happy to know about a makeup artist who can coordinate the makeup for an entire party. Clients at neighborhood beauty salons frequently crave a "look" for a special occasion. And established makeup artists may need assistants.

Makeup artists come from different backgrounds. Some are actors, portrait artists, or even dancers. There are makers of model stage sets among them, and some who were on their way to becoming cosmetologists when they got the chance to do a show.

A college degree is not essential, but a strong fashion sense is. You need to understand theater lighting and possess an awareness of color, facial shapes, character traits, and period.

PROFESSIONAL AFFILIATION

Makeup artists and hairstylists belong to the same union, Local #798 of IATSE, which covers work in films and TV as well as theater. Wages and working conditions differ for each medium. Artist and stylists who earn a reputation for fine work may be paid more than the established pay scale.

FOR INFORMATION, CONTACT:

Makeup and Hairstylists Union Local #798 31 West 21st Street New York, NY 10011

Unlike hairstylists, makeup artists do not need a state license before they can apply to join the union. They must, however, pass an exam by showing their ability to perform standard makeup techniques. Makeup designers —who do not actually apply makeup—are not required to be members of the union.

THE HOUSE MANAGER

Every show plays in a "house"—a theater—that the producer rents from a theater owner. Each house has its own staff of box-office people, ticket-takers, ushers, engineers, cleaners, porters, and stage-door attendants, and its own stage crew.

The house manager, who is employed by the theater owner, is in charge of them all and is responsible for maintenance of the building. He or she administers the theater's weekly payroll—which can be in excess of $50,000, and covers about seven different unions, all of which have different rules for benefits, deductions, holiday pay, and so forth.

In addition to the rent they charge producers for the use of the house, theater owners receive a (negotiated) percentage of the show's gross. That is why both the house manager and the company manager count the box office receipts after every performance, and the house manager's signature goes on every statement of the amount of money taken in.

> You're a trouble-shooter, too. Making sure that people are submitting correct bills for work that's been done—that's just your paperwork. Then there is what you do on your feet: You are there before every show, checking to see if there is enough toilet paper, that all the light bulbs are working. You're there for the fire and police certification. Before every performance the fire department comes and checks—no obstructions to the fire door. You handle everything from leaks to burglaries to ticket problems. People who come on the wrong day, who forget and come on another day. . . .
>
> When they are loading in and loading out, you have all that traffic. You must take care of the house, make sure they are not banging up the walls, chipping the paint. And you don't want broken seats. You have to protect the physical plant as well as serving the patrons, producers, and theater owners. You want people to feel comfortable when they're in the theater. That's part of the experience of enjoying the show.
>
> CAROL FLEMMING, house manager

With the production stage manager, the house manager ascertains how they are going to call the show. Before every performance the stage manager gives the "Okay, go!" cue between the front and the back of the house.

A house manager's effort to add to the audience's enjoyment may increase the theater's income. The manager of the Mitzi E. Newhouse Theater, in New York's Lincoln Center, accomplished that by engaging a home baker to sell fancy cookies and gourmet coffees at the theater's concession stand during intermission. In the twelve minutes, audiences, who had previously spurned the usual soft drinks and candy bars, consumed every chewy brownie and mini-muffin on the young woman's crystal platters.

PROFESSIONAL REQUIREMENTS

House managers are members of the Association of Theatrical Press Agents and Managers (ATPAM). They serve the same apprenticeship as company managers and take the same written test. They take an oral exam, however, that is different.

FOR INFORMATION, CONTACT:

Association of Theatrical Press Agents and Managers
165 West 46th Street
New York, NY 10036

The pay scale for house managers is the same as for company managers—$1,319 per week, with benefits (until the next contract negotiation).

The house manager's job contract is for a calendar year, starting on Labor Day—considered the start of the theatrical season. But that is only if there is a show in the house. If the show closes, then the house manager is out of work along with everyone else.

After six years at the Brooklyn Academy of Music, where there are four theaters, I managed the Virginia Theater for two years. *Jelly's Last Jam* was playing there—one of the most innovative musicals in many years. So I was involved with good people. The next production was *My Fair Lady*, with Richard Chamberlain. Then the theater was closed for renovation, so I started looking around. There are only a finite number of houses!

CAROL FLEMMING

THE BOX-OFFICE STAFF

When theatergoers are at last persuaded by publicity, advertising, critics' reviews, nominations, and awards to buy a ticket to a show, the treatment they receive at the box office colors their perception and expectation of the experience.

Everyone wants the best seats in the house, but the box-office staff can provide only the best seats *available.* Now that ticket sales have been computerized, available seat locations for any performance are readily identifiable on a terminal screen. This does not imply that the box-office person's job has become an easy one. There are people at the window, callers on the phone, and requests via the mail. There are cancellations, exchanges, and sometimes, returns. And everyone is in a hurry.

Fairly large amounts of cash are handled; charges may be billed to credit cards. Some buyers carry away their tickets; some reservations are to be picked up before the performance; some orders must be delivered.

For a hit show, the line at the box office forms in the early morning and never really goes away. The producer loves it, but the staff can get a bit frazzled. Through it all, the box-office personnel—the treasurer and his or her assistants, if the sales are brisk—must remain cool, patient, diplomatic, a public ambassador of good will—for the current show and all the rest to come.

After each performance the amount of ticket sales is totaled by the treasurer, with the house manager and company manager. All three sign the daily income report.

It is a full-time, high-pressure occupation.

NECESSARY SKILLS

A level temperament and the ability to avoid confrontation are obviously essential. The box-office person should be well-organized, able to handle myriad details and have a knowledge of bookkeeping and some computer skills. As always, a familiarity with theater is helpful. A college degrees is not a prerequisite.

It's possible to gain experience by selling tickets for any type of school activity or by working with any local groups that produce special events. These organizations may also provide computer training.

PROFESSIONAL AFFILIATION

Box office personnel on Broadway and throughout the country are members of the Treasurers and Ticket Sellers' Union, Local #751. They work a 40-hour

FOR INFORMATION,
CONTACT:

Treasurers and Ticket
Sellers' Union
Local #751
1500 Broadway,
Suite 2011
New York, NY 10036

Telephone and Mail
Order Clerks Union
Local #B-751
330 West 42nd Street
New York, NY 10036

week, and they must be bonded—investigated and certi-fied trustworthy to handle money. According to the most recent contract, box-office treasurers' assistants are paid $1,006.74 per week, with benefits.

The employment picture is hardly rosy; currently the Broadway theaters are completely staffed. Applicants may nevertheless sign up and get on the union's waiting list. They will be interviewed by the business agent and wait their turn.

The ability to order tickets and pay for them by tele-phone *has* created jobs for telephone ticket clerks. These people do not handle money, but they deal with the pub-lic over the telephone. They work shorter shifts—a plus for those who want time to pursue other theatrical avenues. Turnover is faster here.

This work is under the jurisdiction of Local #B-751, the Telephone and Mail Order Clerks Union. Prior to the latest negotiation, the established pay scale was $484.38 per week.

Film

Hollywood, the Dream Factory
HORTENSE POWDERMAKER

I N THE HALF-CENTURY since anthropologist Hortense Powdermaker spent a year studying filmmakers and used that label as the title of her book about the movie business, no one has come up with a more inspired sobriquet. Turmoil in the upper echelons of the movie business has lately been of gargantuan proportions. Despite the biggest shakeups, executives leap from one salary level to another so much higher that onlookers can only wonder if the numbers have any relation to reality. On departing each luxurious office suite, their announced severance pay frequently exceeds the gross national product of a medium-sized country.

All of which has made producing films more of a gamble (and possibly more expensive) than ever. Will the person who can say "Yes!" to a producer's idea have that same power, or that same office, three days later? Will new management even care to glance at the title page of a script favored by the previous regime? Will the departing executive prove so enamored of the project that he or she will insist on taking it to wherever the next office is?

No one can know, but everyone loves to speculate.

However, the process of making a movie is quite plain, and beyond speculation. No matter who's in charge in the executive suites, once a producer falls so in love with a story idea that it nags and nags and will not go away, there's really only one way to bring it to the screen. Every film progresses from pre-production to production to post-production and requires the cooperation, discipline, and, above all, the talent of many skilled professionals.

THE MOVIE PRODUCER

Most of today's films are made by independent producers, not movie studios.

The basic ingredients are the same as in the theater: the movie producer needs *material* that he or she feels passionately about and the *money* to get the movie made. However, a play traditionally develops when a production is planned; then, once the show opens, it is repeated in live performance for as long as there is an audience to see it.

The film producer, on the other hand, must first develop the material into a script that is saleable enough to attract studio financing for the project. During this developmental preproduction stage, the producer is gambling that funds will become available and the movie will be made. Many projects that are proposed in this way to the movie studios never make it to production, but when a producer succeeds, the resulting film is a tangible product that can be duplicated, packaged, distributed, and sold in numerous ways. The potential rewards are worth the producer's initial risk.

The filmmaking process is far more complicated, and hugely more expensive, than the mounting of a very elaborate stage show. Getting the desired stars and director to commit to the impending project, and then acquiring the material and the money within the time they are available, is a feat. These steps can take the most experienced producers a very long time.

DISCOVERING MATERIAL

The impetus for a film may originate with the producer or someone—friend, writer, director, star—who brings the idea to a producer's attention. The source may be a personal experience, a news event, the recollections of someone living or dead, or simply a notion or an image that triggers a story. All those are original ideas.

If the idea is based on existing work—such as a book, a play, an article in a periodical, a character, a song, or a previously made film—the producer will need to secure permission to use the material. This means locating the original author or owner of the material (or his or her representative or estate) and negotiating to *option* or purchase the property. Material for which the copyright has lapsed is in the public domain and may be used freely. In this category, for example, are the Bible, the novels of Jane Austen and Charles Dickens, and the plays of William Shakespeare (reportedly the world's most popular screenwriter).

Whatever the source, the producer's strong reaction to the material is essential. The idea has to strike him or her as the most fantastic, or funny, or weird, or highly romantic—something to get excited about. Convinced that an audience will be just as excited, and want to see the movie, the producer becomes willing to persevere in seeing the idea make it to the screen.

This emotional response is really all anyone has to go on. In the continuing search for a great story, there are no exact formulas for successful films.

Producer-writer Lynda Obst told TV interviewer Charlie Rose:

> No one knows what will be a sure-fire hit. It can take years to get a project done, and no one can calculate public taste that far in advance.

FROM IDEA TO PROJECT

Unless the idea came from a writer originally, the producer's first task is to connect with a screenwriter who brings additional enthusiasm along with dramatic skill to the project, can flesh out the irresistible idea, and transform it into a compelling script.

Prior to investing personal funds, a producer will try to interest a studio executive in the project by *pitching* the idea—telling only the essence of the story—in hopes that the executive will be intrigued by the idea, will believe it can attract a bankable star and a gifted director and recoup its production costs in its first weekend showings, and will advance the funds for this portion of the work. Such a nod from the executive puts the project into *development*. With this financial investment the studio earns the right to make and distribute the movie.

Failing that, the producer either digs into personal funds, finds a financial partner willing to advance this *front money,* or arrives at some arrangement with the writer that allows them to proceed.

The writer sets to work on the script, which, depending upon their agreement, may go through several drafts and is shown to the studio executive who originally okayed the development. Several reactions are possible:

• The executive will frown and say, "I don't think there's anything to this. Take it somewhere else." This is called *turnaround*—the producer can turn around and seek someone else as a potential buyer of the project (and repay the studio for its initial investment).

• The executive will say something like, "The script has possibilities, but it needs work. There are too many holes. Punch up the lead." That means the studio is willing to invest additional money to get the script sharpened. The project is still in development. Many producers view this as a step that gets the studio heads so committed to the property that they will eventually make the film rather than lose their investment.

• The executive will jump for joy and say, "Yes, yes, we must make this movie!"—in which case the project has been given a *green light.* That's tantamount to winning the lottery.

According to Hollywood lore, the idea for the hugely successful movie *Independence Day* came to director Roland Emmerich during a publicity junket for his film *Stargate*. Asked if he believed in aliens, he said he believed in the great "what if?": "What if you woke up and there were huge spaceships over your town? Wouldn't it be the most exciting thing that ever happened in your life?" Realizing he'd stumbled on a terrific movie idea, he and writer-producer Dean Devlin quickly whipped up a script about an invasion from outer space. Twentieth Century--Fox took all of one week to give them the go-ahead.

Once the studio decides to make the film, the producer brings a director into the package—in some cases the director has been attached to the project, at least in name, while it was being pitched. Now the director's direct involvement will further heighten the emotional content of the material. Together, producer and director study the script in depth—whether it needs polishing, and whether another writer might be more suitable—mull over casting choices, consider where they will shoot, begin to scout locations, and discuss the number of sets and their size, what the characters will wear, and the visual style and scope of the movie.

The PRODUCTION MANAGER, hired by the producer, and the studio's budget department work out an estimate of how much the movie will cost, as well as the number of shooting days in the production schedule. Costs fall into one of two categories:

- *Above the line,* which refers to talent—that is, the salaries for director, writers, actors, and producer.
- *Below the line,* which refers to all the other production expenses pertaining to the physical cost of the movie—including the sets, costumes, location and studio crews, studio and equipment rental, transportation, catering, editing, mixing, music, legal fees, living expenses, and so on.

When the producer and studio reach agreement on the number of dollars and days—and whatever additional details are peculiar to the project—starting dates are set. At this point the producer, in effect, turns the film over to the director, but still keeps watch over each day's work and is ready to be supportive whenever necessary.

ATTRIBUTES OF A PRODUCER

Producers are marked by energy, determination, and an instinct for good story ideas—material that will appeal to a mass audience. As originators of projects for which they seek major financing, they need to be effective at selling ideas, smart about raising cash, and shrewd at making deals. Getting the movie made requires the talent to assemble an effective creative team and to delegate responsibility while remaining on top of all that's going on. It's a singular mix of passion, creativity, and chutzpah that knows no cultural boundaries.

My passion for films started when I was a little boy in Bombay. At school, in my spare moments, I would draw up cast lists of film stars whom I would have in my films. Years later, I wanted a certain actress for a film and her agent said, "No, no, no." But she was playing in Toronto, so I went there with some of our reviews and gave her the script, which she read. She called me later, gave me her agent's home telephone number, and told me to call and tell him that she wanted to do it!

Ismail Merchant, producer

GETTING STARTED

Capable producers have come from all sorts of backgrounds. A great many are film-school graduates who have produced student films that attracted attention and earned them a foothold at a studio or in a producer's office. In addition, veteran writers, directors, and actors have formed companies to produce their own films, all in an effort to gain access to exciting material.

Learning the business has much to do with forging relationships, getting to know scores of writers, directors, and agents as well as other producers. Ideally, these connections can be made through any kind of entry-level position with any company in the business. Such jobs generally fall under the heading of "assistant." If that seems impossible, there are countless related organizations to join, courses to take, and activities to volunteer for that can make it easier to meet colleagues. Novice producers are also advised to spend their time reading scripts of both successful films and unproduced manuscripts so they can learn to recognize good work and talk about it intelligently to the professionals they hope to work with. It's all preparation for the moment when they fall in love with an idea or property. They'll then have plenty of people in the business to call on for help in moving forward with it.

That is really the key: Finding a property and, in the words of so many professionals, "attaching" oneself to it. With no track record and no financial backing, first-time producers either borrow from friends, relatives, and credit card companies to make their movie, or they secure the rights for themselves and then bring the property to someone who *can* get the money to make the film. Either way can be a beginning.

Studio management, if favorably impressed, may offer a deal whereby, for a certain period, the producer has the right to maintain an office on the studio lot, and the movie company has the right to finance and distribute the producer's films.

FINANCIAL CONSIDERATIONS

Everything is negotiable. For producing the film a producer is paid a fee commensurate with the scale of the production. Depending on the deal, there may be royalties and additional payments when the movie reaches certain numerical goals. Producers also receive a (lesser) fee when their property is placed in development. This is an important safeguard for the producer, because studio management may change during that development period; new executives are not likely to green-light projects their predecessors were keen on. The possibility leads many producers to claim, ruefully, that they've made a career out of being in development.

However, when the green light goes on, and the script is right and everything falls into place, producers manage to pay their expenses many times over. Some of them also manage to win awards. Which proves that in addition to being smart deal makers, given the chance, they can also be creative.

In the words of producer-director-actor John Huston: "The experience of making the movie is better and more important than the film itself."

Hollywood is still a predominantly male world. Some studio executives are barely thirty years old—perhaps, then, the field of producing is most hospitable to guys who are young. However, women are gradually building résumés, recording respectable grosses, and making their way as producers of top films.

THE SCREENWRITER

Screenwriters create material for the large movie screen and for the small television screen. The essential ingredient for a successful film, according to producers, directors, writers, and actors is a good story. Whether it's a comedy, drama, or thriller, the audience must want to see *what happens next.*

Writing for the screen is considered more difficult, requiring more discipline, than writing a novel, because a script contains only what the audience sees or hears. The characters' unspoken thoughts, unless they can be revealed in words or action, cannot be described. The medium is, after all, known as *moving pictures.*

Writing for the screen also differs from writing a play, where, as Garry Marshall has said, "The writer can take as long as he wants to tell his story." In movies and TV, a story is told within certain standard time limits. Understandably, writers who can routinely deliver compelling screenplays, given the limitations, are hard to find.

Adding to the difficulty is the enormous number of already-filmed movies—and that the whole world has seen them. So many wonderful stories have been told that thinking up new ones or putting new spins on familiar tales is a challenge. However, the prospect of reaching an audience of millions makes it a challenge that countless numbers of people are eager to take.

BASIC REQUIREMENTS

Training in dramatic writing technique is necessary. A liberal arts degree with a major in dramatic writing is a recommended way to begin.

In addition, prospective screenwriters are advised to immerse themselves in movies, to watch them over and over again, so as to understand and appreciate the ingredients that combine to make good ones. They should develop a good ear for dialogue—understanding how it both resembles and differs from "plain people just talking."

A recommended, and popular, how-to manual for screenwriters is available in paperback at most good bookstores: *Screenplay: The Foundations of Script Writing*, by Syd Field.

Among the many schools across the country that have become well-regarded for preparing students to work professionally, Yale Drama School has a significant share of successful graduates. Other current leaders are the University of California, Los Angeles (UCLA), the University of Southern California (USC), and the Department of Film and Television at the Tisch School of the Arts, New York University (NYU).

FOR INFORMATION,
CONTACT:

The American
Film Institute
2021 North Western Avenue
Los Angeles, CA 90027

TIP-East
c/o National Academy
of Television Arts
and Sciences,
New York Chapter
165 West 46th Street,
Suite 500
New York, NY 10036

Beginning courses in screenwriting—customarily taught in New York and Los Angeles by very knowledgeable professionals—are available to nonmatriculated students at many schools. A number of screenwriters periodically conduct weekend seminars in story structure at cities across the country. Geared toward aspiring writers, these classes are advertised in trade publications.

For writers with a bit more experience, the Center for Advanced Film and Television Studies of the American Film Institute, in Los Angeles, offers classes in screenwriting as well as a Television Writers' Workshop. The New York chapter of the National Academy of Television Arts and Sciences (NATAS), in conjunction with the Writers Guild of America East and To Increase Production in the East (TIP-East) administers a seminar for training writers of situation comedies.

SIMPLE BEGINNINGS

Just as painters have to paint and dancers must dance, writers have to write, regularly. Technique improves with practice. Sitting down to do the solitary work is a necessary discipline.

Writers need to have samples of their work to show so that they can get jobs. They must show them to agents, who will send their work out to prospective buyers and submit their names when new projects are put together.

For a writer with no industry connections, whose work is unknown, an agent is an absolute necessity. No one will read anything that is not a submission from an agent. This is not some Byzantine exclusionary policy, but a protection against any possible charges of plagiarism.

> You need five pieces to show an agent, something he or she can send around with the hope that it hits. Without an agent you need to know *someone*. Getting an agent means only that you can get your stuff looked at. You still have to get your own work.
>
> RENÉE ORIN, writer-actress

> People make the mistake of trying to speculate on scripts for series. That's a fatal mistake. They can't possibly know how to do it well enough to impress anybody. If you send it to another show they're not interested— why would they want to see a script for another series? It is a waste of time and energy. You can't sell it anywhere else.
>
> The way to make it into the TV or movie business is to create original material for a two-hour movie which can be sold as a story. You have a

large number of places where you might sell it. And you might write a movie that sells for $800,000. That's happened more than once.

LAURENCE HEATH, writer-producer, Murder, She Wrote

MOTION PICTURE ASSIGNMENTS

Even if a script does not reach production, producers' favorable reactions to the work can become a selling point. Writers who exhibit talent with a particular genre, fluidity with dialogue, or in-depth knowledge of a hot topic may be noticed by production executives and asked, for example, to do rewrites on another writer's script that is already in production. Unlike *playwrights*, who retain the rights to their plays and must approve any changes, screenwriters are regarded as employees, hired to work on material that is the property of whoever bought the story.

Writers may be asked to do *treatments*—narrative-prose versions in story form of possible movie material. The treatment may be used as a basis for the *screenplay*—the final script containing individual scenes, dialogue, and simple camera instructions.

To secure a major star's commitment to a project, the producer may engage an additional writer to rework the plot or dialogue to make the role more appealing. Changing dialogue, narration, or action is referred to as *polishing* (in contrast to the deeper, more significant structural changes in *rewrites*.) The star, on signing, may want to call in a favorite writer for a few extra touches—scenes, lines, words—additional *polish* so the role will more closely fit the star's persona.

> In the theater, everyone looks to the writer for the answers. What shall we say next? They assume the writer knows the characters. Not so in Hollywood. Most films are written by a committee. There were twenty-seven writers on the movie version of *The Flintstones*!
>
> PAUL RUDNICK, screenwriter and playwright

Understand that such writing assignments are not routinely handed out to new arrivals. Oscar-winning writers do dialogue polish and rewrite jobs. In fact, several very big names are as respected in the industry for their talents as script doctors as for their hit shows. On all levels, competition is fierce.

TELEVISION ASSIGNMENTS

The sheer volume of programming on the small screen promises additional opportunities for screenwriters. Twenty-four hours a day, seven days a week, the networks, independent stations, and cable channels have to fill the screen with something. And for many of those hours what they choose to air is original dramatic material.

A script for a TV movie is always a good audition piece for a screenwriter.

Another marketable type of screenplay is for the relatively new form of the direct-to-video movie.

Every weekly series, live-action or animated, half-hour comedy or hour-long dramatic show, will have writer-producers on staff to whom outside writers, freelancers, submit ideas, usually through their agents. The thing to remember about scripts for video-size entertainment is that budgets will not allow for complicated, drawn-out shooting schedules, elaborate special effects, and scenes of great spectacle.

PROFESSIONAL AFFILIATION

The initial film or television writing assignment brings eligibility to join the Writers Guild of America East (WGA-E), in New York; or West (WGA-W), in Los Angeles. The initiation fee for new members is $1,000. Annual dues are $50 plus 1½ percent of your earnings from the sale of material or from employment in WGA's jurisdiction.

The Guild's agreements cover work in motion pictures, television, and radio. For example, the pay scale for an original screenplay, including treatment, is $42,057 on a low-budget film and $79,656 for a big-budget production. Television compensation is based on length of show, broadcast time period, and whether it's a network program.

FOR INFORMATION, CONTACT:

Writers Guild of America East
555 West 57th Street
New York, NY 10019

Writers Guild of America West
8955 Beverly Boulevard
West Hollywood, CA 90048

Separate payment schedules apply to nontheatrical films and nondramatic television programs—such as news, quiz shows, and audience participation shows. Residual payments (fees for additional uses of the work, such as rebroadcast on TV or cable, and transfer to video-cassette or any other form) and employer contributions to the Guild pension plan and health fund are additional benefits. The complete (31-page) schedule of minimum rates is available from the Guild, as is the *Professional Writer's Teleplay Format Book* and an agents list.

The Guild's manuscript registration service assists writers in establishing the completion date and identity of their property. All writers are advised to register their material—including synopses, outlines, ideas, treatments, and scenarios—with the Guild prior to showing it to producers or agents.

A CAUTIONARY NOTE

The follies of Hollywood have long been chronicled, especially on the stage—from Kaufman and Hart's *Once in a Lifetime* to Mamet's *Speed-the-Plow* and Shanley's *Four Dogs and a Bone*. Today, for example, writers with hundreds of hours of prime-time experience under their belts are unable to get appointments with much less seasoned people who are very young but are running everything—executives whose frame of reference or range of experience may be extremely limited, and for whom events that occurred more than five years ago are ancient history.

One playwright whose work had received glowing notices from the Hollywood press was invited to "take a meeting" with a number of agents, whose enthusiasm over the telephone was boundless. At their offices, their ardor cooled to dismissal when they saw that the anticipated "new" talent was a portly gentleman more than forty years old.

> The buyers today are so young that, the story goes, an experienced writer was pitching projects and came up with the idea of the earth going off its axis and plummeting toward the sun. The young executive was listening intently and said, "Is this a true story?"
>
> RENÉE ORIN

Don't say we never warned you!

THE FILM DIRECTOR

It is the director's job to transform a written script into a motion picture audiences will see, hear, and enjoy. The director is in charge of all elements of production, both technical and artistic, and of assembling them into a cohesive whole. That means identifying the theme of the story, conceiving how each scene fits into that theme, and deciding how best to tell that story in pictures and sound.

In addition to working closely with the producer and writer during development, during production the director must deal with a cast of performers whose personalities, talents, and work habits span a wide range. In collaboration with the director of photography, the director must know how to get the most telling pictures of their performances. During post-production, as the scenes are edited in concert with the film editor, and sound and music are added—a sound effect is introduced, for example, at a precise moment—it is the director's ability to spot the best moments of each take that dictates the movie's final form. The director's involvement with the production is second only to the producer's. On the movie set the director is the one in charge.

> I had directed the play *Jeffrey* and was asked to do the film. I had never been on a film set. The biggest surprise was that we were supposed to shoot ten pages the first day! I had no time with the actors. I had a one-week rehearsal with the leads, but with the day-players, none.
>
> CHRISTOPHER ASHLEY, director

Sidney Lumet, director of more than thirty-eight films, wrote in his book *Making Movies*:

> There are no unimportant decisions in movie making. I must decide what the movie is about. By the time I'm ready to shoot, I have a lens plot. Different lenses tell the story differently. Then I go to movement versus steady shots. With rehearsal the camera work emerges. By the time I go on set the movie is done for me. I shoot it. I am famous for being ahead of schedule and under budget.

ATTRIBUTES OF A DIRECTOR

While the character names may be different wherever this story is told, the punch line is the same in Hollywood, New York, and all points in between:

> X (who is the greatest person in a given endeavor) goes to heaven and is welcomed by St. Peter, who announces proudly that optimum conditions

have been set up to allow X to continue to do what he/she did so superbly on earth. X, visibly disappointed, declines. St. Peter makes an alternative suggestion. X is still unhappy. St. Peter asks what's the matter. X replies, "Well, to tell you the truth, I really want to direct."

The power of the director's position—the idea of so many people waiting to do one's bidding—is surely seductive. However, one has to know what to tell them to do. Skill in communication is probably one of the prime requisites for a successful director. Other distinguishing characteristics are a talent for and love of storytelling; decisiveness; emotional awareness; creativity; humor; energy; attention to detail, coupled with the ability to envision the whole and remember the nuances of every take.

The camera sees the flick of an eyelash. You decide what you are going to show. You do a lot of homework.

LENORE DEKOVEN, director

And, as William Wyler is credited with saying, "The key to directing is to resist the temptation to be a swell fellow."

GETTING STARTED

There are no established requirements for directors. Theoretically, anyone can be hired by a producer to direct a film. Many of today's directors had already demonstrated great proficiency in other areas of the business, so there was little risk in signing them as directors: Actors Clint Eastwood, Jodie Foster, Mel Gibson, Ron Howard, Penny Marshall, and Robert Redford; writers Woody Allen, Michael Crichton, Nora Ephron, Garry Marshall, Elaine May, and Edward Zwick; film editors David Lean, George Stevens, and William Wyler—these names are but a few examples.

For beginning directors, the advice is to become attached to a project you feel strongly about. This can be done by developing a project oneself or by working with a writer who has a track record and has corresponding enthusiasm and reaction to the story.

New directors do get hired, by either a production company or studio, for projects the company may be interested in and for which the producer has no director in mind. The director in such cases will probably have become visible in a related field, such as commercials, industrial films, documentaries, or music videos. The young director may have created an attention-getting short film or, like Christopher Ashley, directed a hugely successful play. David Fincher's stunning use of computer effects in a slew of music videos earned him the chance to direct the movie *Alien 3*.

THE DIRECTOR'S ACTING CLASS

A tall young man with a worried look rose to ask the first question at the

Directors Guild of America seminar at a Show Business Expo. "I'm a director of photography, and I'm going to direct my first movie. I want to know, what do I say to the actors? I know all the guys on the crew, but with these people, I can't figure out what they do. How do I tell them what I want?"

From the back of the hall came a voice: "Talk to Lenore DeKoven!"

An associate professor of film at Columbia University's School of the Arts, Lenore DeKoven is credited with initiating what is now a widely recognized and imitated program of teaching directors how to direct actors. A co-founder of the organization New York Women in Film and Television and former literary manager and casting director of the Mark Taper Forum, in Los Angeles, she has also been a producer. She hired herself as a director.

It was very clear that there were no contemporary female directors. Margo Jones, founder of the Alley Theater, in Houston, Texas, had died. Few people knew about Ida Lupino, who was so good, working quietly on the West Coast. There were no role models, although there had been women directors, even in film, early on.

Working with Gordon Davidson at the Mark Taper Forum was good, in that I got connected with Theater West and chaired their board. I initiated the Conrad Bromberg play *Dream of a Blacklisted Actor,* which was a big success, and as a result I heard about the American Film Institute, which had a directing workshop for women. The actress Marsha Mason and I were among the beginners—the first women to have credibility as directors in film.

While I was out there, I taught in the theater department at the Master of Fine Arts program at UCLA. My first group of students didn't want to leave me. They formed a workshop called Our Workshop West, and that was the beginning of what I am doing now.

I created a course called Collaboration, which also involved dramatic writing. I had been a music major in New York at the High School of Music and Art, and playing in the orchestra seemed to me the height of *collaboration*: Seventy-five people working together under the baton of one conductor. That was very exciting to me.

I was always very discontented by what I saw directors *not* doing. I felt there was something wanting. There was a lot of training for actors, but nobody seemed to be teaching directors to talk to the actors. There was a need. I think directors have to know the actors' craft and the actors' language. They have to work with all the instruments they are playing with, just as the orchestra conductor speaks to the musicians in their language. That's the key. So I try to fill what I perceive as the very large gap in the training for the director—to understand the actor and to collaborate with the actor and the writer. The director is there to accomplish the transition of the writer's words through the means of the actor's instrument into life.

First, we work at establishing a common vocabulary. The directors act. They learn what it feels like physically to do even a very short scene—the length of a take. And what actions go with what feelings. How to ask for what they want to show.

Quick messages are essential. There is so little time to talk to the actors and to work it through. You have to cast for what you want, or cast brilliant actors, and you don't always get those.

LENORE DEKOVEN

Determined to become a full-fledged director, DeKoven learned about a television directors training unit at NBC. She became the the first woman director of *Another World*, a daytime drama, got her Directors Guild card, and was on her way.

DeKoven has been teaching long enough for some of her alumni to have directed major films. One of her best-known former students is Ang Lee, nominated for an Academy Award for his direction of *Sense and Sensibility*. Lee's sensitivity in working with actors was cited in the accolades for his superb 1997 film, *The Ice Storm*.

WHERE TO STUDY

Aspiring directors need training in the use of today's increasingly sophisticated equipment. They need to know how best to work with their team. To understand the sweep and flow of storylines, they need to delve into the works of other directors, other times and places. At colleges, universities, and film schools, it is possible nowadays to do that: study all of movie history, from the oldest primitive black-and-white one-reelers to the latest widescreen, color, digital-stereo extravaganzas and have the opportunity to create one's own films.

Many high schools with theater arts departments now include classes for students interested in film; among these are the schools belonging to the network of Performing and Visual Arts Schools. Accredited film schools advertise in the trade publications, such as *Back Stage*, *American Cinematographer*, *American Theatre*, and even *Premiere*. If these sources seem too remote, there is always the possibility of seeking information from your local film commission; every state has one (see page 228).

In Los Angeles, members of The American Film Institute (AFI) are eligible to register for courses in professional development, including their highly regarded Women Directors Program (see page 218).

Colleges and universities offering courses in film studies are listed in the annual *Princeton Review* (or in the college catalogs). These listings can also be accessed on the Internet. The facilities and the emphases within any a course of study should be examined carefully; some schools are more interested in technical training, others pay more serious attention to script values, and so on.

UNION AFFILIATION

Directors of film, television, and radio are members of the Directors Guild of America (DGA), which represents more than 10,000 men and women working in the United States and abroad. DGA has collective bargaining agreements with motion picture production companies and television networks; these agreements establish minimum wages and working conditions. Rates differ according to a film's budget and length. For example, the current weekly minimum rates for a director are as follows:

- On a low-budget motion picture—$6,189
- On a medium-budget film—$7,034
- On a high-budget film—$9,848.

Separate agreements cover work in television dramatic shows, variety shows, and in commercials. The terms specify other matters of importance to working professionals.

FOR INFORMATION, CONTACT:

Directors Guild of America
7920 Sunset Boulevard
Los Angeles, CA 90046

East Coast address:
110 West 57th Street
New York, NY 10019

TALENT AGENTS AND ATTORNEYS

The tremendous power that agents currently wield in film and television is said to have come about as a result of the demise of the studios beginning in the 1950s. Since then, no longer signed to exclusive long-term contracts, legions of performers, writers, designers, directors, composers, and choreographers have sought professional representation and career guidance and signed with those agencies whose people could deliver the most submissions for the most prestigious projects at the most desirable fees.

In the Hollywood that emerged, every project—they were no longer referred to simply as movies—required a new series of negotiations. Darryl F. Zanuck reportedly resigned as head of Twentieth Century-Fox because he was increasingly frustrated at spending 90 percent of his time on negotiations and only 10 percent making movies, which was what he really wanted to do and where he excelled. It was as if, before each baseball game could begin, George Steinbrenner had to negotiate Doc Gooden's salary and then the salaries of the other players he wanted on the field for that game—all season long. The cost of talent soared and drove up the cost of movie-making.

As in theater, talent agencies are franchised by the various talent unions and guilds and operate within their established regulations. The 10-percent commission that agents receive on a client's salary is paid by the client when he or she has been paid. That is, talent agents are not paid in advance. They make money only when their clients are working. It stands to reason that agents want to represent talent whose 10 percent commission is the greatest; they seek to have signed with them a roster of talent with promising careers.

In the process of *building* clients' careers, an agency representing one or two major stars whose performances are deemed essential to the success of a project might suggest that a third performer, whom they also represent, be included in the cast. Such a request would rarely be denied.

Such packaging of talent affected not only motion pictures but television as it blossomed into a mass medium. Agencies whose client lists included major writers, directors, and performers were able to offer the TV networks a combination of the talents needed to make a complete show—a television package. Rather than serving simply as representatives of talent, agents assumed a creative function—seeking new talents and originating projects to employ their writing, directing, and performing clients.

ATTRIBUTES OF AN AGENT

Agents in film, television, or theater need the same industry awareness as the talent buyers—the casting directors and producers—to whom they want to "sell" their clients. They must know who is at what studio, who needs what, and how they can fill those needs. They must have the imagination to envision or invent project possibilities for their clients, within all areas of the business. They need access, the ability to make the phone calls that translate ideas into action. Whoopi Goldberg credited her agent with the daring idea that she replace Nathan Lane in the Broadway hit, *A Funny Thing Happened on the Way to the Forum*. This talent agent, who also was representing Lane, the departing star, obviously knew whom to call and thereby made sure the agency retained the sizeable income (commission) that role represented.

Talent agents also negotiate contracts. Beyond wages, contracts can include all sorts of conditions, such as the size of a client's name in all advertising; a star's mode of transportation to and from the set; the talent's share of revenues from additional distribution and licensing; what personal assistants will be on staff; any other special working conditions. While the client is the one who gets the job, the agent has to get what the client wants. That requires skill in discerning how far one can go.

GETTING STARTED

Of course, no one begins as a superstar's agent, even if the star happens to be a very close relative. To reach that level takes time—to solidify relationships with producers, directors, casting directors, and talent. While building that trust, prospective agents should be developing taste as well as savvy. In addition to a broad knowledge of film and television, a familiarity with theater and publishing—eternal sources of film and television writing and acting talent—is recommended. College degrees, while helpful, are not absolutely necessary. Stamina, awareness, and energy, coupled with a gregarious personality, are essential.

Jobs come through the grapevine: The operative word is, always, *networking*. Dentists, cousins, pet groomers—any connection can be useful, and everyone is using them. Consequently, a bit of research prior to writing an inquiry letter can make one person's request for a short get-together stand out from the dozens of others that cross the desk of a studio executive. Know something about what that person does, what his or her office does. Hint at how you can be helpful. Humor helps. In this particularly frenetic area of the business, people want to work with people they will like.

One of New York's most respected and successful offices is owned by a woman who first sought part-time employment when her children started school. Hired as a receptionist by another woman who ran a small talent agency, the young mother treated everyone respectfully, paid attention, and learned all she could about the business. She worked long hours, became an agent, and advanced to partner; she now oversees a staff of agents representing prestigious performers, directors, and writers in every medium.

Success is no secret. While each organization works in its own way, news about a bright young agent who works hard, finds talent, confidently contacts people, and knows how to close terrific deals can travel in the business with fiber-optic speed.

Rewards are equally obvious—a large desk in a spacious office, surely, but also opportunities to represent high-profile talents or to assemble prestigious projects. There are seemingly no limits as to how far a truly talented, dedicated agent can travel. Already, studio heads have been chosen from the ranks of "superagents."

ENTERTAINMENT ATTORNEYS

All those cleverly negotiated deals have to be formally written down so that everyone will understand—or at least know—what has been agreed to. So everyone has a lawyer, on all sides of the contract that officially seals a deal. For example, the following deals are commonly made for a motion-picture project:

- The producer's deals with the studio, the director, the stars, the designer, the crew, the composer
- Writers' option and purchase agreements, step deals and credits. (When, as sometimes happens, thirteen writers work on a project over eight years, there will be many contracts, and more than a few attorneys.)
- A deal made for the foreign distribution of the film
- A deal concerning the manufacture and distribution of a videocassette release
- A deal governing the creation and marketing of a soundtrack music CD

BIG DEALS FOR BRAND NAMES

ATTORNEYS MAY MAKE deals to obtain the right to use certain logos, trademarks, or products in a given film. Companies may allow their properties to be shown only in particular circumstances—or not at all. Fans of *E.T.* will remember that the little boy offers the alien bits of candy, which audiences quickly recognized as Reese's Pieces. Sales of the candy zoomed. Producer Steven Spielberg had originally hoped to use M&Ms. However, that candy company had refused permission because their executives assumed that audiences would hate the thought of an alien eating their candy.

Mention of an athletic shoe company throughout the film *Jerry Maguire* was granted because the company expected that the film would end a certain way. When the filmmakers changed the ending, the company complained loudly. Lawyers were called in to settle the matter.

- Deals with the insurance companies
- Deals made with the owners of sites where location shooting will be done

And those are just some of the major ones. If a Kevin Kline character in a movie sits down to breakfast, you can bet that an attorney made a deal that decided what brand of cereal he would pour the milk on—giving that product big-time exposure in cinemas all over the world.

Using a living person as the subject of a film or television show will necessitate *permissions*. Certain sites or famous works of art may be shown only with permission. Photographs, film clips, and bits of music may be used only with permission. Every permission is a deal, which means a contract—or a letter of agreement—and, probably, a payment. Otherwise a lawsuit could be brought against the project.

In many a negotiation, demands for percentages of profits must be dealt with. And, indeed, how does the deal define "profits"? These are matters for the attorneys.

Differences of interpretation often occur concerning what is written in a contract and even about what was said in a preliminary discussion. A star will turn down a script: "Did I say I would definitely make that movie? I don't think so. We were just having lunch." The most perfunctory of agreements become legal matters that need well-qualified attorneys.

PROFESSIONAL OPPORTUNITIES

To practice as an entertainment attorney you must, of course, earn a law degree and pass the bar exam in the state(s) where you will practice. Attorneys' attraction to the industry indicate that they have some emotional or cultural tie to this field and are comfortable with the larger-than-life-size personalities, attitudes, and mores of the population.

The highest percentages of attorneys practice in New York and California. The volume of business in Los Angeles suggests that opportunities are far more plentiful there than in New York—there are so many sides of the deal to represent.

The attorneys who make up the legal departments at studios, agencies, and production companies have their counterparts at the unions and guilds, and all the corporations engaged in buying and selling products or services to the entertainment industry. Moreover, a number of attorneys serve as personal career counsellors or managers for high-profile performers who feel their professional needs are better met by legal professionals who negotiate deals with "escalator" clauses than by agents.

It's not difficult to locate those firms specializing in theatrical law and to judge the size of their practice. Attorneys will be listed in a classified telephone directory—the Yellow Pages—and local bar associations will also have listings. To be considered for an entry-level job, one applies in the same way as at any other law firm. As always, any connection is worth mentioning.

THE UNIT PRODUCTION MANAGER

The unit production manager (UPM) coordinates, facilitates, and oversees preparation of the group of people, or unit, that will make the film. In theater terms, this career would be like a combination of the duties of the general manager and the production stage manager.

Like the general manager, a unit production manager is initially employed by the producer at the start of the project to prepare a script breakdown and estimate of the cost of filming the screenplay—the number of shooting days, locations, scenes, and setups required; how large a cast and crew will be involved; and how much equipment will be needed. The UPM, producer, and director conduct a preliminary location search. This may mean visiting nearby sites, consulting the network of international, state, and local film commissions, viewing slides, film clips, or videotapes—or flying around the world. Using the information they gather, the UPM arrives at a budget.

> The hardest part is preproduction. You must be prepared because enough will happen that you don't expect. You try to have a little "play" in the budget, but that is getting harder all the time. It is a complicated process.
>
> PETER RUMBOLO, production manager and producer

IN PRODUCTION

Once the production gets a green light, the unit production manager has the power to make all the deals for equipment rental and hiring of the crew. For the duration of the shoot, the UPM oversees day-to-day production decisions and anticipates changes, in an attempt to be ahead of the director and avert crises, such as what to shoot if the weather plays havoc with the schedule.

Failure to meet the shooting deadline will mean, at the very least, the significant additional cost of extra shooting days—costing conceivably as much as $100,000 per day on a major project—and, at worst, the possible loss of key people who have been engaged to work elsewhere on specific dates. At the completion of each day's shooting, the UPM supervises the production report, accounting for the day's work.

The UPM deals with transportation of personnel, equipment, and supplies; takes care of insurance permits and security; checks and signs all purchase orders, overtime, and pay vouchers; and is in charge of petty cash. The unions permit a UPM to work on more than one production at a time.

LOCATION MANAGERS

Among the first people to be engaged by the UPM is a location manager, who is sometimes listed in the credits as ASSISTANT UNIT PRODUCTION MANAGER, LOCATION COORDINATOR, or SECOND 2ND ASSISTANT DIRECTOR. Using the script as their blueprint, the location manager, director, and production designer review all the scenes that will have to be shot on location. They check the preliminary search notes and make a final list, which the location manager then sets out to fill. A location may be as simple as a weathered doorway or as complicated as a sprawling mansion on a hill near a lighthouse with a winding road leading to it from the highway.

> Your job is to find locations that work for the creative staff and are within the budget. The terrible thing is when they love it, but it costs $30,000 a day and you need it for fourteen days. Or sometimes you find a great location and you come back with everybody, and it's torn down! We looked at 400 mansions for *Batman*. We settled on the Soviet embassy—spent a fortune for stuff. Then the Soviet government was thrown out. In the end we used a school.
>
> PETER PASTORELLI, location manager and production manager

The location manager finalizes deals for the selected locations, secures the necessary permissions, insurance coverage, and street permits for the shooting days. Then the location manager makes arrangements for necessary parking spaces, catering, housing and dressing rooms. Generators, electrical hookups, and portable toilets are commonly required, along with telephones for everyone. The location manager must also supply all drivers with area maps and directions to each location. If neighborhood businesses (or residents) complain about inconveniences and disruptions caused by the shoot, the location manager is expected to deal sensitively with them so as to avoid any unpleasantness.

> During the shoot of *Sea of Love*, they used a shoe shop on 57th Street, in New York City, which was next to the Baccarat crystal store. They had to pay Baccarat $10,000, because customers couldn't get into their store. Locations are serious business.
>
> PETER PASTORELLI

PROFESSIONAL AFFILIATIONS

The unit production manager is a member of the Directors Guild of America (DGA). To qualify as a unit production manager, one must have had a certain number of days' employment as a First Assistant Director or for a longer term as a Second Assistant Director. The number of days varies according to which regional DGA office has jurisdiction over the work performed.

Location managers working on the East Coast are also members of DGA, with the same salary level as Second 2nd Assistant Directors. In California and the western states, the function is performed by members of the Teamsters Local #399. In Florida, the same job may be performed by a member of DGA, or Local #399, or even by a nonunion employee; it depends on where the show originates, or the company's customary employment practices.

STARTING SALARIES

Guild and union contracts are negotiated every three years. For current wages and working conditions, or answers to any questions, check with the union before signing any agreement.

Minimum terms for unit production managers assume a five-day week for filming in a studio, with a salary of $2,813 for the week; the terms assume a seven-day week for filming at distant locations, with a salary of $3,937 for the week.

For location managers (second second assistant directors), salary minimums are $1,691 per week for filming in a studio; $2,363 per week for filming on location.

ASSISTANT DIRECTORS

The director concentrates solely on shooting the film. Assistant directors are trained professionals who handle all the daily, scene-by-scene production details. As such, it is not a position that is filled by fledgling, or aspiring, directors. Indeed, there is a team of assistant directors that consists of the following:

- The FIRST ASSISTANT DIRECTOR (1st AD)
- The SECOND ASSISTANT DIRECTOR (2nd AD), who assists the 1st AD while also working closely with the UPM
- The DGA Trainee.
- Perhaps an intern.

Depending upon the size of the production, there may be a second 2nd assistant director, as well.

The director chooses the first assistant director. He or she works with the director on a script analysis—sets, props, locations, costumes, makeup, cast availability, necessary special effects or "process shots." Numbered scenes in the script are broken down into exterior or interior, day or night, scenes, then into the number of shots and setups (separate camera placements). In production, scenes are grouped according to location, rather than story sequence. The length of each scene is calculated. For this purpose script pages are measured in eighths (so that a scene may be, for instance, 2⅜ pages) and allotted a portion of the shooting day.

This detailed breakdown yields the *production shooting schedule*. From the first day of shooting, every day is spent making the film according to the schedule.

I read the script, make notes, and highlight any changes. Like the production manager, I break the script down into strips, using different colors to represent interior, exterior, day, and night scenes. That visualization helps me remember what I'm talking about. There are computer programs that do this, but you must do your first one by hand.

The names and numbers of the cast, the background people, vehicles, animals, everything—the better you know it, the more you can shoot in a day.

GLENN TROTTIER, 1st AD

During production, the 1st AD acts as the director's voice on the set and relays all notes to the cast and crew. He or she determines the cast and crew "calls"—the times when personnel must be present and fully ready for filming—and prepares the next day's call sheet (bulletin). The 1st AD serves as a facilitator of each day's work flow.

You must think about what we will shoot *next* and what to shoot *instead* if something doesn't work out. When the producer comes on set and asks, "Why aren't we shooting now?" you'd better have an answer. When the director says, "The crowd goes wild!" that crowd has to be directed. My

THE ASSISTANT DIRECTOR TRAINING PROGRAM

THE DIRECTORS GUILD maintains an employer-funded training program designed to provide opportunities for a limited number of people to become assistant directors. It is a two-year program, consisting of 150 days of on-the-job training, plus regularly scheduled seminars and special assignments.

These trainees work under the supervision of DGA second assistant directors, first assistant directors, and unit production managers on the sets of feature films, series, and commercials shooting in the area. Upon completion of the program, candidates are qualified to be considered for membership in the DGA as second assistant directors.

This is not a training program for would-be directors. It is training in the supervisory, administrative and organizational duties of a lucrative and respected career. The next upward move would be to the career of unit production manager.

While they are employed on a production, trainees are paid a modest salary, which begins at about $450 per week and increases every six months over the two-year period to about $550. The rates have been negotiated by the Guild and signatory producers. During their participation in the program, trainees also receive health insurance, at no cost.

To explore the opportunities this program might offer you, contact:

Directors Guild of America
Training Program
110 West 57th Street
New York NY 10019

reputation is as someone who is able to move people around quietly. Filming *Last Exit to Brooklyn,* the extras in the last scenes not only knew where they had to go, but had characterizations, motivations, haircuts, and clothes.

GLENN TROTTIER

The second assistant director is usually selected by the 1st AD, and assists him or her while also working closely with the UPM. The 2nd AD distributes the daily call sheet to cast and crew, distributes any script changes to the cast, and prepares each day's production report, telling how much of the schedule was fulfilled. He or she collects reports from the camera, script, and sound departments, provides the actors with their schedules as to clothes, makeup, and hair, takes care of day-player and extra contracts, and also does the paperwork for whatever permits and reports may be needed by the production office. The 2nd AD supervises meal breaks, making sure everyone on set gets to eat within the period specified by each union.

Communication is the key, and you are the information center. You handle the call sheet with the UPM and the 1st AD. This is the daily plan, which even tells what actors are *not* working. It is like a subpoena. You are the one the cast asks, "What is the call time?" With forty-six actors and only two makeup artists and one hair person, how do you do it? You go in whatever direction is called for.

PARNES CARTWRIGHT, 2nd AD

The 2nd AD also supervises the work of the DGA trainee or the intern assigned to each film. Knowing how to do the support work that enables the massive production machine to function is learned through on-the-job training and advancement through the ranks.

Movies are the last of the guild-like activities. You really need to do the apprenticeship.

PETER RUMBOLO

I was a production assistant for three years. Then I became 2nd AD. I did that for seven years. Now I am a first assistant director.

GLENN TROTTIER

STARTING SALARIES

At the current rates, first assistant directors working in a studio make a minimum salary of $2,672; filming on location, they make $3,739. Second assistant directors working in a studio make a minimum salary of $1,791; on location they make $2,502. And second 2nd assistant directors working in a studio make a minimum salary of $1,691; on location they earn $2,363.

GETTING STARTED

This career track requires an intuitive sense of organization, careful attention to detail, a passionate dedication to movie-making, and an ability to delegate tasks and oversee their completion. Everyone, from the DGA trainee to the production manager, deals with a broad range of people daily. The ability to get along with all of them is an asset. A major in film or play production is certainly helpful, but not essential.

> As an acting major, I'd taken some technical courses. I got to work on a movie through a friend. When the location manager found it hard to deal with the public, I became his assistant.
>
> PARNES CARTWRIGHT

> I was going to law school. A summer job had me escorting some Teen Tours across the country. That was much more to my liking than office or court work. I discovered the DGA training program. I worked for Sidney Lumet as a trainee. Then I worked as 2nd AD.
>
> GLENN TROTTIER

INTRODUCTION TO THE PROCESS

With more than twenty-five years' experience as a production manager and assistant director, Robert Bordiga is one of the creators and seminar leaders of the DGA Assistant Director Training Program. He has also originated Nuts and Bolts Production Seminars, a weekend intensive course for professionals who seek a comprehensive understanding of the production process in film and television. The program has attracted producers, filmmakers, writers, auditors, attorneys, and segment producers on nondramatic programs.

> FOR INFORMATION, CONTACT:
>
> On Budget Features, Inc.
> 163 Amsterdam Avenue, Suite 315
> New York, NY 10023

Participants in the Nuts and Bolts weekends have a chance to take a screenplay and *almost* make it into a movie—all that's needed is the money. They go through the entire step-by-step budgeting and scheduling process, comparing the methods of preparing low-budget independent features, major studio pictures, and television movies and series. They have mentors at every session who are veteran 1st ADs and UPMs. The seminars are offered in New York, Los Angeles, and Minneapolis.

> To get hired, find out whom you know among the regular crew people on a production, as early as possible. Send, or fax, your résumé. Volunteer to work for free. It is who you know.
>
> ROBERT BORDIGA

THE PRODUCTION OFFICE STAFF

Gearing up to make a motion picture is like starting any new business. Communications have to be sent and received. Bills must be paid. Messages and mail need to be delivered. Permits must be filed. Equipment has to be rented or purchased. Reports, releases, and waivers are submitted in triplicate. Appointments are made, meetings taken. The Production Office handles the daily business of the company, both at the studio and on location.

PRODUCTION OFFICE COORDINATOR

From the preparatory stages to the final wrap-up for a specific production, the production office coordinator (POC) is responsible for the efficient set-up and operation of the production office and acts as the liaison between the employer (usually the producer), the unit production manager, the assistant director, and the script supervisor. A POC covers only one production at a time, even if the same employer has several projects in production.

While every project is unique and the duties may vary, the POC is expected to be familiar with all phases of production activity. He or she works with the producer, director, writer, and heads of all the departments, as well as with suppliers, insurance companies, accountants, and government agencies. Ideally, the POC has some knowledge of budgets, union contracts, and regulations, can fill out disability reports, and decipher the multicolored strips of the production breakdown board, which note the time, place, and characters for every scene. The POC sees to it that the production report, call sheet, shooting schedule, and script revisions are properly prepared and distributed.

ADDITIONAL STAFF

As the term implies, the duties of the ASSISTANT PRODUCTION OFFICE COORDINATOR are assigned by the POC, based upon the needs of the project. The services of an assistant POC are not always deemed necessary.

The PRODUCTION ACCOUNTANT sets up the auditing office, opens the company bank accounts, and oversees cash flow. An alternate job title can be PRODUCTION AUDITOR or LOCATION AUDITOR. The auditor tracks orders, pays the production's bills, calculates salaries according to the various union contracts, writes the weekly checks and, if necessary, cashes them. An ASSISTANT AUDITOR assists the auditor in distributing payments, keeping the books, and writing cost reports.

ASSISTANT TO A PRODUCER

Sharon Waldman describes herself as SLAVE to Laurence Heath, a producer of the television series *Murder, She Wrote*:

> Every job as an assistant is slightly different, but the basic idea is that you do the same things that a secretary would do on a normal job, but you also do things like editing scripts, correcting any mistakes you find—so as to make the producer look good. It turns out to be a career, and it can be a very good career.
>
> What I would say to anyone interested in this career is: First, go to college and take all the film and TV classes you can. Second, learn all the computer programs you can that relate to scripts. There are many. The most important one for this job would be script formatting. When a show is in production, that is very complex and technical.
>
> This can be an entry-level job in the sense that if you already had experience doing a similar job for a small production company, you could conceivably come to a studio and get into this job. The timing would have to be right—like everything else. It's difficult to walk in if you don't know someone.

GETTING STARTED

Sharon Waldman was a very fast typist, and when she needed a temporary job, she got an opportunity through a friend to work for a script-processing company typing soap opera scripts. One thing led to another.

> You start out working for a local company—a small production house—summers, part-time, whatever you can do. Go to them and work and learn as much as you can. Every city where they have to produce commercials or industrial films for local people has one. They are there. Get some background, then go to a large city. Go to as good a school as you can get into and study good writing. They will expect you to know it.

PROFESSIONAL AFFILIATION

On the East coast, the International Alliance of Theatrical and Stage Employees (IATSE), Local #161, organizes production office coordinators and assistant coordinators. The pay scale for production office coordinators is $181 per day, or $819 per week. For assistant office coordinators it is $94 per day, or $468 per week.

In Los Angeles, office and professional workers are covered by Local #174 of the Office and Pro-

---

FOR INFORMATION, CONTACT:

International Alliance of Theatrical and Stage Employees, Local #161
80 Eighth Avenue
New York, NY 10011

Office and Professional Employees International Union, Local #174
120 South Victory Boulevard, Suite 201
Burbank, CA 91502

fessional Employees International Union (OPEIU). Among the fourteen contracts OPEIU administers within the film industry are agreements covering executive secretaries, assistants to producers, directors, writers, accountants, auditors, and entry-level production personnel who are assigned to make copies, collate, and distribute scripts.

> Qualifications for these jobs really vary widely. For some of them, all you need is a high-school diploma. But the higher you go, the more skills you need. And some of our people have advanced degrees.
>
> CHRISTINE PAGE, business representative, OPEIU

Annual wages begin at around $23,000 and peak at $70,000.

THE CASTING DIRECTOR

Once the major stars are committed to a feature film, the producer and director rely on the casting director to study the script, confer with them about the remaining roles to be cast and how they visualize the characters, and come up with a list of suggestions. This work usually has to be accomplished within a very limited time.

> I try to come up with something new and original in every piece of casting I do. When I am at a movie, I am constantly making notes. It's like, "Oh, I have to remember that actor and put him on my new faces list." I have a program on my computer keeping track of when I saw that actor, what I saw the actor do, his or her age, and so on, so I can keep my mind fresh with new ideas.
>
> MARY JO SLATER, casting director

The production manager's schedule lists the number of shooting days for each character, which gives the casting director some idea of the importance of the role. Sometimes an actor whom everyone agrees is ideal for a part may be accustomed to a higher salary than the role is budgeted for. If no agreement is possible, the casting director must suggest alternatives—one reason why casting directors are always on the alert for interesting new talent while maintaining relationships with talent agents.

Casting directors work in both movies and television. In television, with its two-hour made-for-TV movies, miniseries, half-hour sitcoms, and one-hour dramatic shows, the casting director meets with constant pressure over an extended period. A regular series will normally employ an on-staff casting director and assistants. Scripts may come in only a week before an episode starts production.

The casting director reads the script, writes brief character descriptions of the roles to be cast, and sends them to a company called the Breakdown Service, which distributes casting information to talent agents. The agents then submit their clients' photos and résumés to the casting director, who will also call suitable performers from his or her own files, if time permits. From hundreds of submissions from agents, the casting director winnows the field down to a manageable number and schedules appointments. Auditioning and casting noncontract players follows. In TV, network executives, in addition to the producer, must approve the casting director's suggestions.

> I cast a Movie of the Week that became a series. Then we hired a new casting person for that series.

> I like to get involved with a project as early as possible. I want to talk with the writers, offer ideas, assist the development. There may be people I can think of—to see if we can get a valuable performer attached to the project early on. . . .
>
> DAWN STEINBERG, casting director

Daytime dramas, such as soap operas, operate differently. Their storylines are projected far enough in advance to allow time for a talent search when new characters are being written in.

> I may read 250 actors for one role. The philosophy is that if there is someone who might be remotely right, I would rather take the extra four minutes to read that actor than not at all. We really love going to the producer and saying we have five to ten really good choices.
>
> MARK TESCHNER, casting director

ONE CASTING DIRECTOR'S STORY

Dawn Steinberg was a student at Performing Arts High School, in New York City, when Alan Parker was shooting the movie *Fame*. She landed the job of managing the extras—the students who would appear as students in the shots.

> I loved the excitement of making the movie. When I got out of school, I kept on doing that during vacations. I kept working in the business every chance I could. The entry level is to intern, help out.
>
> You have to love to go to the movies, watch TV, and see theater. That was my great training.

She wanted to produce children's television, but finding no way to get into that area, she returned to casting. At CBS, she was director of casting for daytime and prime-time. When her husband's career producing TV movies took them to California, she sought opportunities to assist other casting directors on features and TV films.

> I got to know people, and they trusted me. I was dedicated, energetic, efficient. You have to like actors—you have to like *people*. Believe it or not, there are people in this business who do not. And you have to be a nice person.

In 1995, she became casting director at Big Ticket Television, a division of the Aaron Spelling organization. Part of her job was to look for other opportunities for the actors who work on Spelling shows, to complement their work, expand their reach, capitalize on their visibility, and throw attention back on the shows. The best part of the job?

> Finding the right new talent. To discover someone no one thought would

be good. Helping young talent to get an agent. I had a great victory recently when we were working on something where they needed a black actor to play an executive. Well, I had just met a 29-year-old who impressed me as perfect for that part. I got them to see him, and they agreed. Which is not only good for the project, it's a plus for me—that allows them to trust my judgment.

Shortly thereafter, Steinberg was made vice president of Big Ticket Television. Apparently, plenty of people trust her judgment.

PROFESSIONAL AFFILIATION

FOR INFORMATION, CONTACT:

Casting Society of America
6565 Sunset Boulevard, Suite 306
Los Angeles, CA 90028

Casting directors in film and television, as in theater, are not represented by a union. Their organization, the Casting Society of America, attempts to set standards and gain recognition for the work they do, such as on-screen credit in the opening titles.

ANTICIPATED INCOME

In film, casting directors work on a freelance basis. Casting directors on a continuing television series are usually employed by the production company that does the show for the network. The salaries they are able to negotiate are commensurate with their experience, with the number of roles to be cast, and the expected difficulty in finding the right performers. This generally translates into a salary on a level with that of a member of the design team.

THE CINEMATOGRAPHER
AND RELATED CREW

To translate the written screenplay into the moving images that will captivate audiences is the job of the director of photography, also known as the CINE-MATOGRAPHER, and referred to on the set as the DP. This highly skilled professional has extensive knowledge of equipment, lighting, and optical principles, and a highly developed aesthetic awareness of the ways color, movement, mood, and composition can be used to tell a story.

Chosen by the director and producer early in pre-production, the cinematographer studies the script, makes his or her own scene-by-scene breakdown and, based upon conferences with the design team, decides on the equipment, the lenses, lighting, and film stock (all of which the production manager orders) that will best tell the story. The cinematographer also selects the CAMERA OPERATOR and GAFFER (lighting chief).

Once shooting starts, the DP is second only to the director in authority on the set. Together they decide on camera placement, how and when it will move, and on lighting.

> Once the cinematographer comes on, a bond is made with the director. The designer is running around getting everything ready that you have talked about before. At the director's right arm now is the cinematographer, who says "Change that color."
>
> ALBERT BRENNER, production designer

ON THE SET

The DP tells the gaffer how to light the scene, then explains to the camera crew how to set up for the shot. After the director rehearses with the actors, they run the scene for camera rehearsal. This allows the DP to check camera angles and lighting, plan camera movements, and anticipate focus adjustments. The sound crew (page 147) rehearses at the same time to coordinate microphone moves to avoid a boom shadow or the hint of an overhead mike drooping into the picture.

Prior to shooting a scene, the DP will look through the camera to check the composition of the shot. Video monitors connected to the cameras permit everyone on the set to review a take and judge whether they got everything they were striving for, and what to improve in the next take.

The DP views the prints of the previous day's shooting, or *dailies,* with the director, possibly requesting re-takes if the location and actors are still available, or offering editing suggestions if they're not (for example: "There's a better moment in Take 6 you can use in Take 2—that'll give you the scene.") Most important are the DP's instructions to the film lab on the development, exposure, and printing processes needed to give the film the distinctive visual quality that's wanted.

GETTING STARTED

This profession calls for a thorough apprenticeship. The majority of current cinematographers first learned the equipment working as untitled helpers, taking cameras apart and putting them back together again. After a time they were promoted to assistant camerapersons and, eventually, to camera operators—where many are content to remain—and to cinematographers.

Happily, technical progress and recognition of achievements in film have made it easier for students to learn much more about filmmaking at an earlier age. Thanks to technology, it's possible to study the work of award-winning cinematographers at home, without having to sit through a whole movie just to watch a particular shot. With nearly professional-grade equipment available at a relatively moderate cost, aspiring filmmakers can begin playing with film almost as soon as they are able to point the camera. Music videos and commercials offer early opportunities for graduates of film schools to get working experience using the most advanced products and techniques.

The SECOND CAMERA ASSISTANT is the entry-level position on the camera crew. Under the DP's orders, the second assistant loads and unloads the film magazines (in total darkness to avoid exposing the film), keeping a record of how many feet of film have been exposed and whether enough of the reel remains to complete the next shot. The second assistant prepares the *slate,* the hand-held board that shows the name of the project, director, DP, and the number of every scene and take, and operates the *clapper* at the top of the slate. He or she announces the take number and snaps together the black and white diagonally-striped clapper; the immediate sight and sound (clap) when the halves of the clapper meet serve as a matching point for the synchronization of the audio track and the picture. The second assistant also keeps a written record of every shot and take, as well as a log listing the scenes and takes completed for each day. Familiarity with (and respect for) the equipment and constant attention to the numbers are essential.

The FIRST CAMERA ASSISTANT is known as the *focus puller*—the person who moves the focus ring on the camera lens, so that objects in the shot remain in focus while the distance between the objects and the camera changes. The first assistant measures the distance between the object (or the actor) and the camera at the start of the shot, and writes that distance in his log book, which is attached to the camera for convenient reference. The first assistant may stick bits of colored tape on the floor, to mark the actors' positions. Focus changes are rehearsed prior to shooting the take. According to the DP's instructions, the first assistant fits the proper lenses on the camera, attaches any necessary filters and, most important, always keeps the camera clean and loaded. If the crew has no second assistant, the first assistant may be responsible for loading the camera, threading the film, and making certain that the interior is dust-free. In an emergency, the first assistant should be able to operate the camera—which is the next step on the road to cinematographer.

The CAMERA OPERATOR does exactly that—first, lines up each shot and checks that the correct lens has been placed in position and that the film is threading correctly, and then sits behind the camera, turns it on, signals when the film is running at the proper speed, and smoothly executes whatever camera moves the DP and director have planned. This work is done with plenty of camera rehearsal under the scrutiny of the director and DP. The camera operator peers through the viewfinder and "feels" how far to tilt when an actor stands, how to frame the door the actor walks through, and so forth. After each take, the camera operator tells the DP and director whether the shot was technically correct—no boom shadows, flares, or reflections, all movements done as rehearsed.

Camera operators may also operate special equipment, such as the Steadicam—a harness-like support for a lightweight camera which the operator wears for handheld camera shots—or cameras mounted on cranes, helicopters, or whatever an unusual shot calls for to achieve the desired effect.

Camera operators have total knowledge of the equipment—its maintenance and repair—and of what the other crew members need to do. Camera operators who prefer to remain at this level, rather than moving on to DP, argue that it's the best job on the crew—they only take credit for what's well done.

A STILL PHOTOGRAPHER is employed on each film to take photos that may be used for publicity, advertising, or theater display. The still photographer also takes photos for the continuity, art, costume, prop, and makeup departments. (These departments may use their own Polaroid shots.)

CAMERA CREW

The GAFFER is the DP's choice for chief electrician on the film crew. The gaffer is employed a few weeks before shooting will start. Because this is a key position, many DPs and gaffers work together all the time; the DP relies on the gaffer to understand and get done quickly whatever is needed. Prior to each day's shooting, DP and gaffer discuss the scenes to be shot and the lighting plan for each, either on location or on a set. The gaffer then informs the crew. Before the day's shooting is scheduled to start, the gaffer's staff of electricians will have readied the lighting for the first scene. The gaffer stays with the DP at all camera rehearsals, his or her crew alert to make any adjustments that may be called for—adding scrims, tilting reflector boards, or operating any equipment, such as fans.

The gaffer's chief assistant, the BEST BOY, is as highly skilled an electrician as the gaffer. In a sense, the best boy serves as an advance electrician and prepares all the lighting equipment for the upcoming scene while the gaffer stays to supervise the crew on the set that's in use. The best boy may also be responsible for organizing, labeling, and packing the equipment on the equipment truck.

Working under the supervision of the best boy and the gaffer are several ELECTRICIANS who do whatever is necessary to fulfill the DP's lighting plan. They install wiring so that lamps can work, position cables, and set up and adjust every kind of light, as well as scrims, reflectors, barn door shutters, and so on, as directed by the gaffer and/or best boy. They pack and load equipment, and then unpack and unload at each location.

A company going on location brings its own electrical power generator and an electrician serves as the generator operator.

THE GRIP DEPARTMENT

Nonelectrical work is supervised by the KEY GRIP, who takes instructions from the DP and whose department is responsible for rigging, leveling, and moving equipment. Grips work closely with both the camera and electrical crews. For example, when lamps have to be hung on pipes, the grips rig the pipes.

When a complicated shot calls for the camera to move forward or back, up or down, a DOLLY GRIP lays the boards or tracks upon which the dolly—the wheeled platform upon which the camera is mounted—will have to be pushed or pulled. In addition to running the dolly, the dolly grip reports to the camera department each day before shooting starts, to make certain the camera is mounted securely before moving it to the shooting area. Moving shots may also require another dolly grip to operate a second wheeled platform, which carries the mike and boom operators. These moves are coordinated in rehearsal.

If the camera has to be mounted on a crane and soar vertically or swing horizontally, CRANE OPERATORS—as many as four skilled mechanics, who sit with the camera operator—will rehearse these potentially dangerous moves with the camera and electrical crews.

For supremely complicated moving shots, lightweight cameras can be mounted on a robot crane system and operated from the ground by teams of LOUMA CRANE OPERATOR GRIPS, who use a video monitor that displays the camera image. The camera operator is thus able to remain on the ground rather than try to fly through the air with the camera.

A BEST BOY GRIP is the key grip's assistant, and functions in much the same advance manner as the gaffer's best boy.

THE SOUND DEPARTMENT

When a sound crew does an excellent job, hardly anyone notices their work. At the head of what is customarily a three-person team is the SOUND MIXER. Like the gaffer, the sound mixer joins the project shortly before shooting at the director's invitation, even though the production manager does the actual hiring. Sound mixers want to read the script in advance and break it down scene by scene, to judge the film's sound requirements.

Wearing headphones on the set, the sound mixer controls the volume levels on the tape recording machine—traditionally a Nagra, the industry standard—and tells the director whether a tape is clear, meaning that no external noise—called *disturbance*—has interfered with the dialogue. Lines that cannot be recorded cleanly are recorded separately, as wild lines, and are later edited into the track. After each scene, the sound mixer records, separately, about a minute's worth of ambient noise—in the studio this is called *room tone*—to use as a constant background in editing.

The microphone actually recording the dialogue and sound effects is handled by the BOOM OPERATOR, who also has to be familiar with the script so as to swivel the mike toward the actors who speak and to follow them as the scene progresses. To avoid a boom shadow or any intrusion of the mike at the top of the screen, the boom operator must be familiar with camera lenses and how a scene is being shot. If using a boom is impossible, the boom operator plants mikes where they will not be seen, but where they can provide matching sound. Because different mikes have different recording capabilities and qualities, the boom operator is expected to know which to substitute in any scene.

If actors speak to each other across a wide space, a so-called THIRD MAN, handling a second mike, becomes necessary. The third man is also a cable person and clears all cables out of the way as the camera dollies and the boom operator follows alongside.

PROFESSIONAL STATUS

All these skills are covered by various local offices of the International Alliance of Theatrical and Stage Employees (IATSE), each of which negotiates minimum wages and working conditions for its members. Local #644, the camera union, represents cinematographers, camera operators, assistants, and still photographers. As of the last contract, the weekly pay scale was:

- Director of photography: $2,344
- Camera operator: $1,806
- First assistant: $1,171

- Second assistant: $972
- Still photographer: $1,427

Superstar cinematographers and camera operators (or their agents) will be able to negotiate above-scale salaries.

The American Society of Cinematographers is the respected professional association of directors of photography. Their monthly publication, *American Cinematographer* is available to the public (see page 216).

Electrical and sound crews (and also carpentry crews) belong to IATSE's Local #52, for studio mechanics. The weekly salary is five times the daily rates shown here.

FOR INFORMATION, CONTACT:

International Alliance of Theatrical and Stage Employees Local #644 505 Eighth Avenue, 16th Floor New York, NY 10018

International Alliance of Theatrical and Stage Employees Local #52 326 West 48th Street New York, NY 10036

- Gaffer: $247.11 (negotiable)
- Best boy; electrician; generator operator; key grip; dolly grip; and best boy grip: $230.11
- Grip: $197.23
- Sound mixer: $312 (negotiable)
- Boom operator; third man: $239

Benefits include employer contributions to union health and retirement funds. Acceptance into a local customarily requires payment of initiation fee and annual dues. The autonomous locals set their own rules concerning these and matters of membership and qualifications.

GETTING STARTED

Graduate or undergraduate degrees are not actually required for entry into these professions. Courses in film production present opportunities to gain valuable hands-on experience. Outside the major production centers, local television stations, independent commercial production houses, and theater companies may be willing to hire novices as interns, gofers, or general assistants. Your nearest film commission will have information on incoming film units doing location shooting who will need to hire local crew people.

Working at a camera store has been the starting point for many cinematographers. Talent, attention to detail, energy, patience, intelligence, and dependability are the necessary characteristics.

THE PRODUCTION DESIGNER

Design in film and television provides visual signals that, within split seconds, let the audience know whether a setting is urban, suburban, or rural and supply clues to the social class, sex, education, and income of the characters inhabiting those spaces. The production designer is responsible for everything that you see on the screen that does not move (meaning the actors) and (the designers lament) is usually out of focus.

Albert Brenner, five-time Oscar-nominated production designer, explained it this way:

> The function of a designer is to give the director what he wants. It is his picture, and you are going to try to enhance it. You bring what you would like to see in it, in hopes that it will help the film. I design what I think is right for the film, then go talk to the director about it, and tell him what I've done.

Producer-director Garry Marshall, who had Brenner on his team for the movie *Beaches,* said:

> Albert taught me how we could use different color schemes to express the various phases of the movie—pastels for youth, grays for tough times, reds and golds for success, and muted sunset colors for illness. Albert showed me how art could be used to carry a story.

The designer is brought into the team after the producer, writer, and director have done their pre-production work. Depending on the number of scenes, locations, or sets, that is usually about ten or twelve weeks before shooting is to begin.

> Every time I get a script, I read and panic. How are we going to do this? Then I start breaking it down, scene by scene, shot by shot. You find out it's not that difficult.
>
> Normally, I go look at locations myself. I explain to the location manager that when we all go out to look at a possible location I haven't seen and the director asks me, "How are we going to shoot this?" I don't want to stand there with egg on my face and say, "I don't know." So, I go.
>
> ALBERT BRENNER

> You read the script, you see nothing. You let the words seep in. You work with the director to see his needs.
>
> BRANDY ALEXANDER, production designer

When the director has approved the design concept, SET DESIGNERS (also called DRAFTSMEN) draw the plans, and scenic studios create any necessary sets. Since the dissolution of the major studios with their famed backlot streets, huge scene docks and construction shops have been dismantled, with scores of treasured pieces discarded or sold at auction. With the availability of trained production people outside the major production centers, and with attractive incentives offered by competitive film commissions, location shooting has become the norm. While locations present the opportunity to incorporate startling scenic or architectural elements into a film, designers actually prefer to create their sets.

> You need to provide space for a camera and a crew. Sixty to a hundred technicians will be standing around. You develop "wild joints," which are movable wings of the set, so that you can make room for the action.
>
> BRANDY ALEXANDER

> Building a set gives the director more control and gives the company fewer headaches. And I know the look is better. When you design a set you design for the geography of the screenplay. For example, in *The Goodbye Girl,* there's a scene where Richard Dreyfuss has taken over the bedroom and Marsha Mason hears his guitar music, and she is angry. I read the script and felt those lines should be delivered on the way to his room; she is talking to herself out loud. I designed the set so that her bed was just the dialogue's length away from his door. When she said her lines she reached his door. I told the director, Herbert Ross, what I had done. He walked the set saying the lines and, like all great chefs who ask for just a bit more salt, he said, "Move it a foot more."
>
> ALBERT BRENNER

The production designer will work closely with the set decorator and the propmaster, describing the countless details—furnishings such as books, trophies, souvenirs, art collections, and so on—that will create the visual context.

CREATIVE PROBLEM-SOLVING

The designer remains with the production throughout the shoot. Despite weeks of intensive preparation, the unexpected can always happen, threatening to derail the schedule. For example, on the movie *Pretty Woman,* a serious earthquake meant that a scene in San Francisco's glorious War Memorial Opera House had to be postponed indefinitely. Designer Brenner hung a row of box seats from the wall of the soundstage. Seated in gilt chairs, eight extras in formal dress gave the illusion of an audience of several hundred socialites at a gala occasion.

One scene which was inserted on shooting day called for two actors to meet in a nightclub. Designer Mel Bourne created the effect of a dingy bar by using circles of colored neon tubing against a black background. The director then shot the scene using only closeups.

To establish the leading lady as a singing star, the script called for her to be seen in concert bowing to a cheering crowd. The cost of this half-minute sequence would have been exorbitant. Designer and director agreed that to show her rehearsing on the stage of the empty amphitheater early in the day, with only her musicians, could tell the same story and be shot easily, saving time and money.

In production design, the differences between film and television have mostly to do with time and money, of which there is far less in television, and the need to compress visual elements for the small screen.

> In films, the script has a beginning, a middle, and an end. You know what you have to deal with. You research old magazines, you scout. But in episodic TV you never know what the *next* script will call for. And you are always behind the gun. You have eight days.
>
> BRANDY ALEXANDER

> You have to be more inventive, and the budgets are very tight.
>
> TOM JOHN, production designer

Television offers designers opportunities in several other forms, such as news, interview, and discussion programs, as well as game shows and special-events coverage (see pages 203–206).

THREE CAREER PATHS

After majoring in theatrical design at Yale Drama School, followed by a short university teaching stint in the Midwest, Albert Brenner came to New York City, where he worked on all the live programming at CBS and on commercials and industrial films. After one film job in New York, he was recommended to a producer doing a movie in Florida. That producer recommended him to Clive Donner, a British director shooting his first American film, *Luv.* Donner then recommended him to director John Boorman, for work on *Point Blank.* And Boorman recommended him to his friend Peter Yates for the Steve McQueen film *Bullitt.* Brenner then decided to move to California.

His first Hollywood film brought him his first Oscar nomination, for *The Sunshine Boys,* starring George Burns and Walter Matthau. He explained how he designed the set:

> I designed it as an apartment in the Ansonia [a landmark building on Manhattan's West Side]. It allowed the director to go from one room to another, and to another, and another. All the rooms were linked by doors; you didn't have to enter and exit through the same opening—even in the bathrooms. Ever since, I always put two doors in a bathroom.

Mel Bourne, also from Yale, describes himself as having wandered into live TV. His commercials—work he considers the greatest education anyone could have for film—attracted the attention of Woody Allen, who wanted a specifically New York look for a film he was going to call *Annie Hall*. Bourne worked on seven Allen films, and he designed the disturbing *Fatal Attraction* (working with director Adrian Lyne) and Terry Gilliam's phantasmagorical *The Fisher King*.

Bourne also designed the popular television series *Miami Vice*, which premiered in 1984 and has been credited with redefining the style of TV crime shows—from grimy to stylish. Previously, television backgrounds had been nondescript, so as not to upstage the performers. (It also boosted the entire film business in South Florida!)

> That first show set the visual impact. It was a perfect marriage of many elements: style, sound, clothes, lighting, architecture. The initial work, the conception, was the most exciting part. Miami looked like a set to me from the start, with those Art Deco buildings and the mix of different groups of people.
>
> MEL BOURNE

Daughter of two accomplished performers, Brandy Alexander grew up in Los Angeles and went to work directly in film and television. She began as a draftsperson, drew storyboards, and designed for *The Waltons, Dallas,* and *Hill Street Blues*. For her work as production designer on *thirtysomething,* she earned two Emmy nominations. She advised: "The business of a production designer is to be invisible. The better your work is, the less people notice it."

One aspect of her approach to designing a film set is to do a "history" of the space: "What did it used to be? What kind of story took place before we came here?"

PROFESSIONAL REQUIREMENTS

Sketching, perspective drawing, and rendering techniques are basic requirements, to be augmented by training in design—line, proportion, composition, and color. The design schools—and there are excellent preparatory high schools as well as colleges and universities—are not difficult to find, particularly in large cities. Some schools train people who want to work only in film.

Experienced designers agree that schools can only teach the tools and how to use them; they cannot teach how to be a designer. To achieve that, designers are advised to immerse themselves in the vast world of design—go to museums, read books on design, study pictures, and observe the visual world. If possible, travel in order to absorb as many design influences as possible.

> In my opinion, the person who comes most fully equipped to the job is the designer. He or she has to know art, design, furniture, costume, technical

things about construction, and has to know how to draw. If you want to get this job, learn as many of those things as you can.

ALBERT BRENNER

The ability to sketch is a great advantage. Then it's there—a discussion tool. They may change the sketch, but you get something.

TOM JOHN

CAREER LEVELS

An entry-level position would be as a DRAFTSPERSON (sometimes called SET DESIGNER), moving up to ASSISTANT ART DIRECTOR—a valuable position from which to learn about costs, sources, how to deal with the property and craftspeople. Further advancement would be to ART DIRECTOR and/or PRODUCTION DESIGNER.

SET DECORATORS seek, find, and (usually) purchase the furnishings shown in the production designer's presentation. SET DRESSERS handle the placement of the personal touches for each shot. Of course, some designers like to control every aspect of the environment they create.

The people I work with are very capable. We go to shops together, they arrange for all the paperwork and trucking. They will say they saw a sink we can use, or something like that, but they understand they are not going to dress the sets—I am.

MEL BOURNE

Actual set construction is performed by CARPENTERS and CARPENTER'S ASSISTANTS at a scenic studio, under the supervision of a CONSTRUCTION COORDINATOR. As in the theater, SCENIC ARTISTS paint the sets and do any special artwork, such as signs or backdrops, or they treat walls (and even costumes) to make them appear old and dilapidated. A TOUCH-UP PAINTER is always on hand on location or on the sound stage to do just what the title implies—cover up dents, cracks, scratches, and chips—or paint any replacement props.

MATTE ARTISTS paint artwork that becomes a portion of a scene as it is combined with the live-action photography in the printing of the film. This is how numerous special effects are achieved. The artists also work on the set and then in the technical lab where artwork and film are fitted together.

SPECIAL EFFECTS

Rain-soaked streets, volcanic eruptions, uncontrollable fires, sinking ocean liners, and other common cinema spectacles were formerly the province of studio special-effects departments, which were adjuncts of the design division. Nowadays, they are manufactured by independent special-effects companies. However, the planning of those effects—the sequence of exploding, zooming, burning, or cascading elements in each scene—is another aspect of the production designer's work.

> The special-effects person got a lot of credit for the movie *Backdraft,* and should have. But he didn't *design* the effects. Remember, everything you see in the world of a film had to be put on paper, designed.
>
> I have initial talks with the director about what this is going to look like. I transmit that to the art director (assistant designer), who draws it in storyboard form and shows the producer and me what it will be. The effects house then manufactures the effect.
>
> ALBERT BRENNER

> That wild horse in *The Fisher King* was realized by Douglas White of Make-up and Effects Laboratories. He bathed a white horse in red henna base, then airbrushed fuschia food coloring on the horse's musculature. Cherry red was sponged onto the animal's coat. We added bright red extensions to his mane and tail and blackened his hoofs. Four colors of acrylics were squeeze-bottled onto his body, to look like drippings. The horse was bathed every night.
>
> MEL BOURNE

Effects may be physical, and *stunts* fall into this category—exploding buildings, talking robots, tables that collapse in a barroom brawl. Effects may be optical—double exposures that send fantastic spaceships hurtling to gaseous planets, or dissolves that create an illusion of a disintegrating vampires. Either way, sequences are plotted on storyboards. The designer then collaborates with craftspeople, special-effects wizards, or computer artists to realize the design in terms of the story.

Stan Winston, four-time Oscar winner for special effects, said:

> I create characters for film and I embrace technology. But the dream must come first. It is a balance between art and technology. Effects will not hold our attention without a story.

TO MAIL ORDER:
The Albert and Trudy Kallis Foundation 2310 Canyonback Road Los Angeles, CA 90049

There is a videotape of interest to anyone who wants to enter the magical world of movie special effects: The planning and execution of a blazing fire in a gigantic wheatfield, the dramatic high point of the television film *Amber Waves,* is shown in "The Making of *Amber Waves,*" available by mail order (see box). The videotape costs $25, which includes postage and handling.

SPECIAL-EFFECTS PROFESSIONALS

Experts in special effects may not necessarily have a design background, but they are excellent at drawing—and in imagining.

There is no formal training for this. You get in and do it. I was an actor. I became a makeup artist, then a director, and finally went into crafts. I create *creatures*—characters for films. From *King Kong* to *Jurassic Park* to *Toy Story* and whatever will come next, it's always a guess, because we haven't done *this* before.

It is always getting more refined, more "invisible." But the technology serves the story. If you have an art background you should learn computer science. A computer person should learn art. Beyond that, you need a basic education, and the desire.

STAN WINSTON

The new digital technology makes it possible to produce special effects through highly sophisticated electronic means, usually with computerized equipment. Using software programs such as Flame, elements can be shot separately, then joined through such techniques as compositing, rotoscoping, and warping, and then transferred from the digital tape on which the effects were created to film.

These processes are very expensive. Moreover, the experts agree that while computers make it all sound amazingly easy, without inspiration from creative human beings the machinery just sits there.

You still have to learn the basic philosophy of what you are doing: What is this scene about?

BILL HANAUER, business representative, Screen Editors union

Films such as *Independence Day, Twister,* and *Dragonheart* may have received less than enthusiastic reviews for their story lines, but they earned millions of dollars for their studios thanks to their amazing special effects. In 1997, all three films received Academy Award nominations for the excellence of their visual effects.

Industrial Light and Magic, the special-effects division of Lucas Digital, created the effects for *Twister* and *Dragonheart*. Separate teams of around a hundred computer software and design people worked on each project. Because the films were shot on location on days that were not always sunny, the lighting of the special-effects elements for both features had to be digitally matched to the lighting of all the outdoor shots. For *Twister,* a software code had to be written to control the movement of the millions of spinning particles and dangerous flying debris. For *Dragonheart,* the company developed its own software to synchronize Draco the dragon's facial movements with the emotional vocal readings, supplied by actor Sean Connery.

Most of the effects in *Independence Day* were achieved "the old-fashioned way" using small, painstakingly detailed physical models. Director Roland Emmerich assembled a group of more than 300 freelance artists and designers, many of them students, to work on the project. Each of the film's explosions was storyboarded or choreographed—designed—just as Albert Brenner described above.

THE COMPUTER ARTIST

The record-breaking success of the animated movie *Toy Story* has focussed attention on the advancements in computer-generated film images. Unlike their animated cousins in hand-drawn cartoons like *The Lion King*, the *Toy Story* characters appear to be fully three-dimensional inhabitants of a three-dimensional world—more like puppets. They have been set in motion, frame by frame, by a process known as Pixar.

To Steven Jobs, co-founder of Apple Computers, Pixar represented the ultimate relationship between film and the computer—so he bought the company from its creator, George Lucas. He has described Pixar as an additional entertainment medium.

The Pixar animation technique depends on talented ARTISTS, ANIMATORS, and COMPUTER EXPERTS. The process begins like any other special-effects design: Storyboard sketches depict the film's progress and overall visual tone. Once the sketches are approved, actual sculptures of the characters are made and their images are digitized into the computer. The computer animator then creates the story's scenes on the computer. Using on-screen wire frame–type images as models of objects or characters, he or she manipulates them by marking control points—articulating variables, or *avars*—on the wire frames. Motion sequences are enacted by the computer. Then the animator adds the surfaces and features that cover each model, filling in the wire frames. Finally, "layers" of lighting, color, texture, and other desired visual effects are added to create the total look of the scene.

Shattering the myth that computers will do everyone's work faster and cheaper, this multi-stage process is costly and time-consuming. Every character, set, and prop—an estimated 2,000 of them—was constructed in the computer as a three-dimensional model. Like *The Lion King*, the making of *Toy Story* was a four-year project.

CAREER ADVICE

Don Padgett, of United Scenic Artists, is understandably confident about the outlook for the union's members. Opportunities for computer-proficient artists are apparent. Experts agree, however, that dexterity with computers is only part of it. They advise would-be animators that to successfully capture the physicality of a character, artists need drawing techniques and the instincts of an actor.

In fact, the process of arriving at the specific body characteristics and movements of the *Toy Story* creatures echoes the stories of how the original Disney artists each portrayed one of the dwarfs in *Snow White and the Seven*

Dwarfs: Those artists did not all do a little bit of everything; rather, they animated specific characters, with their distinctive carriage and habitual gestures. In fact, the dwarfs resembled the seven animators who were working in the studio, drawing one another acting out the story. John Lassiter, director of *Toy Story*, refers to himself as "a trained, hand-drawn art person," and had previously worked as a Disney animator.

A good thing for aspiring animators would be to study animated movies, from the earliest to the present. Pay attention to the characters, notice their personal styles. Realize that they are all undergoing emotional experiences—heroic, foolish, sad, or wondrous—which the audience can identify with. Their behavior is what we call acting. Characters whose adventures captivate audiences over decades must be good actors, in good stories. Which is to say that all the technology in the world cannot operate without inspiration from human beings.

FOR INFORMATION, CONTACT:

Walt Disney World
Professional Staffing
Box 10900
Lake Buena Vista, FL 32820

The Ringling School
of Art and Design
2700 North Tamiami Trail
Sarasota, FL 34234

California Institute
of the Arts
247600 McBean Parkway
Valencia, CA 91355

TRAINING PROGRAMS

Potential animators may submit their portfolios to Walt Disney World Professional Staffing. The Ringling School of Art and Design offers courses in computer animation, graphic design, and illustration. It is near the offices of the Walt Disney Company.

California Institute of the Arts was one of the first schools to offer professional training in art and animation, right near the heart of the Hollywood production units.

FOR INFORMATION, CONTACT:

United Scenic Artists
16 West 61st Street
New York, NY 10023

International Alliance
of Theatrical and
Stage Employees
1515 Broadway
New York, NY 10036

PROFESSIONAL AFFILIATION

Production designers, assistant designers, draftsmen, painters, and computer designers are members of United Scenic Artists (USA). Construction coordinators, matte artists, set decorators, and set dressers are members of the International Alliance of Theatrical and Stage Employees.

Technology advances quickly, and conditions change. Questions about wages, working conditions, and benefits for these numerous job areas should be addressed to the nearest union office.

THE COSTUME DESIGNER

One of the production designer's first collaborators is the costume designer. The same talents and training are required for costume design in film and television as for theater, and many of the same designers do splendid work in all three areas.

However, garments are used differently. Theatrical costumes are built to withstand strenuous wear eight times a week, for an extended period of time. Clothing for the large or small screen may be worn only in a few scenes, and sometimes may be seen only in a front view closeup. In such cases, the "costume" may consist solely of the top—which will be perfect for the closeup—paired with an ordinary skirt or trousers not to be photographed. It would be a waste of money to buy more costume than was needed.

The costume designer will establish the period, class, and relationships of all the film's characters and be responsible for everything worn by the principals, day players and, possibly, the extras (especially in a period piece).

> I work with the costume people on the colors we will be using—this color on this set—and then let them go, because they bring their own expertise and talent to it. When we have talented costume designers, there is nothing else I need to do.
>
> ALBERT BRENNER

The designer prepares a scene-by-scene costume breakdown for each character, provides character sketches of each outfit, and shows fabric swatches to the director and producer. (Fabrics that rustle, or shine, or are too stiff to drape well are rarely used.) Once the designs have been okayed, the designer arranges for the costumes to be built, bought, or rented. When an outfit is used in a stunt, or has to be torn or soiled, several copies must be made. Shoes, gloves, handbags, handkerchiefs, jewelry, and any other character accessories are also the designer's responsibility.

Matthew Broderick, appearing on the television program *Inside the Actors Studio* (June, 1996), credited the costume designer's role in the movie *Ferris Bueller's Day Off*: "The costume designer thought of things I never would have, and that helped me a lot. She designed and built that character as much as I did."

The costume designer, like the production designer, remains on set during production, to coordinate the total look and handle whatever emergencies may occur.

THE COSTUME CREW

On complicated productions, an ASSISTANT COSTUME DESIGNER will be employed to handle clothes for lesser roles, do preliminary sketches, and to shop for needed items. The assistant may arrange for the costume rentals and take care of special problems, like making fabrics look aged or stained.

The WARDROBE SUPERVISOR (or COSTUMER) is in charge of the cleaning and pressing—the maintenance—of all costumes and accessories used in the film. The supervisor prepares a separate scene-by-scene costume and accessory breakdown, organizing and labeling each outfit by actor and character name. On shooting day, the supervisor is responsible for each actor being in costume at the scheduled time. Because scenes are shot out of sequence, supervisors are expected to take Polaroid snapshots of the actors in each outfit at the start of a scene and at the end, so that the costumes and accessories can be monitored for their place in the story. For instance, if an actress plays a single woman in some scenes, and her pre-wedding scenes are filmed after the scenes of her character's married life, she might mistakenly go before the camera still wearing a wedding ring; such an error might easily be made without the snapshots as a reference.

FOR INFORMATION, CONTACT:

United Scenic Artists
16 West 61st Street
New York, NY 10023

International Alliance
of Theatrical and
Stage Employees
1515 Broadway
New York, NY 10036

Supervisors frequently act as dressers; women care for the women's outfits; men handle the men's.

Costumes are built by shops (see pages 60–62) that construct clothing for motion pictures and for the theater.

PROFESSIONAL AFFILIATIONS

Questions about wages, working conditions, and benefits for these numerous job areas should be addressed to United Scenic Artists (USA) and the East and West Coast local offices of the International Alliance of Theatrical and Stage Employees, which represent costume designers, costumers, and wardrobe attendants.

HAIRSTYLISTS AND MAKEUP ARTISTS

Qualifications for hairstylists and makeup artists are the same in film and television as they are for theater. However, the focus and demands of the work differ.

In the theater, the curtain goes up on a live show that is performed from start to finish day after day; the assignment is to re-create the makeup, hairstyles, wigs, and special effects for the performers every time. Among the audience in the theater, some people are seated farther away than others; under bright stage lighting and in front of painted scenery, performers' makeup must "read" up in the last row of the balcony. Frankly false eyelashes and big hair are necessary (and acceptable) exaggerations. No one worries much about crow's feet, laugh lines, or even under-eye puffs; they are invisible beyond the first row of the orchestra.

Film and television, on the other hand, are essentially closeup mediums. The camera is the audience. When the image is projected on the movie or television screen, everyone sees what the camera sees. So, the hairstylist and makeup artist must be meticulous in their attention to every hair, eyelash, and pore of any face seen on camera. They remain on duty, on or near the set, for the entire day of shooting. Retakes, changes in camera angle or lighting, specks of dust, or a sneeze—any of these can lead to an assistant director's call for "Makeup!" The face seen in the first take of the day is the one that's expected to be in the last shot, many hours later.

> In movies, continuity is everything. You have to match from shot to shot. And we have to watch. Sometimes there can be days between shots in the same scene, and in between, someone will tell an actress, "Oh, your hair doesn't look good that way, you should comb it different." Well, I have to explain you can't change your look in the same scene.
>
> DAISY CARBEON, hairstylist

LOCATION WORK

Whenever film and television productions use real people's homes rather than studio sets, the hairstylist and makeup artist will be transported to the site and remain with the cast until the day's shoot is completed. Similarly, when scenes must be shot in specific outdoor or foreign places, the cast and crew, including makeup and hair, go on location, sometimes for several weeks. The production company is responsible for everyone's room and board and per diem expenses.

SPECIAL EFFECTS

If aliens appear or corpses awaken, if characters have to age or suffer disfigurement (think of Ralph Fiennes in *The English Patient*), makeup artists and hairstylists get to show their creativity—and have a chance to win awards. They design and apply blemishes and wrinkles, scars, bruises, masks, and possibly a third eye in the middle of a forehead. On camera, it all has to look unquestionably real, in every scene. Challenges like these can require a three- to four-hour makeup session, every camera day.

> The characters in *I'm Not Rappaport* are old, but they talk about their youth and they play those parts. Our days began at 5 A.M.
>
> JEAN BLOCK, hairstylist

Scenes in which the actors' wounds heal as the story unfolds are not always shot in sequence. For example, a character who has just been in a brawl and has a nasty black eye makes a phone call from the booth outside the saloon; the action immediately following, where he has entered the saloon, is shot three days later. Polaroid photos are taken of the actor when the bruise (or any other condition) is brand-new and in all its subsequent stages; these serve as references for the makeup artist and hairstylist.

Makeup artists and hairstylists who create such special effects receive an individual credit.

WORKING WITH A STAR

Wherever a camera is concerned, the relationship between performers and the people who do their makeup and hair can become extremely sensitive. So much is riding on appearance and on how the star feels about the way he or she looks.

Two artists may be equally skillful, and a performer may look just as lovely or healthy, no matter which of the two does the hair or makeup. Yet, one artist will be requested while the other is not. It's a matter of confidence, perception, and rapport: "I just feel my skin has more of a glow when so-and-so does my face," a star might say.

Hairstylists and makeup artists who are requested by a particular performer are given a separate contract and receive an individual credit. Their services may even be part of the negotiation for the star's services in a film.

GETTING STARTED

Makeup artists and hairstylists working on feature films and television are members of the International Alliance of Theatrical and Stage Employees,

Local #798, in New York, and Local #706, in Los Angeles. (Membership in this union described on page 105 in the theater section.) Every local has information on incoming productions. In regional markets, the local film commission should have dates of incoming productions as well as the names of the production manager or location manager, or whoever is staffing the local crew.

The pay scale for makeup artists and hairstylists is the same. In New York, the daily rate is $273.51, plus benefits; and assistants are paid $258.56. Rates will differ in other areas, and will change with contract negotiations.

There is a certain amount of nonunion film and television production, such as independent films, college and university productions, and local industrial material. The film commission may have information about these opportunities also. Otherwise, it's a good idea to consult the classified telephone directory for listings of theatrical or motion picture equipment rental houses; they'll know about upcoming shoots.

Competent, agreeable stylists and makeup artists, who consistently do good work, are certain to be noticed and remembered by production managers who always need capable people they can rely on.

THE TRANSPORTATION CAPTAIN AND CREW

When a movie goes on location, every single item related to the production has to be transported to and from the scene. That includes equipment and personnel. From bobby pins to generators, every item has to be packed into a designated vehicle, and has to be accessible when it arrives. Each time shooting is finished at a location, everything must be packed up exactly as before, to be available for the next morning's shoot at the next destination.

To assemble the necessary fleet of trucks and cars, the production manager engages a transportation coordinator, or captain. During pre-production they determine how many trucks, cars, and drivers will be needed. Their lists could include a truck for every department: camera (with darkroom), electrical, construction, props, wardrobe, makeup, dressing rooms, and specially fitted trailers for each of the stars. A driver is needed for every truck. Two persons are needed for trucks longer than 18 feet.

Daily transportation to and from the shoot for the director, DP, assistant directors, starring actors, costume designer, wardrobe supervisor, makeup artist, hairstylist, script supervisor, production designer, stand-ins, and anyone else whose presence is required on the set. A chauffeur is needed for every car.

Cars or trucks that are *used in the film* also have to be transported, *not driven,* to the location. That requires a special flatbed truck. Another driver is therefore needed.

Before the caravan sets out, cars, trucks, and drivers will usually be needed for local trips to and from supply houses.

PROFESSIONAL REQUIREMENTS

Teamsters Local #817 has jurisdiction over the transportation department jobs. The union takes a certain amount of flak because once their vehicles arrive at the location, the drivers have no other responsibility except to wait until the day's shooting is done and then drive back to the starting point. In his book *Making Movies,* director Sidney Lumet remarks that the drivers always seem to be the first, and hungriest, people on the food line when the folks who have been working hard all morning break for lunch. He does point out that capable transportation captains see to it that all vehicles are parked out of camera range. Sounds easy, but then so does driving.

The pay scale set by the union is as follows:

FOR INFORMATION,
CONTACT:

Mr. Thomas R.
O'Donnell, President
Teamsters IBT, Local 171
1 Hollow Lane
Lake Success,
Long Island, NY 11042

- For transportation captains: $2,637 per week
- For special drivers: $2,176 per week
- For regular drivers: $171 per day, $1,970 per week
- For helpers: $163 per day, $1,886 per week

Employers also contribute to the workers' health, retirement, and scholarship funds.

To be considered for these jobs, one needs a commercial driver's license (CDL) and training in operating tractor-trailers. The union also covers drivers who work on theatrical load-ins and transport touring companies.

To apply for membership, send a résumé and copy of the CDL to the union.

THE SCRIPT SUPERVISOR

One of the most demanding production jobs is that of script supervisor. This has historically been a woman's position, and no matter how elaborate the production, only one person has ever been assigned to do the job on any shoot.

The position is described as liaison between the director, the employer (producer), and the editor. This is not an interpretive position. It requires the most detailed sort of record-keeping. In effect, the script supervisor writes the diary of the shoot, as it happens, take by take.

> You really have to think of yourself as a department of one. You sit by the director, take all his or her notes on each take. It's sometimes hard to get permission to go the bathroom!
>
> RENATA STOIA, script supervisor

The script supervisor uses an advance copy of the shooting script to make a breakdown of the wardrobe and props that figure in the action. The list includes both principal actors and day players, and the scenes in which they have to change costume.

She (or he) prepares a chronological breakdown of the story, noting day and night sequences and every time span—the years, seasons, months, and days that pass in the story, or the hours within one day—and circulates those notes to costumes and props, as well as all other departments needing the information.

She also does her own rough timing of the script, estimating scene by scene how long the movie will be.

On the set, the script supervisor records the action on *continuity sheets*. These tell where the scene is set; whether it is day or night; what characters are in it; how they are dressed; what the props are used in each scene—how much liquid is in the glasses, what time is shown on the clocks and so on; which items are seen again; and which are to be eliminated.

Using a stopwatch, the script supervisor times the master shot and all subsequent takes. She tells the second assistant director the number of each take. She follows the dialogue and records any line or word changes; describes actors' positions and movements.

The script supervisor's report tracks the number of script pages shot and the number of scenes and setups. She notes the time of the company call and the first shot, meal times, and "wrap" time.

Much of the script supervisor's work serves as daily notes for the film editor. For her detailed notes, the script supervisor lines the script. *Lining* refers to vertical lines drawn on each script page where she writes what slates (showing scene and take numbers) cover the dialogue and action, the camera movements, the lenses and filters used, the film footage, and the date of all takes. She keeps track of the director's *disposition* of each take—hold, print, *n. g.* (no good), and the reasons—writing all this information next to the take number. She also notes whether any portion of a take was good, and up to what point.

For the director and editor such records are essential in locating all parts of the film and assembling them in the proper sequence. They also show whether the director has sufficient coverage (reaction shots from different vantage points) for each scene.

In television, a weekly dramatic series, such as *Law and Order*, is usually shot on film, and employs two script supervisors. They alternate: One prepares the upcoming script, the other covers the shoot. Shows that are videotaped work under a different system (see the section on television).

GETTING STARTED

An entry-level position at a production house, or in the office of a producing company, would probably give an aspiring script supervisor an opportunity to acquire skills and eventually do this work. Coming in with secretarial skills would give you an advantage.

> Because the whole thing goes so fast, I've found that shorthand is a valuable skill.
>
> RENATA STOIA

Graduate or undergraduate degrees are not essential to become a script supervisor. Hands-on film courses would be a good way to acquire an ear for dialogue, an understanding of nuance, an eye for detail, and familiarity with the way scripts are written and broken down.

PROFESSIONAL AFFILIATION

FOR INFORMATION, CONTACT:

International Alliance of Theatrical and Stage Employees, Local #161
80 Eighth Avenue
New York, NY 10011

Script supervisors are members of the IATSE's Local #161, serving motion picture script supervisors and production office coordinators. The contract is negotiated in three-year intervals. The current pay scale is $285 per eight-hour day and $1,282 per forty-hour week, plus employer contributions to the union's pension, welfare, and annuity funds. There is considerable overtime work involved in this position.

SECOND GENERATION

Renata Stoia joined the union's Local #161 in 1959 and worked steadily from that time until she decided to retire in 1996.

> It was time to do something else. I was finding the long hours, particularly on location, incredibly demanding.

Now Renata's daughter Barbara carries the stopwatch—as a script supervisor on *Law and Order*. When the show is on summer hiatus, she freelances on films shooting in New York.

"In this job," Stoia said, "we all bounce around."

THE FILM EDITOR

To assemble the thousands of feet of film, containing hundreds of scenes shot out of sequence, and to shape them into a seamless dramatic work that reflects and enhances the vision of the director, writer, and producer, is the film editor's task. As Ralph Rosenblum and Robert Karen, authors of *When the Shooting Stops,* have stated: "When it came into being in 1902, film editing transformed motion pictures from a recording medium into an art form."

> You hope that what you put together is so compelling that the director won't want to change it fundamentally. And you hope that your effort is strong enough, that you really have examined all the choices, and that this really is the right way.
>
> STEVE COHEN, film editor

The work is a collaboration between director and editor that, at its best, is almost like being able to read each other's minds. Director–editor relationships frequently continue through many films; one outstanding example is that of director Martin Scorsese and editor Thelma Schoonmaker, who met in a summer course at NYU's film school.

WHAT EDITORS DO

The editor usually begins working on the first day of principal photography. In the evening, after shooting, the director and editor watch the "dailies," the prints of the previous day's shooting. The editor takes notes on what the director likes, doesn't like, how a scene should be paced, and how a performance has to build. Then the editor goes to work on an initial assembly of the film called the *first cut.*

> The editor makes the first cut of the film pretty much independently of the director. There has been a constant discussion process, but the director doesn't have time to be in the editing room because he's shooting the picture.
>
> STEVE COHEN

Editing is described as an interpretive art. Like the soloist who interprets a composer's musical score, the editor interprets the director's concept.

> My job is to make my work invisible. No one else on the movie has that goal. I want you to think the actors were brilliant, when actually I pieced their performances together from little pieces all over the place . . . I want you to think the director was brilliant, even though his scene originally

made no sense. I want you to think the writer was brilliant, even though we cut out most of what he put in.

STEVE COHEN

Within the past five years, film editing has been transformed from a hands-on craft that required the meticulous attention of many levels of skillful assistants, to an electronic process in which film editors no longer handle any pieces of film. Movieolas, the hand-operated machines editors once used to scrutinize film sequences frame by frame, are gone. (Someone has speculated that they will resurface as hot collectibles at nostalgia conventions.)

Conventionally shot film is transferred to digital tape, and the tape is then used to transfer that visual material to computer hard disks. The editing is then done on a computer screen. At the end, the material is transferred to film for viewing. The editor's quartet of assistants handles the process of conforming the film to the computer data. A SOUND EDITOR works alongside in the initial stages.

The new post-production is expected to become even more digitalized: In the Sony Pictures sound production facility, sound engineers must know digital technology; editors must cut electronically. The current push is to build sophisticated cameras that shoot digitally without sacrificing image quality—thereby eliminating the need to process emulsion film.

It's a very exciting time to be an editor. There are changes every day. I am trying to bring our sound editor in early and gather the sounds at his workstation. As we get closer to finishing there will be six or eight sound editors, a post-production supervisor, and others. I interact with all of them.

STEVE COHEN

Lost in Yonkers, the first digitally edited feature film, was directed by Martha Coolidge and edited by Steve Cohen, who also edited the first two TV movies to be cut digitally. Author of the textbook on how to use the Avid computer editing system, Cohen is now a consultant to Avid.

People were very skeptical. I did weeks of demonstrations, but people didn't think it was possible. Only when the film was finished did people take notice. Martha Coolidge took chances, and she and the Sony Pictures executive, Gary Martin, trusted me.

STEVE COHEN

Currently, an editor has about six months to edit a feature film, which may have had a sixty-day shooting schedule. Nine months used to be the allotted time. In the rush to get product out, schedules are being shortened.

Editors work extremely long hours. Producers assume that because you have a computer you can do it faster and no longer need the people who used to sit next to you. They are trying to do films with shorter turnarounds and smaller crews.

BILL HANAUER, business representative, Local #771, Motion Picture Editors Union

The technology expands our expectations. The thing is, the job has changed, and we have to find new ways of working.

STEVE COHEN

ATTRIBUTES OF AN EDITOR

According to Bill Hanauer, editors are highly skilled, highly educated, and more intellectual than many other colleagues. He commented:

> One of our best editors is a woman with a master's degree in Chinese history. Editors have a mindset that can lock onto technology and do amazing things. People from the old school are not so facile, but they, too, have that attention-to-detail mind. The ability to visualize, remember what is there, and understand it.
>
> Editors look for other editors who can have a sense of the whole project. They don't want someone to be just a technician.

A sharp mind does seem to be the common denominator. Thelma Schoonmaker had studied political science and Russian at Cornell University and was doing graduate work in primitive art at Columbia University when, uncertain about what she wanted to do, she answered an ad that offered job training as an assistant editor. Carol Littleton, an Academy Award nominee for her editing of *E. T.*, was in the UCLA doctoral program when she decided to switch from teaching to a career in films. And Steve Cohen was a science major in high school, majored in art at Yale, and earned a masters degree in psychology. He studied at night while working his way up from messenger to assistant and then to editor. (He is now chairman of the editing department at the American Film Institute Center for Advanced Film and Television Studies.)

> This job demands a lot of concentration, a lot of focus for long periods of time. You have to be willing to work in a dark room twelve hours a day, six days a week. You have to like computers—and you have to like movies. We are a small group—me and about six or seven people working in isolation.
>
> Editing is an addictive process. Everything you do accomplishes something, so you don't want to stop. When you work with film, there's a natural break; you come to the end of a reel, and you take a break. Nowadays, you go on until you are so tired, you say, I *have* to take a break.

STEVE COHEN

GETTING STARTED

Film editors start out by serving lengthy assistantships. Assistants spend long

FOR INFORMATION,
CONTACT:

American Film Institute
2021 North Western Avenue
Los Angeles, CA 90027

Motion Picture
Editors Union,
Local #771
165 West 46th Street,
Suite 900
New York, NY 10036

hours digitizing the footage. Five years is not considered too long a period to "pay one's dues." Within that time, someone generally recognizes the assistant's talent and hires or recommends him or her to someone who needs an editor. Or an editor may be too busy to take on a new assignment, and will recommend the assistant for the job.

I worked as an assistant on several movies for a producer. The editor I was assisting at the time became a post-production supervisor and wasn't available. The producer took a chance on me.

STEVE COHEN

Editors who have long careers become gurus to younger editors. Editor Dede Allen has brought along major editors who started as her apprentices.

BILL HANAUER

With so much home video and editing equipment now available at local stores, at many price levels, a person interested in film editing has a chance at least to begin. For formal training, film schools offer the chance to work on a variety of projects, to be part of a team, and rub shoulders with many different people, all as passionate as you.

Professors ask, "What kind of equipment should I buy?" We answer, "Teach them how to edit. They can always learn how to use equipment. What you are teaching is what it is to be an editor, not a technician who pushes buttons. You have to develop the mind and the heart and the brain for this thing—the *process*."

BILL HANAUER

A great many schools, colleges, and universities offer film courses. It should be noted that the American Film Institute Center for Advanced Film and Television Studies is, at this time, the only accredited school to grant an MFA—Master of Fine Arts—degree in editing.

In addition to their formal schooling, future editors are strongly advised to immerse themselves in the medium. Steve Cohen and Bill Hanauer both advise that you see a lot of films:

It's hard to watch the editing of a movie when you first see it. You are watching the story. You have to see a picture a couple of times to get beyond the story and watch the edits. . . . Study the aesthetics of filmmaking. See *Days of Heaven*—clearly a film created by editing. You learn from really connecting with someone's work. The history of film is important in understanding what you see.

PROFESSIONAL STATUS

Film (including television film) editors are members of IATSE's Motion Picture Editors Union, Local #771 in New York, and Local #776 in Los Angeles. These locals also have jurisdiction over sound effects, music and dubbing editors, assistants and apprentices, and negotiate contracts for film librarians. The current weekly pay scale for editors is $1,855.62; for sound, music, and dubbing editors it is $1,693.77. Employers also contribute to the union health and retirement funds.

There is a great amount of independent filmmaking, some of which is union activity.

POST-PRODUCTION PEOPLE

The film soundtrack almost always requires editing. The location may have been unavoidably noisy, the director may have shot scenes without sound, or the director wants to get better line readings from the actors and turns to dubbing. This doctoring is referred to as Automatic Dialogue Replacement (ADR). Very short segments of film are projected on a screen and the actor, hearing the dialogue on a headset, can lip-sync—say the lines to match his or her filmed lip movement. With ADR equipment, the sequence can be rerun easily, until a satisfactory match is recorded. An ADR editor and assistants customarily prepare the cues and handle the recording sessions.

Sound effects, such as footsteps, crackling twigs, thunder, and complicated, multilevel sounds of car crashes, falling debris, and breaking glass are created by a FOLEY ARTIST, the movies' equivalent of the original radio sound-effects man. Traditionally, the Foley artist creates the sounds and a recording engineer monitors and records them. This is now a digital process.

As editor Steve Cohen explained, these elements of post-production are in transition. Sound editing will undoubtedly be brought into the process much earlier, and dialogue replacement may be accomplished in the film editing studio.

THE COMPUTER STEALS TURF

As digitizing overtakes production, it is expected that more of the work done by trained people will be done by computers. As the industry eliminates film negatives, there are no longer any work prints, and consequently no need for people who work as negative cutters.

Similarly, the services of lab technicians, who scan the film from the first day of shooting to the preparation of the final release form, may not be required.

Color timers have been employed to make certain that the color and density of the images is consistent from frame to frame. They work with the director of photography to learn what the original colors were, and whether the DP wants to modify them in any way. Conceivably, some of this function may eventually be performed digitally.

MUSIC

Music has always provided an emotional backdrop for film and is one of the last elements to be edited into the production. Music cues our responses—creates suspense, enhances romance, provokes laughter—and reinforces what we see on the screen. The composer may consult with the director early in production, but composition actually waits until the film is edited and the musical in-and-out spots are precisely marked and timed.

TRAINING PROGRAM

The post-production field is very specialized, making training a little harder to find, but North Carolina School of the Arts, in an expansion of its professional training program, now has a concentration in Sound Design and Sound Engineering for Theater and Film. Their School of Music even offers a master of music degree program that trains composers in the specialized art of composing and recording music for film and television. This program works in conjunction with student and faculty activities at the same institution's School of Filmmaking.

FOR INFORMATION,
CONTACT:

North Carolina School
of the Arts
Box 12189
Winston-Salem, NC 27199

ADDITIONAL OPPORTUNITIES

Once a project goes into production, the publicity, sales, marketing, and distribution people also go to work. They handle the business side of the business. Like their counterparts in the theater, they must alert audiences to the "product." Their training is the same—it's just that their numbers are bigger. They arouse interest on a global scale.

Are there other careers in and around the movie business? Yes, indeed. Many of these depend upon special ability or training that can be transferable to films. For example, any movie shooting on location needs to provide healthy meals and snacks for cast and crew. CATERERS working for motion picture companies have a lucrative business, but to get into it you should already be in the catering or restaurant business and have a large enough staff to handle such a job.

If you know how to teach animals to behave and do tricks on cue, you might work as an ANIMAL TRAINER. Someone who can handle large groups of animals—one thinks of dog-walkers who calmly stroll about with half a dozen different breeds in tow—could be hired as an ANIMAL WRANGLER. Experience with horses and the ability to show the actor who must ride it how to handle the animal would be useful.

A DIALOGUE DIRECTOR is present on many sets, available to run lines with the actors between scenes. Performers who need individual help hire an ACTING COACH. For these jobs one needs acting training and, in the case of the coach, a lot of experience.

When children under sixteen are cast, state laws require a TEACHER on the set, to help them with their school work. Teachers must be licensed and (in some states) must also be trained welfare workers.

Duels, hand-to-hand fights with swords or knives, and so on are staged by a COMBAT (or FIGHT) CHOREOGRAPHER. The action, first blocked and then slowly rehearsed, gradually attains the required speed. To do this one must be a gymnast with training in stage combat. With the same background one can work as a STUNT PERSON. Stunt people may also double for stars. STAND-INS are the same size and coloring as the movie's major players, and they double for them when lights and camera moves are being set. A stand-in watches his or her actor working with the director, to repeat the action for rehearsal. Acting technique is needed.

A registered NURSE is usually on set, or on call. When stunts and special effects are scheduled, a team of MEDICS will be alerted.

As noted above, numerous people are employed to inform the general public about the business. Member of the Hollywood press report on movie goings-on for a string of newspapers. Trade papers and magazines—*Variety, Billboard, Premiere,* and the like—hire people with journalism experience as reviewers or entertainment reporters, as do the tell-all TV talk shows.

SPECIAL CONSULTANTS are the experts whom producers and writers rely on when their stories deal with topics such as medicine, religion, scientific fields, events in history, and so on, and on-screen accuracy is essential. Experts may work as pre-production advisers and may even continue with the production through its final stages.

A published interview with Dr. Alan Sickles, a well-known specialist in the field of breast cancer, came to the attention of director Chris Columbus, who was preparing to shoot the Julia Roberts–Susan Sarandon movie, *Step Mom.* Dr. Sickles was asked to serve as medical consultant for the film. He said:

> I had meetings with the director and the assistants. They wanted me to go over the script and make sure the language was correct and that they were using the right props. I advised them to change some of the dialogue. I showed them through my facility, explained the kinds of charts and equipment we use and how an office is set up. I may be asked to spend time with the actors when those scenes are being shot.

He fully enjoyed the experience. "Everyone was very friendly," he said.

Some consultants relate so well to the medium that they go on to become the writer–producers of the next movie about their special subject. Which takes us right back to the beginning of the process. . . .

Television

It's kind of like taming lions.
LENORE DeKOVEN, director

THE YEAR 1948 MARKS the humble beginning of television broadcasting on a daily basis in the United States. It is also the year in which a record-breaking 90 million people—half the nation's population—went to the movies every week. Hollywood people referred to television as "radio with pictures" and laughed at the (then) tiny screens. We now realize it was the size of those round screens, plus the fact that what you saw was live—like looking through a window into other people's houses—that made the new medium irresistible. And there was no need to go out and buy a ticket. Best of all, once you bought the set—and they were getting cheaper all the time—TV was "free."

Early television offered a cornucopia that included variety shows; situation comedies; serious music, opera, and dance broadcasts; game and quiz shows; children's entertainment; panel discussions; educational and current events programs; and, carried over from radio, the serial form called soap opera. Add to this breadth the impact of early TV. It's now acknowledged that when Ed Sullivan, on his CBS Sunday-evening variety show, introduced the work of great ballet artists to millions of Americans, many of whom had never been more than 50 miles from home, the artists inspired countless youngsters to aspire to be dancers, and many fine dance companies came into being that now delight audiences across America.

Theater-trained artists were often tapped for early television's dramatic programs, which usually concentrated on domestic themes, stories that took place in simple sets—all easily dismantled and repainted for succeeding shows. These live programs provided opportunities for exciting young dramatists, among them Paddy Chayevsky and Rod Serling; and directors, such as Arthur Penn and Sidney Lumet. For them, producing a television show was very much like working in summer stock, where a season consisted of a new play every week. After the short rehearsal period, the director, cast, and crew moved into the studio, where the play was performed straight through from beginning to end, for an audience of three or more television cameramen, the crew, and millions of viewers watching the live broadcast.

Within a decade, television was so obviously profitable that Hollywood's derisive sneers became smiles of welcome. In Los Angeles there was more than ample studio space—the lack of which was becoming a major liability in the east. Stars became willing to appear on weekly series. Television, and a huge contingent of writers, directors, and performers, became bicoastal.

Today, the greater number of today's television dramatic and documentary programs are produced on film—shot and edited just like large-screen movies, but with shorter shooting schedules and smaller budgets. The audience nevertheless watches a huge amount of live television—news, sports, and special events—as well as taped talk shows and the situation comedies and soap operas for which TV's original multicamera format is an essential production value.

It is still an exploding industry. The major networks' audience share (size) has dwindled in recent years, but the erosion results from increased competition from smaller networks that have aggressively sought (and found) a large and enthusiastic young audience with new shows, as well as from the growing number of cable networks and "niche" channels whose offerings attract special-interest viewers. On both ends of the spectrum there is need for material, which translates into opportunities for talent above and below the line.

TV PRODUCERS

Whereas theater and film producers focus their energy on a single memorable piece of work, television producers are engaged in a recurring process. The TV program is part of a series. Weekly television schedules consist of programs owned and created by the networks (or local stations) and shows created and produced by independent production companies, for which the networks pay a broadcast fee. Therefore, each series will have its executive producer, who oversees co-producers responsible for episodes or segments. In-house programs are handled by network producers. The executive producer on a program created by an independent packager is usually the program's creator and developer, the one who sells the program idea to the network.

Fern Field, a producer and the manager of programming at the USA Network, outlined the producer's job this way:

> The producer does not have to raise the financing for a project, but you have to know the ins and outs, every aspect of the business.
>
> Every project hits a point where the budget is too tight, and if there is no one taking care of the baby, so to speak, sitting down and showing everybody that this is a good project, it won't get done.

Dick Wolf began as an executive script supervisor on *Hill Street Blues.* He was later a co-executive producer on *Miami Vice.* In 1989, he created *Law and Order,* the popular NBC prime-time series of which he is executive producer. His company, Wolf Productions, is the series packager.

Marcy Carsey's first job, right out of college, was as an NBC tour guide. It put her in the right place to meet the people at *The Tonight Show,* who took her on as a gofer. Two production jobs later, she went to ABC, and worked on the situation comedies *LaVerne and Shirley* and *Happy Days.* Within two years she was in charge of the network's comedy shows. Teaming up with Tom Werner, she left ABC to pitch series ideas to all the networks as an independent production company (often called a *packager*). They had little success until she convinced NBC to try thirteen episodes of *The Cosby Show*—one of the most successful programs in TV history, with gross revenues of more than $1 billion. Carsey–Werner is currently the biggest company of its kind in Hollywood.

THE PRODUCER CHAIN OF COMMAND

Every show eventually evolves its own idiosyncratic style, but the process generally works like this: Much of the time, an EXECUTIVE PRODUCER deals with network business and programming executives and with sponsors' representatives. The ongoing task of getting the show done each week falls to a SUPERVISING PRODUCER (sometimes called the LINE PRODUCER), who is in charge of getting the physical production completed on time and on budget; another supervising producer will be in charge of scripts, dealing with staff and freelance writers, having material written or rewritten in time for delivery. There will also be a POST-PRODUCTION PRODUCER in charge of editing, music, sound, and getting prints made and delivered to the network.

The executive producer is actually the SHOW RUNNER the person responsible for it all, who:

- Is the liaison between the network and everyone beneath him or her.
- Decides the order of production.
- Judges which scripts are ready and which need more work (the show runner is often an accomplished writer).
- Approves the casting director's submissions.

And so on. He or she will be involved as necessary to keep the show running.

> And, if anything goes wrong, the executive producer is the one who gets dismissed—by the network.
>
> LAURENCE HEATH, producer

As executive producer of ABC's *Loving*, Jo Ann Emmerich was a network executive in charge of a daytime serial. She observed:

> "Executive producer" is kind of a misnomer in daytime. It's not like primetime or movies, where people can just delegate. In soap opera it is generally a hands-on, full-time job, because the show generally takes twenty-four hours to do. Someone has to be aware of it all to enable the other people to focus on the jobs *they* have to do. It's like being a puzzle master—except that in daytime TV the final piece is never put in place.

A HANDS-ON JOB

At each day's dress rehearsal, the executive producer takes her (or his) place at the rear of the control room, where she watches the show on a personal monitor while the director, associate director, production assistant, and all the department heads focus their attention on the wall of monitors that show all the possible shots from the cameras in the studio (as well as what's being aired on the other networks and local stations).

The executive producer asks why an actor's makeup looks gray, and the makeup artist says he'll check it after the rehearsal. The executive producer gives an acting note: "She has to be like a coiled spring." The production assistant writes it down. The executive producer notices that a child's slippers are very noisy. Should the child be barefoot? the costume designer wonders.

"Socks or ballet slippers," the executive producer suggests. She also remarks that an actress's hair is too neat and her face too clean: "She's playing for sympathy." Hairstylist, makeup artist, and director all take the note, to fix later.

The executive producer requests a different shot: "He should be reacting to her dirty face. That's what he needs to see, and we need to see." The director takes the shot on a different camera.

And so it goes, until the last shot. Between dress rehearsal and taping time, all the necessary adjustments will be made. While each department does its own best possible job, the producer is the one to unite the elements into a more polished whole.

ONE PRODUCER'S PATH

Upon earning her graduate degree in theater from Catholic University, Jo Ann Emmerich came to New York looking for a behind-the-scenes job in theater. Having no connections— she grew up in St. Louis—she worked as an office temp and spread the word that she was looking for a job in the business. A friend heard of an opening at a talent agency; she got an interview.

> I arrived in my dark suit and blouse. The office manager thought I looked too "finishing school" for a rough-and-ready place where secretaries came to work in T-shirts and blue jeans. But he needed a secretary quickly, so I got a three-day trial, at the end of which I was asked to stay. My boss was a true mentor, and within two years I was an agent.
>
> JO ANN EMMERICH

Several of her clients wrote for television, so she became more interested in the production side of the business. She was interviewed by Procter & Gamble, who were expanding their half-hour daytime soaps into hour-long shows, and was hired as an assistant producer on *As the World Turns,* the number-one daytime show at the time. She recalled:

> Again I had a number of generous mentors. I learned a lot working those twelve-hour days. We didn't have to work twelve hours; we were on shifts. But we all loved the job so much, we came in early and just stayed. It was a groundbreaking time for the serials.

Within a year Emmerich's experience in daytime brought her to the attention of Fred Silverman, president of ABC's Entertainment Division, who hired her as the new manager of daytime TV. She stayed fourteen-and-a-half years, eventually moving up to senior vice president of the division.

In a career change, she worked as a consultant to major companies on TV shows. At Lancit Media, she worked on children's programming with many of the people who developed the *Reading Rainbow* series. And then she got the opportunity to produce ABC's *Loving.*

THE CHALLENGES OF PRODUCING

The onus is on television producers nowadays to pass or fail in a short time. Prime-time programs get only a few chances—two, possibly four, episodes—to attract an audience, and that audience had better be sizable. Daytime series are generally allowed a year in which to make their mark.

In the case of a weekly series, the creators have a bit of time, if necessary, to go back to the drawing board, scrutinize the episode's pluses and minuses, and attempt substantive changes (recasting roles, for example) between shows. If a program seems to have promise, there's the possibility of a return engagement later in the season (or in a future period) after additional improvements have been made.

Daytime series require much more fine-tuning before they are even considered for a time slot. That's in some measure because of the significant initial expense of creating all the necessary sets and signing the large number of core performers, and because there will be no hiatus once the daily show premieres. Every weekday for every month of the year, a new show will have to be aired. There is no down time. If something in a story line is not working, the executive producer nevertheless has to move on to the next day's show, relying on instinct and experience to figure out, somehow, what is wrong and how to fix it, and to attract a wider audience.

> The greatest joy is having something that's working and hoping to get the next thing that's going to top it. There are periods when it's wonderful, but that doesn't make the work any less.
>
> JO ANN EMMERICH

CAREER RECOMMENDATIONS

Anyone interested in producing television should certainly watch a lot of TV—not for an entertaining pastime, but for business. There are two ways to observe it: as a member of the vast viewing public seeking amusement, and as a professional. It takes discipline to respond to a show and at the same time be aware of what decisions the producer has made to elicit a desired response. One can learn to notice the elements that combine for an effective moment or a fine show.

One of the most useful resources for aspiring television producers (or writers) is the vast program library of the Museum of Television and Radio, in New York City. There is also a branch of the museum in Los Angeles, with equally impressive facilities. Inexpensive memberships (there are student rates) are available. The municipal library system where you live may also have a video library you can explore.

FOR INFORMATION, CONTACT:

Museum of Television & Radio
25 West 52nd Street
New York, NY 10020

West Coast branch:
465 North Beverly Drive
Beverly Hills, CA 90210

DEVELOPING AN EPISODE

WRITER-PRODUCER Laurence Heath described a fairly typical experience of developing an episode for the series *Murder, She Wrote*. In this case, the star, Angela Lansbury, was also the executive producer of the show. However, the process on any series is much the same as Heath described:

An agent calls and says, "I have a writer who likes your show. Can she send you a script of hers?" I say yes, and the writer sends in a sample. I read it, or my assistant, who has an M.A. in English and has written, will read it. If she likes it, or I like it, I will make an appointment with the writer to come in and make a pitch.

We chat to see whether we are compatible. The writer tells me the idea. It may be immediately disqualified: We may have just done that, or another writer is doing the same thing, or the star has said she would never play a pregnant beggar. But if the idea has possibilities, I say, "Let me check it out and get back to you."

I go to my boss, Bruce, the executive producer. He checks, and we haven't done that idea. Let's run it by Angela Lansbury. I write a page describing the idea of the show for her, with a few complimentary words about the writer. Angela says, "Okay, we'll do the show."

There is no negotiation on price; the $8,500 is standard.

The writer starts to work on the story idea, comes in, and we talk about what she's going to do. She makes a *step sheet* [a skeletal listing of scenes] and gives us a rundown on who the characters are. She comes back for another meeting. We tell her to write the first draft of the *story outline,* which is a scene-by-scene narrative form, thirty pages, double-spaced, with some dialogue—that's unavoidable. We are entitled to two drafts of the story outline. She turns in the first one. No matter how bad it is, we don't end the assignment at that point, and no matter how good it is, we don't leave it alone. We try to embellish it, make it work better.

When the writer hands in the second draft, we have to make a decision, because we are not entitled to any more work for our $8,500. The producers decide the writer is competent. We clean it up a bit before Angela reads it. If she okays the outline, we tell the writer the option is picked up: She gets to write the teleplay and earn another $15,000.

If the original idea has promise but the writer has screwed up the execution, we can stop working with her. But we have bought the story and can still make a plot out of it. There is nothing to shoot yet, no teleplay. If a staff member is able to write it, that's who will do it, and be paid the $15,000 writing fee. Or we might give it to an outside writer who has worked for us before.

We have five people on staff who can write. Not all of them will be able to produce three episodes in the year, so besides theirs we might need eight or nine scripts in a year. More than half the time, writers come in with an idea we can use because they know the show.

The one-hour show is not a movie; so the director doesn't ask for a lot of things he might want in a movie. By the time a script goes into production, it's been looked at by so many people, they've gotten rid of all the problems that involve production—it's pretty straightforward. It has to be. You are preparing one script—having the sets built, the costumes, the score, all those things—*and you're shooting another script,* and *another is being edited.*

Film buffs learn from replaying their favorite old movies countless times, and television has a program history to go back and reexamine also. The shows of the past are receiving increasing study and appreciation. Experienced writer-producers find the video libraries' wealth of recorded material invaluable in researching the background for new series. Students of the medium spend hours watching some of the world's best-written, most affecting, imaginative, zany, or thought-provoking programs—and gain a perspective on human nature that's every bit as valuable as executive management skills. Viewers will discover that, over decades, the most successful programs have been explorations of human nature and relationships.

In additon to studying the medium, would-be producers should try to get hands-on experience as gofers or interns at any local radio or television station or production company. Volunteers are almost always welcome. Even if there are no jobs at the moment, it's possible to ask questions about the business and find out where the next opportunity may be.

> This business is like an addiction. A gamble. There's a dangerous aspect— will it or won't it work? There is something immediate about applause, ratings. Such a shared thrill. It's like a love affair.
>
> JO ANN EMMERICH

WRITERS AND STORY EDITORS

Television's two unique story forms are the half-hour situation comedy and the five-day-a-week daytime serial. The demands of each genre present writers with, arguably, the most challenging jobs in television. A sitcom episode gives the writer twenty-three minutes in which to introduce, develop, and wrap up an amusing situation fifteen weeks or so a year. The soap opera writer has forty-nine minutes to interweave a group of continuing stories in 260 episodes a year. In both instances, scripts must also be constructed to break neatly into acts, which allow time for commercials.

WORKING IN SITUATION COMEDY

Writing for sitcoms requires diverse talents. Most important of these is the ability to understand the humorous potential of the characters' specific universe and tailor script ideas to those characters. You must be able to pitch the plot's premise so adroitly that its potential "clicks" in the producer's mind, and then be able to construct a well-crafted script around that premise.

> A pitch consists of the main action—what we will learn about the character, what will drive the story, the events, and the details of the events. What is going to be funny about the character?
>
> SUSAN SILVER, sitcom writer

When a show has been on the air for several seasons, the characters and their reactions are fully established. The aspiring writer has to create new situations in which they will behave in the ways the audience has come to know and love. The difficulty for the person who wants to break in is that the staff writers know the characters so well that they may have already thought of just about any idea an outsider might present. And yet the only way to get into the group is to try.

> I headed west immediately after graduating. I sold some jokes to comedians and columnists, wrote on spec for three years, and then got hired to write for *Taxi*.
>
> JOHN MARKUS, writer, *The Cosby Show*

> I read plays for a local little theater, then I started to write one-acts. I started sending them out. Somehow, Jay Sandrich, who was then with *The Cosby Show*, saw one of them and told them to use me.
>
> MATT WILLIAMS, writer-producer, *Home Improvement*

Bonnie and Terry Turner, writer-producers of *3rd Rock from the Sun,* had started out as members of a theater group in Atlanta, where they collaborated on material for a revue. That opened enough doors to eventually lead them to *Saturday Night Live* producer Lorne Michaels, who hired them as staff writers. His constant questioning—"Is that the kind of laugh you want to get?"—forced them to think in terms of making a story point, rather than just "throwing comedy at an audience."

Situation comedy, accomplished writers agree, must be based in reality. Being able to string together a lot of gags is not enough. Funny dialogue is usually character-driven.

> The performers have distinct personalities, usually a strong point of view. Many of them are stand-up comedians who have spent ten to fifteen years honing that persona.
>
> CARMEN FINESTRA, writer-producer, *Home Improvement*

> Look at the relationships, and be funny.
>
> PHIL ROSENBERG, sitcom writer

Staff writers pitch ideas among themselves every week. And everyone quotes Bill Cosby, whom they all revere as The Master: "Words on a page are not enough. Actors have to figure out what to do with them."

GETTING STARTED

The recommended route is to get a job on a show—any job at all.

> Then work your tushy off. Work your way up. Then the networks will open their doors to you. This is a writer's market.
>
> JOHN MARKUS

If you do not succeed in landing such a job, then the next best route is to send in ideas for episodes—thereby getting to know the people who work on the shows and getting an "in." Focus on the show you think you'd like to write for. In other words, study it:

> Read a script, or several. Then, look into yourself. Your own experience will always be original.
>
> SUSAN SILVER

> What happens to you could possibly happen to the characters on the show.
>
> JULIE POLL, sitcom writer

Or you may wish to try writing an entire script for the show. Opinions differ as to the advisability of sending in a script to that show "on spec." It may be more useful to use it to try getting an agent. At the very least, it is a sample of your work in the genre and may win you a chance to pitch an episode to the writing staff. When that opportunity comes, have ideas beyond the one that you love best.

> Sometimes you love an idea, and it just doesn't fly. If it doesn't work, don't try to save it. Have another idea. We spend a lot of time on the outline. If that doesn't work, the show won't go.
>
> CARMEN FINESTRA

Find out who is on the writing staff. In sitcom writing, the entry-level position would be STAFF WRITER. Good work at this job brings promotion to STORY EDITOR. From there, one moves up to EXECUTIVE STORY EDITOR. The SHOW RUNNER breaks down the season's scripts into plots, works on each sequence, deals with the network, and, as explained on page 180, oversees the entire staff—which includes the director, cast, and line producer in addition to the writers.

> You'd be amazed: There are maybe fifty people on the staff before we begin a show.
>
> LAURENCE HEATH

Show runners are writers with a great deal of experience, and they frequently carry the title of EXECUTIVE PRODUCER. That's because successful writers can continue up the ladder, to CO-PRODUCER, SUPERVISING PRODUCER, and EXECUTIVE PRODUCER.

CREATING A TELEVISION SERIES

The chances are remote for anyone with no track record to sell a pilot episode for a series to the networks. More conceivable is the possibility of bringing a fully articulated series idea to a packager—such as Carsey–Werner—who does have a track record. Someone in the organization may be able to help develop the idea and interest a network in investing in the shooting of a pilot episode.

> For a pilot you should write a "bible" that establishes the "backstory" for all of the characters. That material gradually unfolds as we go along. It's the first year of a series that is hard.
>
> PHIL ROSENBERG

> Many successful pilots are the third attempt to sell an idea. It is easier to do a movie or write a novel than to write a pilot.
>
> SUSAN SILVER

She adds, as a matter of professional advice: "You can get the scripts of pilots."

Not only is sitcom writing difficult to do well, not many people are teaching it on a regular basis. In New York, TIP-East, a professional organization dedicated to increasing production on the East Coast, periodically sponsors a

FOR INFORMATION,
CONTACT:

National Academy
of Television Arts
and Sciences
165 West 46th Street,
Suite 501
New York, NY 10036

Script City
8033 Sunset Boulevard,
Suite 1500
Hollywood, CA 90046

comedy writing program, mentored by many of the professionals whose words are quoted here. The program is administered by the National Academy of Television Arts and Sciences (NATAS). Classes are small; work is intensive. Applicants are asked to submit samples of their work.

A business called Script City sells television scripts, as well as script-writing software, screenplays, and other related materials. Their catalog is available through the mail.

For an understanding of the fundamentals of dramatic writing, the most frequently recommended book is *The Art of Dramatic Writing,* by Lajos Egri. Despite its age—the book was published in 1946—it is considered the essential text. Copies should be available at any large bookstore, your local library, or from the Drama Book Shop, 723 Seventh Avenue, New York, NY 10019. A newer work, mentioned earlier, that merits attention is *The Playwright's Process* (see page 17); crammed with advice from leading dramatists, it should be available at the same sources.

WORKING IN DAYTIME DRAMA

To write hour-long episodes for a daily soap opera requires learning a different technique. Soaps have been compared to sweeping, old-fashioned novels, in that they deal with many characters and interweave several plots over extended periods. But in a novel, all the threads are tied together for a stirring finale. Soap opera is an endless narrative, with a core of permanent characters and a scattering of new people who wander in for a while, disrupt the lives of the main group, and then fade into the background or disappear.

The creator of a soap first writes a bible, which gives the minute history of all the core characters—the backstory, present status, and future possibilities of each one—and describes all of their relationships. The initial situations are scripted in detail, and major story lines are projected for as long as two years. The painstaking work of constructing a bible whose characters have appealing, long-term story potential can take several years. Once the show goes on the air, the soap creators are its head writers, at least during the beginning years. Then, established shows may call in new head writers to give a story or characters new energy.

> A story can suddenly flop when you had great expectations for it, and vice versa—something you thought might merely be charming turns out to be a great ratings success.
>
> JO ANN EMMERICH, producer

Long-term story lines and leading character descriptions are conceived by the HEAD WRITERS. Generally, these are done for a three- or six-month period.

Incidents have to be paced so that parallel story lines rise and fall at different times. The BREAKDOWN WRITERS work out the day-by-day plot developments with the head writers:

> Usually, the head writer comes in with an idea of what you're going to do for the week in general. Then, in the meetings, you start plotting out what is going to be done each day.
>
> NANCY FORD, writer

Each day's breakdown is assigned to a scriptwriter—of which there may be five or more on staff—who follows the daily plot outline as he or she supplies the dialogue, stage directions, and a certain amount of emotional direction. This is the entry-level position.

> Very bright, intelligent people do not do this automatically. Writing has to be precise in terms of choosing the exact words. First scripts are usually god-awful. I ended up doing three samples before Agnes Nixon [creator of *All My Children*] said one was okay, and it went on the air.
>
> JACK WOOD, writer-director

A high proportion of soap writers have gained extensive experience in the genre as actors or directors. They understand the inherent rhythm of the form. Others were captivated as viewers.

Martha Nochimson teaches writing at Mercy College and at New York University. At one point, with two small children to care for and a dissertation to write, she found it necessary to work at home:

> I got hooked on one particular soap. I was so involved that I wrote a long letter to the producer, with detailed notes for the characters and plot suggestions. He called and asked if I wanted to write for the show. I said, "Sure." I loved it.

Nochimson subsequently wrote for five shows, in New York and in California.

> I really started to write for soaps because I loved them. I like stories. When I was in high school I would lie out on the grass, getting a suntan, and listen to the soaps. My mother would say, "Now, really, is there any value in that sort of thing?"
>
> NANCY FORD

At Indiana's DePauw University, Ford majored in music theory and composition and—to broaden her horizons—she became active in theater. (Collaborating with her college classmate Gretchen Cryer, she has had five shows produced in New York, including *I'm Getting My Act Together and Taking It on the Road*.) When she arrived in New York, hoping to become a Broadway composer, she found work as a secretary at an advertising agency for the sponsor of a number of soaps. Eager for a job that she could do at home and that would permit her to compose, Ford asked for script breakdowns of some of the shows the commercials appeared on and submitted a sample.

They said my work showed promise, but I wasn't good enough. So I just kept trying. I wrote seven sample scripts. Once I got my foot in the door, I was hired to write one script every two weeks. Within a few weeks I was writing three scripts a week for that same show. And ever since I've been fortunate that I've been able to work when I wanted to.

I am turned on by collaborating. Being a scriptwriter is almost like being an orchestrator. The composer gives you the melody and harmony. You find the themes and clarify and elaborate on them.

NANCY FORD

GETTING STARTED

As with situation comedy, writing for soap opera, ideally, should be taught by people who have done the work professionally. There is not a huge reservoir

---

A WRITER SELLS HER FIRST SCRIPT

RENÉE ORIN IS AN ACTRESS with an impressive list of theater credits whose husband, Tony Award–winning composer Albert Hague, played a part in the movie *Fame*. He continued in the role when the movie became the basis for an NBC television series, which prompted Renée and Albert to sell their New York apartment and move to Los Angeles where the series was made. She was torn:

"I was a working actress in New York and knew no one in L.A. I was worried about how to get a foothold there. The answer seemed to be to write a part for myself. The only people I knew were the people at *Fame*. But I had no writing experience.

"While Albert was in L.A., I had dinner with his collaborator, lyricist Lee Adams, and his wife Kelly Wood Adams, who also is an actress. It turned out that Kelly had been studying scriptwriting for a year, and she had an idea for a script. So we began to write.

"I got copies of Albert's scripts, to know how to format for television. We put in a lot of time on the story and then sent it to Bill Blynn, the producer, via Albert. He said it was good but needed work, and he suggested changes.

"We rewrote it three times over many months. And I wrote a role for myself. Once I ran into Bill Blynn, who said, 'Your part is getting so big!' Scripts by freelance writers are always rewritten by the show's staff writers, so I thought: 'If it gets any bigger they'll never let me play it—they'll want a star.' Which is exactly what happened. The part was played by Betty White, who was wonderful. As a writer, I loved it.

---

of former soap writers. The good ones are writing for one of the current shows, or are hard at work developing new ones, so courses in writing screenplays and teleplays provide the next best form of training.

Anyone not familiar with daytime dramas should certainly study them. A new viewer finds them difficult to follow at first; it's like walking in on the middle of a movie. It usually takes a month of viewing to sort out the relationships.

To get into this business, you should learn as much as possible about literature and drama, but you have to burn to do it—and not have anything else that you are burning to do.

NANCY FORD

If there is anyone you know who has any connection with a writer, a producer, a soap actor, tell him or her that's what you want to do, and ask for help.

MARTHA NOCHIMSON

I think the amount of competition shouldn't deter you. If you send your work to enough people, someone will choose it.

JACK WOOD

"We got the final credit—written by Renée Orin and Kelly Wood Adams, and I got into the Writers Guild instantly. Within a month I had a fancy writer's agent.

"Cross-country collaboration was difficult for Kelly and me, but I needed a collaborator. I'm good at dialogue, not situations, and I am not a self-starter. Through the organization Women in Film I met an ex–New Yorker, a former singer who was now a writer, Marilyn Anderson. She and I collaborated for seven years. We won a Luminous Award from Women in Film for a script called *Self-Defense,* and for NBC we wrote *Sunshine Again,* which starred Betty White and Nancy Walker.

"Marilyn is great at pitching ideas. She could do ten at a clip, which is what you have to have. Your major ideas have to be fully formed and written on two or three pages. Lesser ideas can be just a paragraph or two. The process is as follows: First, the story idea is written as a narrative. Then, you outline it, doing the research to fill in all the questions about the story line—the central characters, what they each want, how they change in the course of the story, and what causes the change. Do they achieve their goal?

"Then you do the screenplay. The first ten pages of the screenplay—description—must get people's attention. You have to have exciting characters. Then you need to plot the first turning-point and spring into the story. Several additional turning points which pull them down another path. You need to describe the protagonist, the antagonist, the secondary characters.

"You've got to have fun with it and love it. Once you like what you've done and it's on paper, it's done; you don't have to prove yourself every day, like actors. And it makes money for you."

A strong two-hour TV movie script can still serve as an excellent sample. Many writers introduce themselves by submitting short stories or plays, or by inviting producers and head writers to see staged readings of their work. The ability to tell a dramatic story or to write believable dialogue is what's wanted.

PROFESSIONAL STATUS

All writers for television are members of the Writers Guild of America, which is divided into two membership corporations, one on each coast. Membership on either coast is equivalent to membership in a national organization. The Guild agreements establish minimum fees and payments, protect rights to material, ensure credits, and provide for employer contributions to the Guild pension and health funds.

The new member initiation fee is $1,000. Basic dues are $50 per year, plus 1½ percent of your earnings in a form of employment within the Guild's jurisdiction. The script fee for a non–prime time show, such as a daytime drama, is:

- For a 60-minute serial: $2,361
- For a 30-minute program: $1,278

Fees for writing comedy-variety shows depend upon whether or not the program is aired in prime time, and upon whether it is seen on a network, independent station, or cable channel. There are separate payment schedules for writing the story, for writing first and final drafts of a script, and for completing both story and script. The Guild's established rates for a thirty-minute prime-time network program are as follows:

- For the story: $5,526
- For the first and final drafts of a script: $11,891
- For completing both the story and the script: $16,579

There is additional payment for reruns. The Guild also provides a script registration service.

Subscriptions to the WGA West monthly magazine, *The Journal,* are available to nonmembers; the annual rate is $40. Writers Guild of America East publications include a newsletter, a rate book, an agents list, and a format book.

> FOR INFORMATION, CONTACT:
>
> Writers Guild of America West
> 8955 Beverly Boulevard
> Los Angeles, CA 90048
>
> Writers Guild of America East
> 555 West 57th Street
> New York, NY 10019

THE DIRECTOR

The following story is true: A Hollywood movie director and a visiting television soap director meet in a studio commissary.

THE MOVIE DIRECTOR: Say, I saw that show of yours. It's pretty damn good.
THE SOAP DIRECTOR: Thank you.
THE MOVIE DIRECTOR: How much do you shoot in a day?
THE SOAP DIRECTOR: How much do you see each day?
THE MOVIE DIRECTOR: Well, that show of yours is an hour.
THE SOAP DIRECTOR: That's how much we shoot in a day.
THE MOVIE DIRECTOR: But that's not possible!
THE SOAP DIRECTOR: We know, but we do it anyway.

The Directors Guild of America defines movie and television directors as creative individuals who interpret and enhance the ideas and emotional values of the writer's script. They preconceive a vision of the completed project, and then work to assemble all the other elements of the production into a cohesive dramatic (and aesthetic) whole. That the television director's work is quite different from the film director's is a matter of technology; that the television director's work is frequently viewed as a lesser accomplishment is a matter of time—they have so little of it in television.

A NEW MEDIUM

In the beginning, during television's live-broadcast days, the revolutionary use of multiple cameras with variable focus capability gave the director the opportunity to block complete scenes—establish the setting, move in for closeups and pan for reaction shots—and, at the same time, to cue the music, sound effects, whatever lighting changes and special effects were possible, and to select which camera's pictures would be "punched up" during the broadcast. The television director was therefore able to shoot the picture and edit it simultaneously. With no film to develop, it was like making instant movies. And everyone was a pioneer.

Bit by bit, the system became more sophisticated. During the 1960s, videotape machines were added. Everyone marveled at the huge reels of thick, shiny 2-inch tape. Their invention made it possible to record a program for broadcast at a later date.

None of this was accomplished with ease; shows had to wait their turn for access to the videotape recorders. When they were taped, an episode had to begin and go straight through, leaving blank time on the tape for commercial inserts. There could be no retakes or edits—unless there was a technical malfunction, which meant the whole show had to be done again.

Within a decade, *live on tape* performances (that is, performed straight through as if live, but with the video cameras recording it) had become the standard. Using a thinner, narrower videotape, shows were able to record at the end of a very long day's rehearsal. Retaping was permitted when deemed really necessary. Marie Masters, a leading lady on the daytime drama *As the World Turns*, remembered:

> I was supposed to storm out of the house in a rage. I turned to go, and the doorknob came off in my hand! Thank heaven for tape! What would I have done if we were still live? Climb out the window?

Programs like the soaps that aired five days a week were soon taping six shows a week, which meant that director, cast, and crew could look forward to a week's vacation every few months. For weekly prime-time shows, reruns became a midsummer way of life. To a long-running hit series with a hundred or more recorded episodes, syndication—replays in other markets—was the end of the rainbow.

HOW DAYTIME WAS DIRECTED

As the World Turns and *The Edge of Night*, the first half-hour serial dramas, debuted in 1956. Until that time, television soap operas, like their radio forerunners, had been fifteen-minute programs. Everyone in the business was astonished at the seeming ease of the doubling of the air time.

Director Ted Corday (*As the World Turns*) had devised a rehearsal schedule that became the standard: Each afternoon, the cast was called for a read-through of the next day's script. The ASSOCIATE DIRECTOR (A.D.) timed each page. If the script was long, cuts were made. Short scripts were rarely a problem. After discussion, the cast would be released to go home and learn the lines. The director, A.D., and PRODUCTION ASSOCIATE (P.A.) would then meet with sound, music, lighting, wardrobe people to make sure everyone knew what was required for the next day's episode. The director would study the designer's floor plan, examine whatever sets would carry over to the next day's shooting, and talk to the props department. And then the director would retire to devise the staging and prepare the camera blocking.

Early the next morning, everyone assembled for the dry rehearsal in an empty rehearsal studio, with the outline of the set taped on the floor to exact scale (the A.D.'s job) and folding chairs arranged to represent all the furniture. This was the director's and A.D.'s time to work with the cast on performance, which they considered the priority. They ran each scene twice, with the A.D. timing. Then the actors were released to have lunch and see the makeup and wardrobe people. The director and the TECHNICAL DIRECTOR

(T.D.) reviewed the camera operators' shot lists. The A.D. briefed the STAGE MANAGER (or floor manager) as to who needed a cue for an entrance or exit, on where cameras and booms should be, and on what props would be used. Over a public-address system, the stage manager called cast, cameras, and crew to the set for camera rehearsal.

A television studio is divided into two parts: the control room, where behind a wall of monitors all the technical work is handled, and the studio floor, where the performance goes on. The stage manager is in charge of the studio floor and acts as liaison between the people in the control room and the people on the floor, relaying instructions from the director or A.D. Everyone communicates via headsets.

This technical rehearsal—known as *fax*, short for the expensive studio *facilities* then in use—was the camera crew's first chance to see the action. While each camera person was given the director's planned list of shots for that camera, things could change once the actors were in the set—a shot might turn out to be impossible, or the director or the camera operator might suddenly see a better picture. Directors worked in one of two ways: some preferred to watch the monitors in the control room and ask for modifications based upon what they saw. Others chose a moving lectern, with a personal monitor on the studio floor, so they could see the shot and look at all possible choices. It also allowed them a more direct view of the performances.

After this technical rehearsal, the director gave notes. The actors were released to prepare for dress rehearsal. The stage manager took charge of seeing that the set was ready. The director and A.D. checked off their notes, and set the music, sound, and light cues.

The stage manager called cast and crew for dress rehearsal. After that, the director assembled the cast—usually in the makeup room—to give the producer's notes (comments the production associate had written down during the rehearsal).

After a mandated rest period (to allow the big cameras of that time to cool off), the stage manager would call everyone to the studio and count down to the broadcast or taping signal. Thirty minutes later, the show was over.

Director and A.D. took time for lunch, and then repaired to the conference room, where the cast was assembled to read through the next day's script. As time went on, alternate directors were trained and brought in.

HOW IT'S DONE TODAY

Today's soaps, expanded to an hour, have rotating teams of directors and A.D.s. The pre-rehearsal script-reading day has been eliminated. Actors are expected to come to dry rehearsal with their lines memorized, or close to it. There are larger casts, grander effects, and a greater reliance on post-production.

With further technical advances, shooting scenes out of sequence permits a more efficient work flow than following their order in the script. Cameras and booms work all the scenes acted on one set before moving on to another. With smaller hand-held cameras, location shooting in exotic locales has become affordable—providing sequences that can be used in dozens of episodes. Everything can be electronically edited and timed after the fact. The push is to reduce *fax* time, the costliest item on the production budget.

THE DIRECTOR'S JOB

From the outset, the director has been the one to adjust to the demanding technical nature of daytime serials.

> You feel wonderful when you've done it because it is so incredibly, horribly difficult. And you feel so great when it is over. But you are exhausted. It's all rush, rush, rush.
>
> LENORE DeKOVEN, director

> A director can be brilliant, but if he can't do it in that time frame, the money is not there—every hour of overtime is extraordinarily expensive.
>
> JO ANN EMMERICH, producer

The director may now get the script about two weeks before camera day. He or she blocks the script on paper, which can take at least six hours. At the show's weekly production meeting director, designer, and producer discuss the floor plans for the sets to be used in the episode. Depending upon their ideas about the material, the director may request a particular alignment, or more space in a certain area. With the floor plan and script, he or she retires to plan the shots. On an hour show, there can easily be 500 shots—wide shots, closeups, two-shots, outside the window, tilt-ups (to the top of the stairs), and so forth.

A few days before camera day, in the studio again with the lighting director, the director shows him or her the floor plan and where the action will flow, what needs to move, and where the boom mikes need to be.

> If the director is not prepared when he comes in in the morning, it's a disaster.
>
> DAVID PRESSMAN, director

Early in the morning on camera day, the director arrives at the studio to check the sets and tell the props department what will be needed and how to arrange the furniture to accommodate the staging of the episode. At 7:30 A.M. the two-and-a-half-hour dry rehearsal with the actors begins. After a short break, the director goes to the studio to block the actors and cameras for another two and a half hours. There's a half-hour lunch break, and then it's time to dress and tape the show.

Scenes are rehearsed by location; all the action in one room is blocked, rehearsed, and taped. Then the cameras and booms move to the next set.

Afterward, the A.D. edits them into proper sequence.

Director David Pressman made the big point for anyone considering a directing career—that if you can master the tough challenges of directing the daily serial, you can handle the job in other forms.

> A daytime director who's been on a show for a year can do a film tomorrow. A guy who's only done film could not come in and do a soap.

THE PRIME-TIME WEEKLY SHOW

Situation comedies have embraced the multiple-camera technique. Their weekly routine also begins with an around-the-table read-through, followed by discussions regarding the script, costumes, and directions. The next day is given over to a morning blocking rehearsal, with a late-afternoon run-through for the producer, writers, network executives, and related personnel. Afterward, there are notes.

The following day, the director and the actors rework sections that have been rewritten and arrive at a run-through at the end of the day. The next day is for camera blocking, followed by notes.

On the fifth day, the cast goes to makeup, hair, and wardrobe, while the director prepares for a camera rehearsal. Discussions with designers, lighting, props, and boom people take place. Shortly afterward, there will be a dress rehearsal, which is taped, followed by the "broadcast" taping. A studio audience is present for both tapings.

While this sounds like a life of relative ease for director, cast and crew, the facts are that the script is continually being reworked; jokes are changed, cut, put back. In these situations, the ensemble feeling that develops within the company, becomes vital to a show.

> Directing is more than just the nuts and bolts and technical process. That can be learned. It's also about people, which is difficult to master. Part of working with actors is learning to understand their processes.
>
> GARRY MARSHALL, producer

OTHER FORMS

With twenty-four hours of the day to fill, seven days a week, the more than 1,200 television stations and growing number of cable channels in the United States offer additional forms of live, or live-on-tape, programming. News programming is live—local and network news, and the morning "magazine" shows. Directors of these shows, always working with the same camera and technical crews, in the same set, develop a formula for shooting. Daily variations will relate to the length of segments and timing of on-location news story inserts.

Sports coverage is also live, but taped simultaneously so that instant replays can be viewed, especially when there's a dispute on the field. The coverage is used later as inserts on post-game wrap-ups and news shows. Here the director works with a fleet of cameras and able camerapersons whose sharp eye for a shot can be amazing.

Awards shows and spectaculars, such as the opening day ceremony for the Olympic games, are live, with inserted pre-taped segments. Here, again, the director works with a multitude of cameras, as well as battalions of stage managers and technical staff. These shows require minute-by-minute preparation and as much rehearsal as the production can afford.

Game shows and talk shows are customarily taped in batches of five, so the host, director, and crew presumably work only a few days a week. Once the director and camera people establish the pattern for the program's opening, body, and close, the shows proceed seamlessly. *Jeopardy!* is an example.

> Doing talk shows, you don't carry the work home with you. There's not the constant preparation that you must do on a dramatic show, particularly a soap.
>
> JACK WOOD, director

THE DIRECTOR'S TRAINING

In television, as in theater and film, the directors who work best with actors have either done some acting or had some of the same training. Anyone who expects to direct dramatic material needs this background. As actress Meg Ryan told an interviewer:

> I want a director to do more than tell me, "Now, in this scene, you're happy," or "In this scene, you're sad."

In addition, the director should acquire knowledge of dramatic literature, study script analysis, and participate in all the facets of play production.

To that mixture add training in the use of the television camera. Introductory courses are available from the high school to the postgraduate level throughout the country. The basics are not hard to learn; the skill lies in making the decision—what you are going to show—and calling the shots to make it happen. That comes with practice.

> I did children's shows, talk shows, everything. I was the first director for *All My Children*. It was the joy of my life to create it myself, not follow another director and inherit the cast, however wonderful.
>
> JACK WOOD

THE ASSOCIATE DIRECTOR

Certain aspects of the associate director's (A.D.) job resemble the work of the production stage manager in theater: Via headset, the A.D. cues the camera operators and relays instructions from the director to the T.D., the stage manager, and the sound, music, and lighting departments. The A.D. is the one who makes sure that every person and thing is ready for the director's "Go" command.

She (or he) notifies cast and company of any script changes, and distributes copies of the director's shooting script to all concerned department heads. The A.D. also prepares the final telecast reports and the script "as broadcast" to be put on file. The job keeps you busy.

> It's kind of like being asked to pat your head and rub your tummy at the same time.
>
> JOANNE GOODHART, associate director

The A.D. sits at the director's proverbial right hand throughout rehearsals, timing each scene, and noting the director's staging and camera choices; she organizes this material for the T.D. She makes the individual *shot cards* for each camera operator: Shots are numbered, and each card carries the numbers and descriptions—close-up, two-shot, and so on—that camera operator must make. During run-throughs and at taping time, the A.D. warns the operator of the upcoming shot, "Camera 2, ready shot 53."

> Because there is so little time for rehearsal nowadays, timing varies greatly from one run-through to the next. We are afraid of over-cutting, so we leave in many scenes or sections that may have to be deleted in the editing room. We mark those "possible cuts." With electronic "time code" we can edit by the numbers rather than by sitting around the table at rehearsal.
>
> JOANNE GOODHART

The A.D. can then align scene and time-code numbers, and, working with the videotape editor, electronically rearrange sequences to follow the written script.

An A.D. is commonly considered a director in the making. Jo Ann Sedwick served many years as an A.D. on *The Edge of Night* before earning her promotion to the team of directors on *Guiding Light*.

On the other hand, her predecessor, Joanne Goodhart, given a similar opportunity, opted to remain an A.D. Compulsive, energetic, and highly creative, whenever she substituted for a vacationing director she found herself planning elaborate tracking shots that had the sweep of a movie and calling them perfectly. "I loved the idea of pulling them off with our TV cameras," she said. "Then I realized directing could take over my whole life—and I had three children, plus a husband."

CAREER PREPARATION

This detail-oriented position also requires an understanding of dramatic values and the ability to work calmly and authoritatively with people from every department—from talent to engineering. A drama major, with television training, supplemented with work at a local TV station or theater company would provide a good foundation.

THE STAGE MANAGER

The television stage manager is in charge of what takes place in the studio and serves as liaison between the director, associate director, and all personnel in the control room and the other facilities in the studio. He or she calls cast and crew to the set for each run-through, and at the end of rehearsal announces when everyone is due back. The stage manager "slates" each episode—prepares the slate and announces show name, date, and number—at the start of the taping.

On dramatic shows, the stage manager cues performers to enter, speak or start any activity; an actor whose character is regaining consciousness will need a gentle tap on an off-camera toe before beginning to moan or move. The stage manager also marks actors' positions as requested during run-throughs, and supervises placement of scenery, furniture, and props.

Multiset shows requiring large studios will employ two stage managers— one to oversee each half of the studio. And on the heaviest days, the stage manager may recommend that extra persons be brought in.

On continuing shows or series, the stage manager is a regular member of the staff who knows how the show works and understands the personalities of everyone in the company. Day players rely on the stage manager to assign their dressing rooms, direct them to makeup and lead the (often labyrinthine) way to the set. The stage manager designates locations for costume changes and gives that information to the wardrobe department.

Stage managers on nondramatic shows all do the countdown and opening cue, but their other responsibilities may differ.

> In TV, your boss is sometimes the star, sometimes the director, sometimes the producer. You do whatever the boss wants. You are the person next to the boss.
>
> You have to be savvy, demonstrate your skill as a team player, and know when someone *else* needs to solve the problem.
>
> ANDREA NAIER, stage manager

> In TV, you don't deal with pre-production. You come in last, at the same time as the talent. You must know the heads of the departments, be a mediator, have diplomacy skills.
>
> HOWARD COLLINS, stage manager

By their very nature, awards shows and special events are live programs that employ as many stage managers as the director believes necessary. Stage managers are stationed at key points in the studio or wherever the televised action will take place. Everyone communicates via headsets and mobile phones.

> You have an area to oversee. For the Macy's Thanksgiving Day parade, I am the stage manager of 35th Street. The NBC producer said, "If Andrea wasn't at 35th Street, nothing would get to 34th Street!"
>
> ANDREA NAIER

> I went from theater to the MTV Music Video Awards. I've done the Times Square New Year's Eve event, and I do advance work for press events at the White House.
>
> LOREN SCHNEIDER, stage manager

> The event may be big, but on show day your responsibility is narrow. There is no luxury of getting to know one another, so you have to be fast at learning what you have to do.
>
> HOWARD COLLINS

GETTING STARTED

The necessary skills are organizational ability, communication skills, and a talent for anticipating problems and solving them quickly. Dramatic shows require veterans, most of whom have worked in the theater. Aspiring stage managers should look to local events as opportunities to get started.

> Jobs come via the grapevine. So show up, volunteer.
>
> LOREN SCHNEIDER

> When you read in the news that something will occur in three to six months, assume they will need you and find out who to talk to, who is the head honcho.
>
> STACEY FLEISCHER, stage manager

Experienced stage managers can eventually move up to assignments as producers.

PROFESSIONAL AFFILIATION

Directors, associate directors, and stage managers working in television are members of the Directors Guild of America. Employment confers membership eligibility.

The Guild's live- and taped-TV contracts establish pay rates for network and local programs from five minutes to two hours in length, in prime time or non–prime time. The rates for directors are as follows:

- For 30-minute weekly network prime-time dramas and sitcoms: $15,358 per show
- For 30-minute non–prime time daily dramas: $1,529 per show
- For 60-minute non–prime time daily dramas: $2,667 per show

Pay scales for associate directors are:

- Prime-time: $2,712 per week
- Non–prime time: $1,667 per week

Stage managers earn:

- Prime-time: $1,907 per week
- Non–prime time: $1,537 per week

These figures are supplemented by benefits and contributions to the Guild's health and retirement plans. Contracts, which are negotiated every three years, contain numerous additional details. Always check with the Guild before accepting an assignment.

PRODUCTION ASSISTANT

Responsibilities for this entry-level job vary. In soap opera, the production assistant takes the producer's and director's notes during run-throughs and assists the director in giving the notes to the cast and crew after each run-through. On some shows, the P.A. does scene breakdowns, keeping track of time of day, performers, costumes, props, sound, and music cues. The P.A. may also be expected to time scenes during dry rehearsal.

Getting these jobs is frequently a matter of being in the right place at the right time and in asking the right person for the job. A liberal arts education with a major in theater or communications is advised.

P.A.s can move up to the position of stage manager or associate director.

THE DESIGNERS

As designer Albert Brenner pointed out, "Everything you see is designed."

In television that includes the sets for every local and network news, weather, and interview show, and whatever format comes along next. Design even extends to ceilings and floors. The eye-filling sets and flashing lights of game shows are virtuoso design performances.

Distinctive style is not confined to trend-setting series. Entire TV channels have been built around a "look"—think of MTV. Someone designed it.

THE SET DESIGNER

Carnegie Mellon alumnus Alan Kimmel won a Metropolitan Opera set-design contest when he was a sophomore at New York's High School of Music and Art and went on to create acclaimed, innovative scene designs for major musical-theater companies (he did the clever jigsaw-puzzle scenery for the original onstage world of *You're a Good Man, Charlie Brown*). A two-time Emmy winner for his work in television news, Kimmel recalled:

> I was the designer on a bio-drama about Harriet Beecher Stowe for PBS. We were using ABC's big studio, TV One, and it was my first chance to work with Tom Donovan, who then produced *A World Apart* for ABC. He asked me to design that show. That led me to join the ABC staff. Ordinarily that meant you did a whole range of shows, but the high-tech look of ABC's football coverage was so successful that the network's chief, Roone Arledge, decided the newsrooms should be standardized, too.
>
> And that's what they sent me to do. I went to Tel Aviv, Frankfurt, Los Angeles, and London, where Peter Jennings was the London correspondent. When he was brought to Washington to do *Nightline* with Ted Koppel, I did that set too.

In 1984, Kimmel was asked to put the ABC stamp on all local newsrooms for the presidential election year. That was exactly his design solution—to use wallpaper with the ABC logo in three different sizes. Also, he designed a three-hour special on the forty years since World War II. It earned him his first Emmy nomination.

"The first award I actually won," he said, "was only a little Emmy, for a local morning show with Regis Philbin that became *Live with Regis & Kathie Lee*."

Later, when Iran invaded Saudi Arabia, a special newsroom was set up to do a news special on the Gulf War.

They called me because they wanted a gigantic map of the area to fill the studio, a 40- by 50-foot space. I thought if we had the map on the walls, we'd have to see it *all* the time. Better to put it someplace else—the floor! So I had huge blowups made of the map. We transferred them to plywood-backed muslin, painted each country a separate color, and attached the pieces to the studio floor. In the first shot, it looked like a map of the Middle East—until Peter Jennings walked into the shot, and then it looked as if he was standing right where it was happening, each foot in a different country. It was sensational, and for that I won a big Emmy.

ABC later had Kimmel redesigning news desks again. "This time," he chuckled, "I have an assistant. I do all the measuring, and he does all the drawings and floor plans."

A DAYTIME DRAMA SET DESIGN

Boyd Dumrose, also an ABC designer, was called upon to create an urban set for *The City,* the network's re-do of *Loving.* The producer's idea was to have all the characters living in one apartment building.

Suddenly, it was announced: I had to deliver the set in four months. We didn't have a story. No design scout had been hired. I started with a theoretical design model—it had to be a place that included an office, a model agency, a bar, a clinic, roommate space, and places to be private. By making it an apartment house, with each apartment decorated differently, we'd be able to use interchangeable architectural details—walls, windows, and columns—and bring in different props without trucking sets back and forth from the warehouse. The flexible set saved money on building and setups.

BOYD DUMROSE

The new set design made it possible for the camera to do almost a full-circle pan around the apartments. The openness called for new lighting and new ways of miking the set; there was no place to locate the boom platform. The production design was regarded as a triumph, but the show itself was unable to capture a sufficiently large audience and was canceled early in 1997.

NEW TECHNOLOGY

The latest design advances unveiled by set designer Catherine Spencer may eliminate sets altogether. Virtual scenery, backgrounds created with a computer program, are in experimental use exclusively at ABC. Working on *Good Morning, America,* Spencer explained that the virtual backgrounds could be used for guest interviews, when the guests needed a special area. "The computers are now fast enough to adjust to people moving within the space," She said.

Only two years out of Carnegie Mellon, she started as an assistant at ABC.

"It took four interviews to get the job," she recalled. The timing was right: Shortly after she was hired, *Good Morning, America* needed someone, and she was promoted to that show. Her next promotion made her the show's designer.

While studying at Carnegie Mellon, she worked during vacations to gain experience. She also learned Autocad, the software program that set, lighting, and architectural designers use. Doing temporary designer jobs, she was able to earn from $20 to $40 an hour.

GETTING STARTED

Designers can begin by assisting other designers—doing drawings, models, floor plans, and measurements. They can do gofer jobs at local production houses or apply for jobs painting sets at scene construction companies, and work with community theater companies and at architectural firms. They can seek work at local television stations or with the video production departments of local advertising agencies. Some corporations produce in-house educational videos—you can look for such leads in the Yellow Pages. Businesses you may want to work for will have a listing. As noted, local film commissions and production houses can be excellent sources of information and, sometimes, employment.

> You have to be able to ask for a job. You have to have your résumé to leave with people. And then you have to be good at what you do.
>
> JASON KANTROWITZ, designer

FOR ORDERING, CONTACT:

Ross Reports Television
1515 Broadway
New York, NY 10036

MPE Publications
432 West 45th Street
New York, NY 10036

Ross Reports Television is a monthly publication that lists active production studios in New York and California. It is sold at newsstands and at bookstores near production centers, or you can contact the publisher.

The Motion Picture, TV, and Theatre Directory is another useful guide to industry products and services. Published semiannually by MPE Publications, this pocket-sized sourcebook lists production houses, ad agencies, and support service companies throughout the United States, Canada, Great Britain, Europe, and Japan.

THE DECORATING TEAM

With or without virtual sets, real people sit on real furniture and handle real objects. As in film, these are shopped for and gathered by the SET DECORATORS and property masters. A decorating team usually stays with one show. A standby PAINTER is always present, to take care of chips, tears, and scratches.

COSTUMERS AND WARDROBE SUPERVISORS

Most of the clothing worn on television is contemporary. Few things are made to order. The designer, in this case, creates an overall look for the characters, based upon the script and character description. The designer will meet with a performer who is signed to a long-term contract to discuss the preferences and thoughts each of them have about the way the performer's character dresses.

The wardrobe department of an ongoing show is like an in-house costume collection, laundry, and dry-cleaning establishment.

The wardrobe supervisor, with one or more assistants, studies each script several days in advance, checks with the designer, and has the necessary outfits cleaned and pressed two days before the show. The outfits are labelled and hung on garment racks, with their accessories. On the day of performance, they are placed in the performers' dressing rooms. Shirts are laundered and pressed. Alterations are made. Rips, hems, and buttons are checked. These tasks are usually regular, full-time jobs.

HAIRSTYLISTS AND MAKEUP ARTISTS

Usually the same people work the show on a regular basis. To maintain the characters' look, hairstylists frequently act as the performers' personal hairdresser, trimming and coloring as needed.

Different products are sometimes used for film and television makeup, depending on location, time of day, whether a shot is in or out of doors, whether a performer's skin needs special care because of blemishes, acne scars, or an unscheduled weekend at the beach. The makeup artist is expected to know how much coverage is necessary and, depending on the role, what tones, highlights, and shadows will work best with a performer's complexion and facial structure. The artist is also expected to be able to adjust a performer's makeup if, because of lighting or costume color, the regularly used base tone somehow doesn't look right on the control-room monitor.

Historically, innovative makeup artists have created their own products to cope with these changing conditions. If their special mixtures are particularly effective, other artists, and then performers and models, become their loyal customers. This is how some product lines become industry favorites and then go on to be mass-marketed. Max Factor and the Westmore brothers were Hollywood makeup artists whose unique products wound up at cosmetic counters across the land. The current and highly successful MAC (Makeup Art Cosmetics) and Bobbi Brown lines were created by makeup artists working in TV and fashion who demanded more flexibility than existing colors offered.

PROFESSIONAL STATUS

Designers working in television are members of United Scenic Artists. Wardrobe supervisors and assistants are members of Local #764, IATSE. And hairstylists and makeup artists are members of Local #798, IATSE. Pay scales are on a par with salaries in film (see page 162, or contact the union).

THE TECHNICAL STAFF

Among those seated in the control room are the TECHNICAL DIRECTOR (T.D.), the VIDEO OPERATOR, and the AUDIO ENGINEER. All are skilled engineers, concerned with monitoring the quality of the image and sound signals that beam out to millions of homes. The T.D. is responsible for the performance of the entire group of technicians: In addition to the video and audio engineers, that includes CAMERA OPERATORS, SWITCHING TECHNICIANS, BOOM OPERATORS, AUDIO and SOUND-EFFECTS TECHNICIANS, and CABLE PUSHERS.

When the T.D. announces, "Cameras and booms, please," it's the camera operators' cue to line up their cameras. In turn, they focus on a color-coded rectangular pattern while the video operator, seated before the bank of monitors, adjusts the levels on the control board to attain uniform color and tone on all the cameras.

The technical crew in the control room and the camera crew on the studio floor communicate through headsets. During dress rehearsal and taping, the T.D. will be the one to call, "Take 1" or "Take 3"—which refers to the camera number. The switching technician, or switcher, presses the button that selects the image coming from that camera to be transferred to the tape.

Cameras and microphones are connected to the electrical power source via heavy cables. As the cameras and booms follow the actors back and forth along the studio floor, cable pullers stand close by to keep the camera and mike cables from getting crossed or snarled.

The movable pedestals television cameras are mounted on give enormous flexibility to the director and camera people. They can use the metal ring encircling the top of the pedestal to push or pull the camera into the corners of a set to cover the action. Waist-high adjustment dials allow for rapid changes of lens or focus; they can easily tilt up as an actor climbs stairs and then pan to catch a face at the window. Through the viewfinder, the camera operator sees the same picture the director sees on that camera's monitor in the control room.

Each camera operator receives a list of the shots for that camera before the run-through. During run-throughs and broadcast or taping, they receive directions from the director or T.D. through their headphones. They also hear the A.D.'s cueing of the upcoming shots.

In preparing for tapings in soap opera, directors generally prefer to work on the studio floor and watch an overhead monitor. This allows them to modify shots more quickly. The camera operator marks any changes on the shot list. Changes are also recorded by the A.D. in the control room.

AUDIO AND SOUND EFFECTS

The sound equipment in television is the same as that used in film and theater. The work is basically the same: The audio operator gets the script in advance, and determines what personnel and equipment will be needed for each show. During run-through, dress rehearsal, and taping, the audio engineer in the control room balances the sound coming from the set and communicates with the technicians on the studio floor via headset.

After an episode is taped, the A.D., working with the VIDEOTAPE EDITOR, arranges the shots in their desired sequence and edits the show to meet its proper time slot. No tape is handled. Instead, the tape reels are time-coded, and the entire process is accomplished electronically, using machines that play back and record with no loss of picture quality.

WORKING CONDITIONS

Many of the technical jobs in television are stressful, particularly on dramatic shows. So many things are going on at the same time, with so many on-the-spot adjustments, that the technical staff must have stamina and agility. These positions call for concentration, communication skills, an eye for detail, and an intuitive "quick-study" talent. They learn it, tape it, forget it.

As one of *The Guiding Light*'s original camera crew shouted into an overhead boom during a heavy taping day: "You folks in the control room are all sitting down. Us fellas out here are standing up!" Which happens to be true— camera and boom operators are always on their feet for run-through, dress, and taping. Besides the physical demands, camera people must be doubly alert, listening to the voices in their ear and watching the actors they follow on the set.

Nondramatic shows usually develop a formula for program opening, body, and close. People take their accustomed places in their usual set. Guest appearances may call for adjustments in camera position or focus, but major shifts are rare.

Emergencies, such as a sudden camera breakdown, will be apparent on the control room monitors. The T.D. and director quickly invent and call new shots through the headphones.

RECOMMENDED TRAINING

Camera operators should take courses that teach the basic production processes. They need to understand the elements of pictorial composition, and camera angles and placement. They should also understand lighting and perspective in relation to the TV picture, because the TV camera, which is for recording an electronic image onto videotape, is not the same as the motion-picture film camera; the skills are not immediately transferable.

For technical directors and video operators, an electronic engineering degree or similar training is necessary. As already noted, this part of the business is changing radically. Leaders agree that learning the basic principles is important if one is to have a career as a creative person in this field, rather than as a video button-pusher.

GETTING STARTED

There is a lot of competition for openings in these fields. You should seek out local production houses, local TV stations, or any corporation with an in-house audiovisual department. Volunteer to do anything, just to be exposed to the way the real work is done. Visit equipment rental houses, see how current broadcast-standard machinery actually works, and become familiar with it. In fact, working in a rental house can be a way to get one's foot in the door of a production facility. Jobs, after all, may come through the grapevine.

Once you do land a job on an audio or video or camera crew, if you are working on a regularly scheduled program it can be like working on a long-running Broadway show.

FOR INFORMATION, CONTACT:

The International Brotherhood of Electrical Workers Broadcast Department 1125 15th Street, N.W. Washington, DC 20005

New York address:
Local #1212
230 West 41st Street
New York, NY 10036

The National Association of Broadcast Employees and Technicians 5034 Wisconsin Avenue Washington, DC 20016

New York addresses:
Local #11
888 Seventh Avenue
New York, NY 10019

Local #16
1865 Broadway
New York, NY 10023

PROFESSIONAL AFFILIATION

TV technicians, who belong to the International Brotherhood of Electrical Workers (IBEW) and The National Association of Broadcast Employees and Technicians (NABET) make salaries that begin at roughly $350 per day for camera operators. Technical directors are paid more.

Local and network union agreements are the deciding factors in which union has jurisdiction over your position. For information, write to the national headquarters for information about local practices, and for job descriptions, in your area.

AND REMEMBER

Beyond the control rooms and studios, many people work in or around television. Their skills and training are different. Publicists inform and excite audiences about new programs, long-running shows, and entertainment highlights. Columnists, reviewers, and interviewers for the press play a part in satisfying or generating audience curiosity about the programs and the players.

Because television is a commercial medium, the clients of advertising agency executives ultimately finance production by buying time to run their commercials. These executives, as the sponsors' representatives, interact with network sales and marketing executives. Licensing specialists explore tie-ins and ancillary product possibilities. Audience research executives try to discern who's watching or why they aren't. Executives in charge of daytime, prime-time, late-night, news, sports, and special events coverage hunt for good material and try to arrange it in a magical, audience-grabbing schedule.

And, behind the scenes, a lot of people help them do their jobs.

Closing Shot

WE'VE COME TO THE END OF OUR journeys through the show business communities. Like substitutes for the company regulars, we've "trailed" in theater, movies, and television. Your decision about a show business career should be made only after serious self-examination. This exploration has surely demonstrated the discipline and determination that exist on almost every level of the business. So many people speak of their passion for an idea, a project, even a color of fabric or light. There is a lot of energy driving all these machines. There is also a great deal of pride and not a little ambition.

How do you view yourself in relation to all those factors? Ask yourself if you are ready to do the necessary work to become a professional. Evaluate your own talents—what you like to do, what you do best—and fantasize about how you might apply those attributes to aspects of the production process.

Investigate every possibility in your own locale for employment and instruction. Research skills are universally useful. Be open to possibilities: A local event may be a chance for a would-be stage manager, a production assistant, a sound engineer, a lighting person, or a producer.

Whatever you do, get the best training you can afford. Tracing his path from actor to writer to producer, James Lipton, who now heads the school of the Actors Studio, in New York, and also hosts *Inside the*

Actors Studio, a program on the Bravo cable network, spoke about the teachers he'd studied with when he came to New York:

> Stella Adler, Robert Lewis, Hanya Holm for dance, Arthur Lessac for voice, Harold Clurman, who gave me my first directing assignments. . . . When you work with people of that caliber, talent, and enthusiasm, you are hooked! Creativity is all around you. You must make the most of it.

What does the future hold?

More.

All one has to do is be ready, and begin. Certainly there is anxiety about the new technologies and their potential impact on jobs. Change is coming, but change is always coming. It's inevitable. You need only learn the business and adapt.

In the opening pages, we told a story about George Abbott, producer, director, Pulitzer Prize–winning playwright, and quintessential man of the theater. In 1990, at the celebration of his 102nd birthday, Abbott was asked what he considered "the greatest thing that happened in all your years in the theater?" His immediate answer: "Electricity!"

May the electricity light up your future, whether your show business career is in theater, film, or television.

Appendix

T HINK OF THE FOLLOWING reference lists as a set of keys to learning more about show business and acquiring the know-how for pursuing a career.

The **Recommended Reading** list contains a selection of entertaining success stories, instructional works, and chronicles of the theater, film, and television professions. Leafing through them will inspire you to find out more. They should be available at your local library or bookstore.

Rely on **Relevant Publications** for news about what's happening in the business now. Reading the so-called *trades* can be like taking a crash course in which you quickly absorb enough information to form opinions about the people and events in your field of interest. Then you may think up new, effective ways to propel your career.

The **Frequently Mentioned Schools** lists institutions that offer standout courses in theater, film, and television. Study their catalogs and compare their programs with those of local colleges. And go further: Consult the latest information in the various comprehensive college guide books published annually and accessible on the Internet.

Getting in touch with **Organizations and Associations** can open doors for you. A polite request for information or advice is usually answered. Most people will gladly share the benefit of their experience, particularly with an eager newcomer. When you ask questions, talk to professionals, volunteer, or join, you begin an all-important networking process. And it's as easy as saying hello.

Film Commissions are an underused local job resource. For someone intent on a career in production, they're good places to network. You never know whom you'll meet or where your inquiries may lead—perhaps all the way to your future *working in show business.*

RECOMMENDED READING

Abbott, George. *Mister Abbott.* New York: Random House, 1963.

Auletta, Ken. *Three Blind Mice.* New York: Vintage Books, 1995.

Bartow, Arthur. *The Director's Voice.* New York: Theatre Communications Guild, 1988.

Behlmer, Rudy. *Behind the Scenes: The Making of 16 Classic Films.* Hollywood: Samuel French, 1990.

Breimer, Stephen F. *Clause by Clause: The Screenwriter's Legal Guide.* New York: Dell, 1995.

Canemaker, John. *Before the Animation Begins.* New York: Hyperion, 1996.

Charles, Jill, ed. *Directory of Professional Theatre Training Programs.* Annual Publication. Dorset Theatre Festival and Colony House, Box 519, Dorset, Vermont 05251.

_____. *Summer Theatre Directory* (See above).

_____. *The Regional Theatre Directory* (See above).

Clurman, Harold. *The Collected Works of Harold Clurman,* edited by Marjorie Loggia and Glenn Young. New York: Applause Books, 1994.

Egri, Lajos. *The Art of Dramatic Writing.* New York: Simon & Schuster, 1946.

Farber, Donald C. *From Option to Opening: A Guide to Producing Plays Off-Broadway.* New York: Limelight Editions, 1993.

_____ and Viagas, Robert. *The Amazing Story of* The Fantasticks, *America's Longest Running Play.* New York: Citadel Press, 1991.

Field, Syd. *Screenplay: The Foundations of Script Writing.* New York: Dell, 1994.

Gabler, Neal. *An Empire of Their Own.* New York: Anchor Books, 1988.

Goldman, William. *Adventures in the Screen Trade.* New York: Warner Books, 1983.

_____. *The Season.* New York: Limelight Editions, 1984.

_____. *Four Screenplays.* New York: Applause Books, 1995.

Hart, Moss. *Act One.* New York: Random House, 1959.

Hayward, Stan. *Computers for Animation.* Boston: Focal Press, 1984.

Henderson, Mary. *Theatre in America.* New York: Abrams, 1986.

Kaye, Deena, and LeBrecht, James. *Sound and Music for the Theater.* New York: Back Stage Books, 1992.

Kelly, Thomas A.. *The Back Stage Guide to Stage Management.* New York: Back Stage Books, 1991.

Lazarus, Paul, III. *The Film Producer.* New York: St. Martin's Press, 1992.

Loring, Ann, and Kaye, Evelyn. *Write and Sell Your TV Drama.* New York: Alek Publishing, 1984.

Lumet, Sidney. *Making Movies.* New York: Knopf, 1995.

Mandelbaum, Ken. *Not Since Carrie.* New York: St. Martin's Press, 1991.

_____. A Chorus Line *and the Musicals of Michael Bennett.* New York: St. Martin's Press, 1991.

Marshall, Garry. *Wake Me When It's Funny.* Holbrook, Mass.: Adams Publishing, 1995.

McLaughlin, Buzz. *The Playwright's Process.* New York: Back Stage Books, 1997.

Morrow, Lee Alan, and Pike, Frank. *Creating Theater.* New York: Vintage Books, 1986.

Obst, Lynda. *Hello, He Lied.* Boston: Little, Brown, 1996.

Pecktal, Lynn. *Costume Design.* New York: Back Stage Books, 1993.

Reznick, Gail, and Trost, Scott. *All You Need to Know About the Movie and TV Business.* New York: Fireside, 1996.

Rose, Frank. *The Agency.* New York: HarperCollins, 1995.

Schickel, Richard. *Intimate Strangers.* New York: Doubleday, 1985.

Shanks, Robert. *The Cool Fire.* New York: W. W. Norton, 1976.

Sheward, David. *It's a Hit! The Back Stage Book of Longest-Running Broadway Shows.* New York: Back Stage Books, 1994.

Surmanek, Jim. *Media Planning.* Lincolnwood, Ill.: NTC Business Books, 1995.

RELEVANT PUBLICATIONS

Trade publications make it easy to keep abreast of current developments in the business and of the people whose work consistently receives attention or applause. Pay attention to notices of upcoming projects. Search for names you recognize. School and college libraries customarily subscribe to publications the faculty consider worthwhile. If your teachers are not receiving current material, let them know about magazines and articles you have found interesting and helpful.

American Cinematographer, published monthly. Subscriptions available from ASC Holding Corp., 1782 N. Orange Dr., Hollywood, CA 90028.

American Theatre, published monthly, except for double issues in May/June and July/August. Available through membership in Theatre Communications Group, 355 Lexington Ave., New York, NY 10017.

ArtSEARCH, the National Employment Bulletin for the Arts, published biweekly by Theatre Communications Group, 355 Lexington Ave., New York,10017.

Theatre Directory, published annually by Theatre Communications Group. A guide to more than 300 nonprofit professional theaters across the United States.

Back Stage, published weekly by BPI Communications, 1515 Broadway, New York, NY 10036. Available at newsstands, in theater bookstores, or by subscription.

Back Stage West, published weekly by BPI Communications, 5055 Wilshire Blvd., Los Angeles, CA 90036. Available at newsstands, in theater bookstores, or by subscription.

The DGA News, published bimonthly by the Directors Guild of America, Inc., 7920 Sunset Blvd, Los Angeles, CA 90046.

The Hollywood Reporter, published daily by BPI Communications, 5055 Wilshire Blvd., Los Angeles, CA 90036.

Hollywood Script Writer, published monthly by the Writers Guild of America West, 8955 Beverly Blvd., Los Angeles, CA 90048.

The Motion Picture, TV, and Theatre Directory, published semiannually by MPE Publications, 432 West 45th St., New York, NY 10036.

Ross Reports Television, published monthly. For subscriptions, write to Ross Reports, 1515 Broadway, New York, NY 10036.

Screen, the Chicago Production Weekly, 720 N. Wabash Ave., Chicago, IL 60611.

Stage Directions, the Practical Magazine of Theater, 3101 Poplarwood Ct., Suite 310, Raleigh, NC 27604.

TCI (Theatre Crafts International), published monthly, Box 470, Mount Morris, IL 61054-0470.

Theatrical Index, published monthly by Price Berkley, 888 Eighth Ave., New York, NY, 10019.

Variety, published weekly in New York; daily and weekly in California, by Cahners Publishing, 5700 Wilshire Blvd., Suite 120, Los Angeles, CA 90036.

Variety's On Production, published monthly. For subscriptions, write to Cahners Publishing, 5700 Wilshire Blvd., Suite 120, Los Angeles, CA 90036.

FREQUENTLY MENTIONED SCHOOLS

Many of the people I interviewed were enthusiastic about the training offered at the schools they had attended. They were also happy to mention programs they had heard good things about from their colleagues.

While these are the names that came up most often, they are by no means the only places to consider.

American Film Institute
Center for Advanced Film & Television Studies
2021 North Western Avenue
Los Angeles, CA 90027

California Institute of the Arts (CalArts)
24700 McBean Parkway
Valencia, CA 91355

Cinema/TV Department
Brooks Institute
School of Photographic Art & Science
2190 Alston Road
Santa Barbara, CA 93108

Film Division, School of the Arts
Columbia University
513 Dodge Hall
116th Street and Broadway
New York, NY 10027

Film Studies, Drama Department
Dartmouth College
Hanover, NH 03755

Institute of Film & Television
New York University
65 South Building
New York, NY 10003

Tisch School of the Arts
New York University
721 Broadway
New York, NY 10003

Director of Admissions
North Carolina School of the Arts
Box 12189
Winston-Salem, NC 27117

Radio–TV–Film Department
School of Speech
Northwestern University
Evanston, IL 60201

Film & Creative Arts Interdisciplinary Department
San Francisco State University
1600 Holloway Avenue
San Francisco, CA 94132

Filmmaking Department
School of the Art Institute of Chicago
Columbus Drive & Jackson Boulevard
Chicago, IL 60603

Theatre Arts Department
University of California at Los Angeles
405 Hilgard Avenue
Los Angeles, CA 90024

Entertainment Studies
University of California at Los Angeles
10995 LeConte Avenue
Los Angeles, CA 90024-2883

Division of Cinema/TV
University of Southern California
School of Performing Arts
University Park
Los Angeles, CA 90007

ORGANIZATIONS AND ASSOCIATIONS

Job information frequently travels through the grapevine. The following organizations may offer opportunities to learn about them through networking.

Symbols: **C** conferences; **M** meetings; **N** newsletter; **P** publication; **S** seminars

Academy of Television Arts & Sciences
6255 Sunset Boulevard
Hollywood, CA 90028

Actors Equity Association
165 West 46th Street
New York, NY 10036

The union for professional stage managers (as well as actors).

Alliance of Resident Theatres/New York
131 Varick Street
New York, NY 10013
C P

Alternate ROOTS
1083 Austin Avenue
Atlanta, GA 30307
M N

ROOTS is the Regional Organization of Theatres South.

American Alliance for Theatre & Education
c/o Department of Theatre
Arizona State University
Box 873411
Tempe, AZ 85287-3411
C P

For theater artists and K-12 educators who work with young people.

American Arts Alliance
1319 F Street NW, Suite 500
Washington, DC 20004

American Council for the Arts
1 East 53rd Street
New York, NY 10022
P

American Federation of Television and Radio Artists
260 Madison Avenue
New York, NY 10016

American Theatre Critics Association
c/o The Tennessean
2200 Hemingway Drive
Nashville, TN 37215
M

Arts International Program
Institute of International Education
809 United Nations Plaza
New York, NY 10017
P

ASSITEJ/USA
2707 East Union
Seattle, WA 98122
C P S

ASSITEJ/USA is the U.S. center for the sixty-nation International Association of Theatre for Children and Young People. This membership organization promotes development of professional theater for young audiences and families.

Association for Theatre in Higher Education
200 North Michigan Avenue, Suite 300
Chicago, IL 60601
C P

Represents university and college theaters and professional training programs.

Association of Theatrical Press Agents & Managers
165 West 46th Street
New York, NY 10036

Authors Guild
330 West 42nd Street
New York, NY 110036

The sister organization to the Dramatists Guild.

Black Theatre Network
Box 11502
Fisher Building Station
Detroit, MI 48211
C P

The Directors Guild of America, East
110 West 57th Street
New York, NY 10019

The Directors Guild of America, West
7920 Sunset Boulevard
Los Angeles, CA, 90046

The Drama League
165 West 46th Street, Suite 601
New York, NY 10036
N P S

A very helpful organization for directors.

The Dramatists Guild
1501 Broadway
New York, NY 10036
N P S

The professional association of playwrights, composers, and lyricists. All writers of scripts are eligible for membership.

Eugene O'Neill Memorial Theater Center
305 Great Neck Road
Waterford, CT 06385

The Foundation Center
79 Fifth Avenue
New York, NY 10003

A source of information on possible grants and on the grant-making process.

The Independent Feature Project
104 West 29th Street
New York, NY 10001
P S

An organization for young filmmakers, with tie-ins to related organizations around the world.

Institute of Outdoor Drama
University of North Carolina
CB3240 Nations Bank Plaza, Suite 201
Chapel Hill, NC 27599
P

International Alliance of Theatrical Stage Employees
1515 Broadway
New York, NY 10036

International Brotherhood of Electrical Workers
1125 15th Street NW
Washington, DC 20005

International Network of Performing and Visual Arts High Schools
5505 Connecticut Avenue NW #280
Washington, DC 20015

International Theatre Institute of the United States
47 Great Jones Street
New York, NY 10012

The League of American Theaters and Producers
226 West 47th Street
New York, NY 10036

The professional trade association of the legitimate theater.

League of Chicago Theatres
67 East Madison, Suite 2116
Chicago, IL 60603
P

The League of Chicago Theatres Foundation is at the same address.

Literary Managers and Dramaturgs of the Americas
Box 355-CASTA
CUNY Graduate Center
33 West 42nd Street
New York, NY 10036
C M N P

This national membership organization has a student-member category.

National Academy of Television Arts & Sciences
111 West 57th Street
New York, NY 10019

There are branches of the Academy in cities across the country.

National Alliance for Musical Theatre
330 West 44th Street, Lobby B
New York, NY 10036
N P

National Assembly of Local Arts Agencies
927 15th Street NW, 12th floor
Washington, DC 20005
C N P

A service organization offering information and technical assistance.

National Assembly of State Arts Agencies
1010 Vermont Avenue NW, Suite 920
Washington, DC 20005
C P

National Association of Broadcast Employees & Technicians
5034 Wisconsin Avenue
Washington, DC 20016

Local offices can be found in cities across the country.

National Foundation for Advancement in the Arts
ARTS Program
800 Brickell Avenue, Suite 500
Miami, FL 33131

The ARTS Program is the foundation's arts recognition and talent search effort.

New Jersey Theatre Group
Box 21
Florham Park, NJ 07932
C M P

New York Public Library for the Performing Arts
40 Lincoln Center Plaza
New York, NY 10023

A circulating and research library, with the most comprehensive theater collection in the United States.

New York Women in Film and TV
274 Madison Avenue
New York, NY 10016

Non-Traditional Casting Project
1560 Broadway, Suite 1600
New York, NY 10036
C N

An advocacy organization involving all theater artists.

The Players
16 Gramercy Park
New York, NY 10003

A membership organization of actors, writers, and theater people.

Public Relations Society of America
33 Irving Place
New York, NY 10003

Screen Actors Guild
1515 Broadway
New York, NY 10036

West Coast address:
5757 Wilshire Boulevard
Hollywood, CA 90036

The union for stand-ins and stunt artists, as well as actors.

Society of Stage Directors & Choreographers
1501 Broadway, Suite 1701
New York, NY 10036
N

*A labor union representing directors and choreographers in all areas of profes-
sional theater and choreographers working in film, TV, and music video.*

Theatre Bay Area
657 Mission Street, Suite 402
San Francisco, CA 94105
C N P

Theatre Communications Group
355 Lexington Avenue
New York, NY 10017
C N P

The national organization for the American theater, founded in 1961.

Theatre Development Fund
1501 Broadway, Suite 2110
New York, NY 10036

Theatre LA
644 South Figueroa Street
Los Angeles, CA 90017
N S

United Scenic Artists, Local #829
16 West 61th Street
New York, NY 10023

*A union representing scenic designers, art directors, costume designers, lighting
designers, stylists, and associated craftspersons working in theater, film, and TV,
with offices in New York, Chicago, Los Angeles, and Miami.*

United States Institute of Theatre Technology
6443 Ridings Road
Syracuse, NY 13206-1111
C

An organization for design and production professionals.

University/Resident Theatre Association
1560 Broadway, Suite 903
New York, NY 10036

Volunteer Lawyers for the Arts
1 East 53rd Street
New York, NY 10022
C P S

Women in Film
6464 Sunset Boulevard, 5th Floor
Los Angeles, CA 90028
S

The Writers Guild of America, East
555 West 57th Street
New York, NY 10019
P

The Writers Guild of America, West
8955 Beverly Boulevard
West Hollywood, CA 90048

FILM COMMISSIONS

Film commissions are in the business of attracting production activity to the states, cities, or towns they represent. They know that show business means business for local merchants, and one of their primary goals is to make it easier for incoming productions to function—to navigate the territory of permissions, fees, taxes, and paperwork.

To anyone aspiring to a career in show business, visiting companies present an opportunity to see how professional production works. For countless people they have been the way to gain entry into the business.

Arrangements for location production are almost always made in advance. The commission office will have the production schedule, names of people to contact, and descriptions of any special talents (if any) they seek for the staff or crew.

The following is a partial list of film commissions. For additional information, contact:

Association of Film Commissions
5820 Wilshire Boulevard
Los Angeles, CA 90036

ALABAMA
Alabama Film Office
410 Adams Avenue
Montgomery, AL 36130

Mobile Film Office
150 South Royal Street
Mobile, AL 36602

ALASKA
Alaska Film Office
3601C Street, Suite 700
Anchorage, AK 99503

ARIZONA
Arizona Film Commission
3800 North Central, Building D,
Phoenix, AZ 85012

There are fifteen additional film offices in the state, among them:

Flagstaff Film Commission
405 North Beaver Street,
Building A, Suite 3
Flagstaff, AZ 86001

City of Phoenix Film Office
200 West Washington, 10th Floor
Phoenix, AZ 85003

Scottsdale Film Office
3939 Civic Center Boulevard
Scottsdale, AZ 85251

Tucson Film Office
32 North Stone Avenue, Suite 100
Tucson, AZ 85701

Yuma Film Commission
2557 Arizona Avenue, Suite A
Yuma, AZ 85364

ARKANSAS

Arkansas Motion Picture Office
1 State Capital Mall, Room 2C-200
Little Rock, AR 72201

CALIFORNIA

California Film Commission
6922 Hollywood Boulevard, Suite 600
Hollywood, CA 90028

*There are thirty-eight additional film
offices in the state. In the larger cities
are the following:*

Berkeley Film Office
1834 University Avenue, 1st Floor
Berkeley, CA 94703

Fresno Convention & Visitors Bureau
808 M Street
Fresno, CA 93721

Kern County Board of Trade
2101 Oak Street
P.O. Bin 1312
Bakersfield, CA 93302

Entertainment Industry
Development Corporation
7083 Hollywood Boulevard
Los Angeles, CA 90028

The Inland Empire Film Commission
310 East Vanderbilt Way, Suite 100,
San Bernardino, CA 92408

Sacramento Area Film Commission
1421 K Street
Sacramento, CA 95814

San Diego Film Commission
402 West Broadway, Suite 1000
San Diego, CA 92101

San Francisco Film &
Video Arts Commission
Mayor's Office,
401 Van Ness Avenue, #417
San Francisco, CA 94102

San Jose Film & Video Commission
333 West San Carlos, Suite 1000,
San Jose, CA 95110

COLORADO

Colorado Motion Picture &
TV Commission
1625 Broadway, Suite 1700
Denver, CO 80202

Mayor's Office of Art, Culture
& Film
280 14th Street
Denver, CO 80202

CONNECTICUT

Connecticut Film, Video
& Media Office
865 Brook Street
Rocky Hill, CT 06067

Danbury Film Office
46 Main Street
Danbury, CT 06810

DELAWARE

Delaware Film Office
99 Kings Highway
P.O. Box 1401
Dover, DE 19903

DISTRICT OF COLUMBIA

Mayor's Office of Motion Picture
& TV
717 14th Street NW, 12th Floor
Washington, DC 20005

FLORIDA

Florida Entertainment Commission
505 17th Street
Miami Beach, FL 33139

*There are thirteen additional film
offices, among them:*

Jacksonville Film & TV Office
128 East Forsythe Street, Suite 505
Jacksonville, FL 32202

Miami—Dade Office of Film,
    TV & Print
111 Northwest 1st Street, Suite 2510
Miami, FL 33128

Metro Orlando Film &
    Television Office
200 East Robinson Street,
Suite 600
Orlando, FL 32801

Tampa Film Commission
111 East Madison Street,
Suite 1010
Tampa, FL 33602

GEORGIA

Georgia Film & Videotape Office
285 Peachtree Center Avenue,
Suite 1000
Atlanta, GA 30303

HAWAII

Hawaii Film Office
Box 2359
Honolulu, HI 96804

Big Island Film Office
25 Aupuni Street, Room 219
Hilo, HI 96720

IDAHO

Idaho Film Bureau
700 West State Street
Box 83720
Boise, ID 83720

ILLINOIS

Illinois Film Office
100 West Randolph, Suite 3-400
Chicago, IL 60601

Chicago Film Office
1 North LaSalle, Suite 2165
Chicago, IL 60602

INDIANA

Indiana Film Commission
1 North Capitol, #700
Indianapolis, IN, 46204

IOWA

Iowa Film Office
200 East Grand Avenue
Des Moines, IA 50309

Cedar Rapids Area Film Commission
119 First Avenue SE
Box 5339
Cedar Rapids, IA 52406

KANSAS

Kansas Film Commission
700 SW Harrison Street,
Suite 1300
Topeka KS 66603

KENTUCKY

Kentucky Film Commission
500 Mero Street
2200 Capitol Plaza Tower
Frankfort, KY 40601

LOUISIANA
New Orleans Film &
  Video Commission
1515 Poydras Street, Suite 1200
New Orleans, LA 70112

MAINE
The Maine Film Office
State House Station 59
Augusta, ME 04333

MARYLAND
Maryland Film Office
217 East Redwood Street, 9th Floor
Baltimore, MD 21202

MASSACHUSETTS
Massachusetts Film Office
10 Park Plaza, Suite 2310
Boston, MA 02116

MICHIGAN
201 North Washington Square
Victor Centre, 5th Floor
Lansing MI 48913

MINNESOTA
Minnesota Film Board
401 North 3rd Street, Suite 460
Minneapolis, MN 55401

Minneapolis Office of
  Film/Video/Recording
323M City Hall
350 South 5th Street
Minneapolis, MN 55415

MISSISSIPPI
Mississippi Film Office
Box 840
Jackson, MS 39205

Natchez Film Commission
422 Main Street
Box 1485
Natchez, MS 39121

Vicksburg Film Commission
Box 110
Vicksburg, MS 39180

MISSOURI
Missouri Film Office
301 West High, Room 770
Box 118
Jefferson City, MO 65102

Kansas City Film Office
10 Petticoat Lane, Suite 250
Kansas City, MO 64106

St. Louis Film Office
330 North 15th Street
St. Louis, MO 63103

MONTANA
Montana Film Office
1424 9th Avenue
Helena, MT 59620

NEBRASKA
Nebraska Film Office
700 South 16th Street
Box 94666,
Lincoln, NE 68509

Omaha Film Commission
6800 Mercy Road, Suite 202
Omaha, NE 68106

NEVADA
Motion Picture Division /C.E.D
555 East Washington, Suite 5400
Las Vegas, NV 89101

NEW HAMPSHIRE
New Hampshire Film & TV Bureau
172 Pembroke Road
Box 1856
Concord, NH 033002

NEW JERSEY
New Jersey Motion Picture/TV
   Commission
53 Halsey Street
Box 47023
Newark, NJ 07101

NEW MEXICO
New Mexico Film Office
1100 South Street & Francis Drive
Box 20003
Santa Fe, NM 87504

NEW YORK
New York State Governor's Office
   For Film & TV Development
633 Third Avenue
New York, NY 10017

Mayor's Office of Film/Theatre/
   Broadcast
1697 Broadway, #602
New York, NY 10019

NORTH CAROLINA
North Carolina Film Office
430 North Salisbury Street
Raleigh, NC 27611

OHIO
Ohio Film Commission
77 South High Street, 29th Floor
Box 1001
Columbus, OH 43216

Greater Cincinnati Film Commission
632 Vine Street, #1010
Cincinnati, OH 45202

OKLAHOMA
Oklahoma Film Office
440 South Houston, Suite 304
Tulsa, OK 74127

OREGON
Oregon Film & Video Office
121 SW Salmon Street, Suite 300A
Portland, OR 97204

PENNSYLVANIA
Greater Philadelphia Film Office
1600 Arch Street, 12th Floor
Philadelphia, PA 19103

Pittsburgh Film Office
Benedum Trees Building,
Suite 1300
Pittsburgh, PA 15222

RHODE ISLAND
Providence Film Commission
400 Westminster Street, 6th Floor
Providence, RI 02903

SOUTH CAROLINA
South Carolina Film Office
Box 7367
Columbia, SC 29202

SOUTH DAKOTA
South Dakota Film Commission
711 East Wells Avenue
Pierre, SD 57501

TENNESSEE

Tennessee Film/Entertainment/
   Music Commission
320 6th Avenue North, 7th Floor
Nashville, TN 37243

TEXAS

Texas Film Commission
Box 13246
Austin, TX 78711

*There are seven additional
regional film offices.*

UTAH

Utah Film Commission
324 South State, Suite 500
Salt Lake City, UT 84114

VIRGINIA

Virginia Film Office
901 East Byrd Street, 19th Floor
Richmond, VA 23219

WASHINGTON

Washington State Film Office
2001 6th Avenue, Suite 2600
Seattle, WA 98121

WEST VIRGINIA

West Virginia Film Office
State Capitol
Building 6, Room 525
Charleston, WV 25305

WISCONSIN

Wisconsin Film Office
123 West Washington Avenue,
6th Floor
Madison, WI 53702

WYOMING

Wyoming Film Office
I–25 and College Drive
Cheyenne, WY 82002

INDEX

LYNNE ROGERS' extensive acting career includes appearances on Broadway, in touring companies, in films, and on radio and television. For seven years she was a leading lady on *Guiding Light*. She has also been the "voice" of a slew of nationally advertised products and was Procter & Gamble's first product spokeswoman, appearing on radio and TV talk shows across the country.

Her first book, *The Love of Their Lives,* is a behind-the-scenes look at the soap opera industry. She has since written about the theater for *American Heritage* magazine and is co-author (with Mari Lyn Henry) of *How to Be a Working Actor.* She has served on the national and local boards of AFTRA and is the recipient of the Distinguished Service Medal of the National Academy of Television Arts and Sciences.

A native New Yorker, Lynne Rogers is a graduate *magna cum laude* of Queens College and an alumna of Yale Drama School.